Praise for *Breakthrough*

An Immensely valuable book! There are plenty of books out there on creativity, but none like this... an essential read for anyone who is seeking inspiration about the creative life.

—Laura Pritchett, winner of the PEN USA Award for Fiction, author of *Stars Go Blue*

I've been relying on Breakthrough *almost daily... Breakthrough has helped me sit back and remember that my hands and feet are soaking in a creative pool that has no bottom.*

—Emily France, author of *Zen and Gone*, a *Washington Post* Best Book for Young Readers

Breakthrough *is brimming with compassion and wisdom. ...a dazzling foray into the worlds of creativity and the human experience. Whether you want to improve your creativity or you want to gain insight into how to flourish as a human, this book is for you.*

—Nich Krause, creator of *The Scientific Philosopher*

Every creative soul out there should read this book! ...With empowering suggestions spanning the spiritual to the practical, Breakthrough *will help readers reflect, connect, and find renewed joy in their creative endeavors.*

—Laura Resau, Américas award-winning author of *The Queen of Water*

BREAKTHROUGH

How to Overcome Doubt, Fear, and Resistance
to Be Your Ultimate Creative Self

TODD MITCHELL

OWL HOLLOW PRESS

Owl Hollow Press, LLC, Springville, UT 84663

This is a work of literature that depicts some of the author's personal experiences. Quotations, information, and events are used for educational purposes, are attributed whenever possible, and represent how the author encountered them in the public realm. Incidents and conversations are depicted as accurately as the author can recall, although memory is a subjective, imperfect thing. Some names of people and places have been changed. The author and publisher expressly disclaim any liability, loss, or risk, personal or otherwise, that is incurred as a consequence, directly or indirectly, of the contents of this book.

Breakthrough: How to Overcome Doubt, Fear, and Resistance to Be Your Ultimate Creative Self

Copyright © 2021 by Todd Mitchell

Lynda Barry images are copyrighted material and used with permission from *Drawn & Quarterly*.

All rights reserved. No part of this publication may be reproduced, distributed or transmitted in any form or by any means, without prior written permission.

Library of Congress Cataloging-in-Publication Data
Breakthrough / T. Mitchell. — First edition.

Summary:
Breakthrough goes where no other books on creativity dare to tread—exposing the toxic success myths that hold people back and revealing radical, perspective-shifting solutions.

Cover design by Shahbail Shabbir

ISBN 978-1-945654-88-6 (paperback)
ISBN 978-1-945654-89-3 (e-book)
LCCN 2021948431

For all those who create without recognition,
and for my daughters, Addison Story and Cailin Elizabeth,
may you always be wildly creative.

CONTENTS

Start Here 5
A Quick Note on How This Book is Organized 9
Part I 11
Not Another Annoying Success Story 13
Hold Up: Who Am I to Talk About Success? 17
The First Problem with Success Stories: They Focus on the Wrong Things 21
Problem Two: Success Stories Can Cause Us to Focus on the Wrong Things 25
The Comparison Game Will Crush You (It Nearly Destroyed Me) 29
The Comparison Game is Bigger Than You Think 35
The Trouble with Chasing Success: A Brief Word from Monet 39
The Question My Wife Asked Me That Caused Me to See How Irrational Chasing Success Is 41
What is Success Anyway? 45
A Better Notion of Success 49
Why Changing Your Notion of Success Isn't the Whole Answer 53
Four Common Ways to Beat the Comparison Game (and Why They Don't Work) 55
How to Really Beat the Comparison Game 61
Okay, But... 65
Part II 67

What Does it Mean to Love the Process? 69
Your Ego is Holding You Back 73
What is the Ego Anyway? 77
Why the Ego Makes You Feel Bad (And Why Making it Your Enemy Won't Help) 81
What is Creativity? 89
What Creativity Really Is 93
When You Create, You're Not Alone 99
On Visualizing Creativity 101
The Paradox of Creativity, Control, and Intention 105
A Brief Excursion into the Difference Between Trying and Being 111
The Gift of Failure 115
How I Failed 117
How Failure Can Be Your Friend 121
Twelve Practical Ways to Get Past Doubt, Procrastination, and Other Ego Blocks 127
Tyrants, Artists, and the Ego 135
Enough About the Ego and Long Spoons, I Want to Publish 139
What About Talent and Intelligence? 141
Why Perseverance Matters More Than You Think 145
The Study That Will Forever Change How You Look at Commercial Success 147
Take Away Two: Undiscovered Van Goghs 153
But Perseverance Isn't Fun 157
To Surf or to Swim? 161
Part III 165
A Tale of Two Paths: Struggle vs. Surrender 167

The Transformative Journey 173
Transform Your Characters, Transform Yourself 177
Facing the Ordeal 181
The Dark Night of the Soul 185
Apotheosis and Reward 189
How I Died and Found a Better Way to Be 193
The Dark Tunnel of Nihilism 199
The Far Side of the Tunnel 203
The Ego Mind is a Box 209
Developing Observer Consciousness 215
The Benefits of Observer Consciousness 217
On Writing Your Life 221
The Practical Power of Observer Consciousness 225
A Simple Practice for Unlocking Observer Consciousness
.... 229
On Reading Yourself: The Famous Life 233
Surfing the River 237
Scouting the River 243
Wait… Why So Much Existential Stuff? Isn't This Book About Creativity? 249
Who Are You Really? 251
What the Heck Does Being "the Knowing" Mean? 255
On Acceptance 259
The Power of Radical Acceptance 263
When to Worry 269
Hearts Get Broken Open 273
The Secret to Completely Beating the Comparison Game
.... 279

Slay the Comparison Game with Mudita 283
What About Competition? 289
Three Fun Ways to Experience Essential Connectedness and Expand Consciousness 291
The Ego Strikes Back 295
Revision and the Hero's Return 299
A Confession 305
Steps on the Path to Lifelong Creativity 307
Some Mantras 311
The Cup in the Flames 315
Addendum 319
Want to Take Things a Step Further? 321
Meditation Quick Start Guide 325
Acknowledgements 339
About the Author 341
Notes 343
Thank you for reading! 361

Start Here

This book is for creators, which might encompass everyone. After all, life is fundamentally creative, and living well requires relentless creativity. As the writer Madeleine L'Engle put it, "Unless we are creators, we are not fully alive."

More specifically, this book is for writers, artists, musicians, actors, entrepreneurs, innovators, and others who know what it's like to struggle with bringing something new and significant into existence.

Most specifically, this book is for writers. Why? Because writing is the creative practice I know the most about. However, from what I've seen, the challenges of creating are similar in almost any endeavor where you send your creations out into the world to be admired, criticized, or ignored.

It's no secret that the creative path can be brutal. Examples of struggling writers, artists, and other creators are common enough to have become cliché. But if you're drawn to creativity, then you probably also know that creating can be a deeply satisfying and transformative practice.

To create is to conjure into existence new worlds, characters, images, inventions, and experiences. It's a god-like undertaking that requires both vision and ambition. Such ambition inevitably makes the creator vulnerable to criticism and heartbreak.

By the time I started writing this book, I'd had four novels published by major houses and I'd taught creative writing for twenty-three years. Many of my students have become friends who've kept in touch. I have friends (some who are past students, and some who I met elsewhere) who've written best sellers and had their books made into blockbuster movies, and I have friends who've received National Book Awards, Newbery Awards, and heaps of other honors.

I also have friends—some of the most naturally talented writers I've known—who got discouraged and stopped writing. A writing professor told me decades ago that the ones who publish and win accolades aren't necessarily the most talented. They're the ones who stick with it. At the time I thought he was merely being encouraging to struggling young writers like myself who feared we didn't have enough talent. Now, after decades of teaching creative writing and working with hundreds of writers, I know that what he said is absolutely true: the ones who publish and find success are the ones who stick with it.

For those of us taking a creative path, perseverance matters more than talent. In fact, the most important secret to creative success is actually quite simple. It can be summarized by the Japanese proverb, "Fall down seven times. Get up eight."

But how do you keep getting up? How do you persevere when things get rough? **How do you stay creative and hopeful through the many years of doubt, struggle, and failure that almost every creator experiences?**

The answers to these questions aren't what most people think. They certainly weren't what I'd thought they'd be, and they weren't things that other success books had prepared me to see. Nevertheless, there are powerful ways to transcend the suffering artist paradigm and realize your immense potential while enjoying the creative process more.

It would be a terrible waste not to enjoy your creative life. The techniques outlined in this book are designed to help you love every step of the creative process, because when you love what you're doing, you're far more likely to keep going and attain the success you seek.

Creativity is the territory this book focuses on, but the radical perspective-shifting solutions explored in these pages apply to a great deal more than writing, art, music, and other creative endeavors. They're about moving beyond what's holding you back so you can experience life more fully while becoming the wondrous creator you're meant to be.

Fall down seven times, get up eight.

Here's to giving each other a hand up.

A Quick Note on How This Book is Organized

My goal in these pages is to express transformative concepts in as clear, direct, and useful ways as possible. Although many chapters function on their own as brief meditations on creativity, it's understanding the whole that really matters. With this in mind, it might help to know how the three main parts of this book build on each other:

> **Part I: Understanding the Problem**
> **Part II: Exploring Solutions**
> **Part III: Enacting the Cure**

If Part I seems to be focused on the negative, that's because recognizing and understanding a problem is the first step to resolving it. In Part II, we'll explore the reasoning and research behind potential solutions. And in Part III, we'll focus on specific ways to apply those solutions.

Ultimately, the creative paradigm shifts this book describes must be experienced to be understood. Therefore, it's vital to apply concepts to your own experiences and creative practices. To encourage this, several chapters include questions to ask yourself, activities to try, and ways to take things further. I've also included footnotes if you'd like a deeper explanation of a concept mentioned in the text (and if you really want to get wonky and learn about the research that informed chapters, there are endnotes too).

The more you apply the concepts in this book, the more you'll get out of it. Enjoy the experience!

Part I

"You look like a god sitting there.
Why don't you try writing something?"

—James Tate

Not Another Annoying Success Story

Somewhere on this earth right now there's a writing conference taking place. People are sitting in an air-conditioned hall sipping lukewarm coffee and pushing the pallid remains of a cheesecake around a plate while listening to a famous author give a keynote speech.

This speech is the centerpiece of most writing conferences, and you only need to hear a few of them to detect a common formula for such inspirational talks—one where the writer tells the story of their writing journey with a clever mix of humor and confession. The story often depicts some sort of adversity before lightning struck, the Muse descended, or a donkey kicked the frustrated writer in the head, motivating him to finally write the book he always wanted to write and then BAM!—a new best seller was born.

I bet you've heard such stories before. In fact, I bet you know such stories so well that you won't have much trouble matching the author to the success story. Let's play:

Guess the Success!

A) Single mom on welfare has book idea come "fully formed" into her mind while waiting for a delayed train. It becomes the most successful series of all time and makes her richer than the queen of England.

B) Mathematician who wrote down a story he once told a friend's child. It becomes an immediate (and lasting) commercial and literary success.

C) Bored lawyer who, for fun, writes a novel based on a case he witnessed. Ends up selling over 300 million books.

D) Stay at home mom, who "never even wrote a short story," gets a $750,000 book deal for a book she wrote in three months, based on a dream she had.

Answer Key:
A) J. K. Rowling
B) Lewis Carroll
C) John Grisham
D) Stephenie Meyer

I could keep going, telling you about the editor of my first book, David Levithan, who wrote his first best seller, *Boy Meets Boy*, during the weekends as a Valentine's Day gift for his friends. Or Markus Zusak, who wrote five novels, including the international best-selling novel and blockbuster movie *The Book Thief,* well before he turned thirty. Or S.E. Hinton, who wrote *The Outsiders,* one of the top-selling books of all time, during high school when she was seventeen.

I like a good success story as much as the next starry-eyed dreamer. I've been amazed and entertained by them. But inspired to write? Hardly. Instead, such stories often cause me to think, "Wow! What an amazing talent that person must have." And, a moment later, "What the hell am I doing? Why did I ever think I could be a writer?" Then I wash down a bar of chocolate with a beer while fantasizing about being a lawyer.

Success stories have their purpose—they show us that great things are possible. But most of us already lug around a heavy suitcase full of such stories, and this suitcase can weigh us down when the great things promised don't happen for us.

Rather than being inspirational, society's lopsided focus on success stories often stifles creativity. It's akin to telling a depressed person, "Cheer up! Other people are incredibly happy." Not only does this approach fail to help us when we're struggling, it can send us into damaging cycles of self-blame and despair.

If you hear enough success stories, you might think it's normal to hit a home run the first time at bat. Or the second. Or the third. And if you don't hit a home run, or write a best seller, or meet whatever ambitious goals you've set for yourself, then what? How do you keep going?

There are two main reasons why success stories can be problematic for creators:

1) They focus on the wrong things.
2) They cause us to focus on the wrong things.

Let's explore these reasons further.

Hold Up: Who Am I to Talk About Success?

Good question. On the one hand, I'm not extraordinarily rich or famous. Although I've gotten several novels published, chances are you haven't heard of me (and if you have, hello friend!). There aren't any blockbuster movies made of my books (yet). I haven't earned millions selling my work. I'm in a band, *The Squirrels of Rock,* with my two young daughters, but our top songs, "Mustaches" and "Warts," have only been performed before a handful of astonished patrons at a few local breweries, and those lucky souls would probably prefer never to hear our ballads to facial hair and skin conditions again.

On the other hand, I feel extremely fortunate to have a job teaching creative writing that I enjoy, two awesome daughters, a loving relationship with an amazing partner, a roof over my head, and a dog who does my taxes (she's a wickedly smart Aussie, but I suspect she still missed a few deductions last year).

Along with my novels, I've published short stories, essays, comic books, and a few poems. Some of my books have won awards, critics have said kind things about them, and every now and then I get a letter from someone who tells me that one of my books made a difference in their life, which is, for me, the greatest accomplishment.

One thing I've learned from these experiences is that the high of achievement doesn't lead to long-lasting satisfaction or happiness. On the contrary, for years the more apparent success I had, the more I felt I needed to achieve, and the further I drifted from real happiness and success.

Don't get me wrong—I'm deeply grateful for all that I've experienced. But the more I chased after what I *thought* was success, the more frustrated and exhausted I became.

I kept up with my achievement addiction for twenty-five years, constantly struggling to achieve "enough" to feel satisfied. Even though I knew I was fortunate and should have felt happy, anxiety and depression consumed me. Until, after decades of doing everything society told me to do to be successful and happy, I hit rock bottom and couldn't continue.

Then I got lucky. During a nasty breakdown (more on that later), I finally heard the message all my suffering and perceived failures had been trying to tell me. I finally understood what I'd spent most of my life missing. Breakdown then became breakthrough, and what I learned radically improved my life and my approach to creativity.

That's what led to me writing this book—not my achievements, but what I discovered when I failed again and again until I fell apart. The transformation that I eventually experienced, and the changes in awareness that accompanied it, have made my life significantly more fulfilling, enjoyable, and creatively vibrant.

Many of the concepts in this book are supported both by current research and philosophical and spiritual traditions that go back thousands of years. Nevertheless, they're counterintuitive secrets. "Counterintuitive" because they run counter to how our ego-driven society often encourages us to perceive things. And "secrets" because even though these concepts aren't hidden, most people haven't noticed or truly grasped what they are. Some of these counterintuitive secrets are things I knew about for years but didn't comprehend. I only thought I understood them, which was part of the problem. From what I've seen, few people are fully aware of these counterintuitive secrets, and even fewer have applied them to the creative process.

As a result, many of the writers, artists, and creators I've met are seeking success in a way that's limiting their potential and causing them to suffer. I recognize this because I did it for decades. It doesn't have to be this way.

You might feel that the approach you're currently taking to create things is the only option. It might even seem good enough for now. But if you could make your creative practice even a little more effective, fulfilling, and enjoyable, wouldn't it be worthwhile to do so?

The call to create is a potent gift. It's about far more than writing stories, drawing pictures, or finding ways to express yourself. To bring something new and significant into existence requires connecting with the creative source where new things come from. When we do that, we open our minds to much bigger discoveries while expanding our conscious enjoyment of life. Unfortunately, we're often blocked from effectively engaging creativity's transformative power and unlocking our full creative potential.

To understand why this is, it helps to examine how creativity is commonly presented in our society, starting with success stories and some of the ways they lead us astray.

The First Problem with Success Stories: They Focus on the Wrong Things

Often, when we hear creative "success stories," such stories focus on people who've sold millions of books, made famous paintings, won Oscars, directed blockbuster movies, or composed Grammy-winning albums. There's nothing inherently bad about commercial success. The trouble is, if you only hear commercially successful people talk about their journeys, or if the commercial success story becomes the dominant narrative about the creative path that you carry with you, this can distort your sense of what the creative path entails and how to establish a healthy, sustainable relationship with creativity.

In the writing world, for instance, best-selling authors (or even authors who earn a modest living entirely through their creative writing) are extremely rare.[1] They're the black swans and the white squirrels of the forest. If you approach writing poetry, fiction, and creative-nonfiction with the belief that significant financial rewards are the norm, you're most likely going to be disappointed. Worse, for reasons we'll explore in the next chapter, you're going to make realizing your own unique creative potential more difficult.

That said, the best way to succeed is to keep creating. Which is why it can be problematic to only hear commercially successful people talk about their creative journeys. Usually in such "success stories" the most important part of the story is something that the teller, by the very nature of their success, is unqualified to address: **how to keep going when success doesn't come**.

Not only are commercially successful people often not well-equipped to give fellow creators insights into how to persevere in the absence of success, because "success sells," people are encouraged to emphasize their own "success myth." It's a potent feedback loop for those who can use it: be successful, or be born with wealth, fame, and advantages most folks don't have, then talk about how you "gained" success and your success will grow.

The unfortunate result of such success feedback loops is that stories that focus on creative struggles, doubts, and failures are frequently discouraged or ignored. However, there's great value in hearing about other creator's experiences with struggle, doubt, and failure. Such honest stories, that risk vulnerability, can help us feel less alone when we encounter similar challenges, and learning about how others dealt with setbacks can help us gain crucial insights into how to overcome our own difficulties. Researchers have even shown that failure is essential for

---

[1] This doesn't mean it's impossible to make a living as a writer. Almost every business needs good writers, and there are countless ways to turn writing skills into a career if you approach it creatively.

productive learning to take place, and that experiences of failure generally result in more growth and learning than experiences of success (more on this in Part II).

Of course, one can also learn from success. But when success myths become our primary guide, we're left with a distorted, and often misleading sense of the creative path.

Here's an example of one commonly espoused success myth. When I was first trying to publish a novel, I spent years working on several books that weren't very good. *I didn't even want to read them, not to mention send them off for others to read.* After many years of writing books that I felt weren't good enough, I became deeply discouraged. So, I looked to new authors for inspiration. But every time I found a book written by a debut author, it said the same thing on the book jacket: "This is their first book."

First book? I thought. *I've written multiple drafts of three different novels, and they're all terrible. What made me think I could ever be a writer?*

What I didn't know then (what the feedback loop of success kept me from seeing) was that "first book" didn't mean it was the first book they'd written. It meant it was the first book they'd gotten published. There's a big difference.

It wasn't until a friend of mine, who at that time had written several best-selling novels, confessed to me that she'd written **seven practice novels** before she ever got one published, that I realized writing practice novels was a normal part of the publishing journey.

This seems obvious to me now, but the success stories I'd heard (and the book jackets I'd read) never mentioned writing "practice novels." As a result, I not only didn't know that writing "practice novels" was normal, I overlooked the benefits of creating practice novels. I'd only seen my three attempted novels as failures, rather than valuable learning experiences.

A novel is an incredibly complex creation. It takes many years to learn how to plot, pace, and develop multiple character arcs while holding a reader's interest for 300+ pages. True, some folks get lucky and manage to do this on their first try, but they're the exceptions, and having an early success like that might not even be a good thing. It's often much easier to develop your skills and explore your artistic identity *before* stepping into the public spotlight.

Since my friend's confession, I started asking other published authors how many "practice novels" they wrote before they got one published. Some authors will only admit this in private (perhaps because they don't want to undermine their own "success myth"), but the record so far is thirty books.

You read that right—one extremely popular best-selling author I spoke with says she wrote **thirty** practice novels before she ever got one published.

Of course, this says nothing of the practice novels most authors write *after* they get published, because there's nothing about getting published that ensures every book you write afterwards will be great or marketable. **If you want to keep learning, keep growing, and keep creating new things, then you need to be willing to risk failure and embrace your failures.** The problem is, when we're surrounded by success stories that aren't giving us the full picture, seeing failure as a normal and useful part of the process becomes extremely hard to do.

Problem Two: Success Stories Can Cause Us to Focus on the Wrong Things

Whether we're aware of it or not, we frequently internalize the unspoken message of success stories—a message that centers around **extrinsic rewards** (the millions of books sold, movies made, money gained, awards won, etc.). When we're surrounded by such stories, it's natural to want to achieve similar rewards. But the hard reality is that such rewards are few and far between. Inevitably, those who create primarily for extrinsic reasons end up disappointed and struggle to keep going.

It's far more effective and sustainable to engage creativity for **intrinsic reasons** (growth, enjoyment, the bliss of connecting with creativity, increasing awareness, etc.), yet few success stories encourage us to do this. Over the long run, engaging creativity for deeper, intrinsic reasons is not only more gratifying, it's a more effective way to turn your passion into a viable career.

To see why this is, imagine a fruit tree. The typical success story focuses on branches that are full of fruit. The fruits in this case are what success stories depict as the sweet rewards of a creative endeavor—the fame, fortune, or other remarkable achievements. Success stories often work backwards from such achievements to describe how the fruits started out as small buds that developed into blossoms that soon grew into the delightful fruits we know and love. Amazing!

Inspired, or maybe envious, folks who hear such stories might think, "If I do what they did, I'll be successful." Initially, such thinking might seem like inspiration. The success story is giving you hope and a possible path forward. But as you walk this path, more comparisons often sneak up on you ("If they did this, I need to do it too").

Perhaps in the business world, where success stories are also frequently touted, there are tried-and-true steps that make following the paths of successful people an okay bet, but writing isn't like that. Art isn't like that. Creating something new and significant rarely happens by imitating others.

The more you attempt to do what the person in the success story did, the more likely you are to focus on *their* path rather than *your* path. Focusing on what they did might cause you to stray from discovering what only you can do—and for creative endeavors, discovering what only you can do is essential.

To return to the fruit tree analogy, it's akin to trying to coax your branches into giving you the exact same fruit as someone else's tree. Frustrated, you might even cut off the branches and bring them inside so you can obsessively tend the buds while eagerly waiting for fruits to emerge. But cut branches soon die, and those who focus solely on getting fruit from a bud seldom succeed.

The way to get a tree to produce fruit is to nurture the roots. It's what happens underground, in the dark, loamy soil, that determines what fruits will eventually appear. Not only that, your tree is likely a different kind of tree from the ones you're comparing it to. It produces different fruits and has different needs.

Comparing your tree to someone else's makes it easy to miss seeing your tree's potential and what it needs to flourish. That's one of the wicked ways success stories get us tangled up in creativity-crushing knots. Unfortunately, this gets worse the more successful people you know, and the more you play the comparison game.

The Comparison Game Will Crush You (It Nearly Destroyed Me)

Sooner or later, the comparison game will find you. Every professional writer I know has struggled with some version of it. It might start off in small, seemingly benevolent ways, such as taking inspiration from someone else's achievements ("If they can do it, I can do it!"). But it soon develops into something more serious and creatively damaging ("Why them and not me? What's wrong with me?").

I've met extremely popular writers who make themselves miserable by comparing themselves to writers who've won prestigious awards. The comparison game torments them with thoughts like: "If they're winning awards, why aren't I? What am I doing wrong?"

The funny thing is, I also know award-winning writers who torment themselves with the opposite comparison: "If her books are best sellers, why aren't mine? What am I doing wrong?"

Not only does the comparison game often engender feelings

of inadequacy, when a bad case develops it can cause you to unconsciously (or even consciously) abandon your artistic vision to chase after what you think you "should" be doing based on who you're comparing yourself to. And when you're trying to bring something new and significant into the world, abandoning your artistic vision is disastrous.

Here's how the comparison game entered my life and began to lead me astray. When I was eighteen, I bought a used first edition copy of David Foster Wallace's short story collection, *Girl with Curious Hair.*

I loved this book and found it profoundly inspiring. It was around this time that I decided to pursue being a writer despite the fact that I was dyslexic and struggled with writing. (I've always been drawn to difficult challenges, from kayaking class V rapids, to doing a record number of pullups, to spending one very long, cold night in ninth grade stealthily transporting all the glowing Christmas yard decorations from every yard in my neighborhood to one yard for an epic Christmas scene. Sorry neighbors—I was young and bored.)

I learned many things from DFW's writing. Emulating his prose taught me about dialogue, character development, and engaging a reader. When I learned that DFW had published his first book at the age of twenty-five, I decided to emulate him there as well. I made it my goal to publish my first book by twenty-five. Otherwise, I figured I wasn't cut out to be a writer.

I didn't mind playing the comparison game then. I thought it was a good way to spur myself on. However, when I turned twenty-five and still hadn't published enough stories (or even written enough stories that I liked) to get a book deal, I felt like a failure and a phony. I questioned what I'd been doing for the last seven years.

I kept writing because it was the one thing that truly satisfied me, and because I'd already defined myself as a writer, but deep down the sense that I was an imposter persisted. The joy I'd once gotten from writing gave way to a constant struggle to prove that what I was doing was worthwhile. Or more accurately, that *I* was worthwhile.

I knew, even then, that I didn't want to write DFW's stories. I wanted to write different stories. Still, I held myself back and tormented myself for years by playing the comparison game.

I also played the comparison game with Hemingway (who published *In Our Time* when he was twenty-six), Zora Neale Hurston (who wrote *Their Eyes Were Watching God,* one of my favorite novels, in just seven weeks), and Stephen King (who wrote so voraciously that he took on a pen name so he could publish more than one book a year).

Obviously, comparing yourself to some of the most critically praised and commercially successful writers of all time is an idiotic thing to do. It's a rookie mistake. As I became more experienced and skillful as a writer, I also became more skillful at playing the comparison game, and the new versions I played were even more pernicious.

One common version of the comparison game is something one of my friends calls the "if onlys," as in: "If only I could write a best seller like my friend did…" or "If only I could get a movie deal like that person did…" or "If only I could win a National Book Award…"

The second half of these "if only" statements (which is rarely spoken aloud because doing so might reveal how ridiculous such statements are) goes something like this, "…then I'll be happy/fulfilled/able to relax and enjoy my life."

Case in point: for years I thought, "if only I could get a book published by a major publisher, then I'll be happy."

Imagine my surprise when my first book came out with Scholastic Press and it didn't bring me the happiness I sought. Sure, I celebrated (for about five minutes), then more "if onlys" barreled in to replace the one I'd achieved.

"If only I could get a second novel published…"

"If only I could win this award…"

"If only one of my books would sell a million copies…"

There is no end to the "if onlys" your mind will come up with. It's like the mythical Hydra of Lerna that Hercules fought—cut off one head and two more grow back. Nearly every professional writer I know is plagued by "if onlys." Think of the most famous writers or artists you can, and I bet they still have "if onlys."

The trouble is, **when you stake your happiness on achieving "if onlys," the happiness you seek will perpetually be out of reach**. Instead of focusing on what you can control (being happy), you're making your happiness contingent on something that's largely beyond your control (achieving "if onlys"). Even if you get lucky and achieve an "if only," you'll immediately come up with others, so the happiness you experience will be fleeting at best. Motivating yourself by depriving yourself of happiness means that most of the time you're unhappy, and it becomes increasingly difficult to keep creating when you aren't enjoying what you're doing.

Getting my first book published didn't make me happy. Neither did getting my second, third, or fourth novels published, or publishing comic books, or getting audio books made of my novels, or winning awards. Although each of these achievements had once seemed like a golden finish line, none of them led to the breakthrough success and happiness I'd been seeking. Instead, they each spawned new hurdles and anxieties (Would my new book sell enough? Would my publisher drop me?). With every book I published, both my fears and my "if onlys" increased.

I was proud of what I'd achieved, but pride isn't very useful, and it can even be harmful (there's a reason why Greek gods punished those with hubris, or excessive pride). I took very little pleasure from what I'd accomplished, and I certainly didn't feel successful. Instead, I'd gotten stuck in an addictive cycle of achievement.

To make matters worse, I'd started to play a much more damaging version of the comparison game—comparing myself to people I knew personally (because, by this point, I knew several extremely accomplished writers).

Psychologically speaking, the more perceived similarities we have with a person, the more powerful comparisons to them become. We might not compare our earnings to Warren Buffet's (unless we go golfing with him every Sunday and also manage a hedge fund), but we probably do compare our earnings to people we work with every day whom we see as our peers. Hence, Warren Buffet making hundreds of millions more than us isn't likely to bother us nearly as much as a co-worker making millions more than us for doing similar work.

The more writers I knew who appeared successful, the worse I started to feel about myself.

Not surprisingly, I also knew plenty of writers who were struggling to get published, but I rarely (if ever) compared myself to them. And I rarely considered how unhappy some of the highly successful writers I knew were. Since comparing was a habit I'd developed to spur myself on, I always compared myself to people who'd achieved what I thought I needed to achieve, and I only focused on the success I believed they had.

Early in my writing career, I sensed that the comparison game was poison. I even gave a couple keynote speeches about avoiding it. But I couldn't stop playing it. I kept finding new writers to compare myself to and new "if onlys" to torment myself with. There is no end to the comparison game.

Instead of giving me motivation and inspiration, playing the comparison game was wearing me down. Worse, I wasn't enjoying writing much anymore. Every project I began brought with it an undertow of dread since I knew the hope I felt at the beginning would eventually turn to disappointment, frustration, and heartbreak.

Fortunately, there's a way to beat the comparison game and step out of this creativity-crushing cycle, but it's not what you might think. It wasn't at all what I thought it would be, and finding this solution led to far greater changes than I'd anticipated.

It turns out the comparison game is connected to a much bigger problem. And it's a problem that people have grappled with for thousands of years.

The Comparison Game is Bigger Than You Think

Maybe the way I described the comparison game and "if onlys" sounded familiar to you. Or maybe the comparison game has manifested differently in your life. Still, I'm betting you've experienced the comparison game in some form because there are powerful biological and social reasons for why we constantly compare ourselves to others and torment ourselves with "if onlys." Researchers have even called this human proclivity for comparing ourselves to others "fundamental" and "ubiquitous."

Our brains evolved to help us survive, not to make us happy. For much of our history as a species, our survival depended on being part of a group. Those who were kicked out of the group didn't last long on their own.

According to many social comparison theorists (yes, there's a whole area of psychology dedicated to this), in order to improve our chances of staying in a group, we developed mechanisms to constantly compare ourselves to others to ensure that our place in the group is secure. If someone seems to be contributing more than us (killing more deer, gathering more nuts, earning more praise from the leaders) we instinctively feel threatened. We might fear losing our status or being seen as a burden and getting kicked out of the group.

For thousands of years these comparison mechanisms served us fairly well because our groups were relatively small. In a small group, it's easier to secure your place and become a valued member. But now our groups (or what we might see as our groups in this digitally connected world) are spread out, fragmented, and larger than they've ever been. We have millions of people to constantly compare ourselves to. And, thanks to social media, TV, and the internet, we regularly hear about the most successful members of our massive groups. In such a situation, it's easy for people to feel like they don't stack up and aren't needed. It makes sense that many of us fear we're not good enough, aren't doing enough, and aren't valued.

That's where the "if onlys" come in. On a survival level, the "if only" impulse is there to keep us doing more and getting more so that we can prove to the group that we're useful and improve our chances of survival. Spurring ourselves on with "if onlys" makes sense when surviving is the main concern. However, in our large, fragmented, digital-age society, our primal brains go haywire because there's no way to ever do or get enough. Someone will always get more "likes" than us, and there will always be more "if onlys."

These instincts to compare ourselves to others and to want to accomplish more are further amplified by a consumer culture that's learned to capitalize on such impulses to get us to buy more stuff. The message that we must "get more" to be successful surrounds us all the time, as does the message that we're not good enough as we are. People who feel miserable make great consumers because the solution to our misery can be pitched as something we need to buy, and success is always on the horizon, just a few purchases away.

All too often, our desire for success, especially "success" as our consumer culture encourages us to see it, causes us suffering. Which is why it's important to consider what success actually is.

The Trouble with Chasing Success: A Brief Word from Monet

Toward the end of his life, Monet wrote in a letter to a friend, "My whole life has been nothing but a failure."

Think about this: Monet is one of the most famous and influential painters of all time, achieving both critical *and* financial success during his lifetime. He pioneered impressionism and inspired countless artists, writers, and thinkers. He stayed creative throughout a long life (many of his famous water lily paintings were done when he was in his 70's and 80's), and he gave rise to several new artistic movements. By almost any measure, Monet was incredibly successful. Few people have ever accomplished more or had as profound and lasting of an impact. And yet, Monet felt like a failure. So, what does that mean for the rest of us?

On the one hand, if Monet succeeded in numerous ways and still felt like "nothing but a failure," then maybe success isn't the antidote to failure that people might think it is.

On the other hand, failure might not be what we think it is, either. Instead of seeing failure as something to avoid, perhaps failure is an essential part of the creative process. I admire Monet for being able to admit that he felt like a failure—it's a sign that, despite his many successes, he remained humble. Such humility probably helped him stay highly creative.

It would be nice if we could ask Monet what he meant by "failure," but it's over 90 years too late for that. Nevertheless, Monet's statement about seeing his *whole life* as "nothing but a failure" suggests that **accomplishments, no matter how significant, don't result in a lasting feeling of success.**

The Question My Wife Asked Me That Caused Me to See How Irrational Chasing Success Is

I used to trouble myself with thoughts that I wasn't successful enough. I'd tell myself that my books weren't selling enough, I wasn't earning enough, making a big enough difference in the world, or achieving success in the ways I'd learned to think of it. This bothered me constantly. Maybe you've experienced similar worries. For me, it was a weight I carried around, until one day my wife asked me, "Why do you worry so much about being successful?"

Several reasons immediately came to mind. Popularity. Influence. Proving myself. But all of these seemed shallow, silly concerns when I examined them. I knew they wouldn't make me happy.

The most important reason I could come up with was that I thought the financial rewards of commercial success would allow me to have more time to write and be creative. But the more I examined this reason, the more flimsy it seemed.

Some of the most prolific artists and writers in history lived modestly. Van Gogh owned few possessions, lived in small apartments most of his life, and barely had two guilders to scrape together. Yet he created over 2,000 works. Many other writers, artists, and musicians had their most creative periods *before* achieving any sort of significant commercial success.

Not only that, there are numerous writers, artists, and musicians whose creative output plummeted *after* achieving commercial success. Fame brings with it many distractions. From a strictly productive perspective, commercial success certainly isn't a prerequisite for being highly creative, and it can even be a detriment.

Of course, it's hard to create when your basic needs aren't met, or when you have to work fourteen-hour days to keep a roof over your head. But beyond having food, shelter, and security, being creative isn't dependent on large amounts of money.[2]

Van Gogh received a stipend from his brother that kept him from being homeless. Since paints were expensive during his lifetime, he spent most of this money on art supplies and barely had enough left over for food. Fortunately, these days the tools needed to paint or write are much more affordable.

In addition, even though I wanted more time to write, I had to admit that there were benefits to having a day job. The need to earn a steady income forced me to leave the house and talk with other humans, which was something I didn't do when I had days off to write.

The more I thought about it, the more I realized that the real

---

[2] To be clear, I'm not saying that artists, writers, and creators don't deserve payment for their creative work, or that, as a society, we shouldn't do more to support creators (especially new creators). My point is that thinking that commercial success is necessary to keep creating is one way people hold themselves back.

reason I wanted commercial success—the reason that kept me up at night with anxiety about not doing enough to make my books successful—was that I was afraid of not being able to write more books.

When I told my wife this, she cocked her head and replied, "You don't need to be successful to do that. You do that already."

Imagine that. My big fear was that someone or something would stop me from doing what I was already doing and had always done. Since as far back as I could remember, I'd made up stories. When the stories filled my head, I'd written them down. For decades no one paid me to make up stories or write them down. Nevertheless, I'd enjoyed writing and creating things just as much then as I do now.

If you write, you're a writer. If you create things, you're a creator. What difference does it make if ten people see your work or ten thousand? The process of creating, discovering, and sharing is the same.

True—I worried that if my books weren't commercially successful enough, big publishers wouldn't want to publish me anymore. But there are other ways to share one's work, and publishing with big houses had never been all that enjoyable. It was the part of the process that filled me with the most anxiety and led to the biggest distractions.

The more I thought about it, the clearer it became that what I'd sought from publishing was approval. I wanted a big plaque that said I was a "real" writer.

How ridiculous is this? Would we call Van Gogh less of an artist because he only sold one painting during his lifetime and never had a successful show or exhibition of his work? It deserves repeating: if you write, you're a writer. If you paint, you're a painter. If you act, you're an actor. If you sculpt, you're a sculptor. Fill in the blank with whatever your creative passion is—be it street magic, haunted house building, making videos, or performance art. **If you create, you're a creator.**

I was afraid of losing something that was fundamental to my being. I'd always created stories because of who I was. Even if I were imprisoned, I probably would have made up stories. And if I had pen and paper, I would have written those stories down or scrawled them onto the walls of my cell. I wrote and created because it was what I was called to do. If I stopped, it wouldn't be because a book wasn't successful enough. It would be because I felt called to do something else.

By staking my ability to continue doing what I wanted to do on a sense of success that was beyond my control, I'd created my own torment. As Hamlet lamented, "I could be bounded in a nutshell and count myself a king of infinite space, were it not that I have bad dreams."

I was causing my own bad dreams, and I could change them. It started with changing how I saw success.

What is Success Anyway?

I know what you're thinking: here's where I redefine success and call it a day.

Yes and no.

Is success achieving wealth, fame, or even just a bit of recognition? For many of us the answer is "Hell yes!" To avoid confusion, let's refer to this as "commercial success."

Most of us want some form of commercial success because, deep down, we believe it will make us happy. We might believe that selling a bunch of books, becoming popular, having more influence, winning awards, making heaps of money, or simply having our work get praised and acknowledged is what we need to live a great life. Oddly enough, we'll chase after this notion of success even in the face of considerable evidence that it won't bring us lasting happiness at all.

It's no secret that many commercially successful people aren't very happy. We could compile a long list of famous writers, artists, actors, musicians, and others who, at the apparent peak of their commercial success, succumbed to depression, drug-addiction, or suicide.

Every time this happens, people question why. It goes against our core belief about commercial success. If achieving wealth, fame, influence, and recognition are what we're supposed to want to be happy, then how could extremely successful people be so miserable that they destroy themselves?

The reason for this is fairly simple: **commercial success and happiness are entirely different things. Chasing after one doesn't bring you any closer to the other**.

Imagine how disappointed you'd feel if you sacrificed twenty, thirty, or forty years of your life chasing after commercial success thinking it will make you happy, only to achieve it and discover that you're even less happy *after* attaining such success than you were when you first began your quest.

Rationally, it's not hard to accept that fame and fortune don't bring lasting happiness. Neuroscientist Richard Davidson has even shown with brain scans that some of the happiest people—including the "world's happiest man" ever recorded—are Buddhist monks who live modestly and own almost nothing (seeking the opposite of fame and fortune).

Nonetheless, the myth that commercial success brings happiness continues to call out with its siren's song. And this myth is further reinforced by a consumer culture that holds up rich, famous, commercially successful people (instead of genuinely happy, aware, compassionate people) as the ones to admire. We're surrounded daily by messages urging us to chase after more money, things, followers, fame, and greater achievements to attain happiness. Despite the cognitive dissonance this creates, people keep seeking aspects of commercial success, believing that if they can only achieve the next thing, they'll feel satisfied.

Essentially, it's an addiction. Chasing after such shallow, external notions of success might bring us short-term pleasure when we achieve something and are rewarded. But, like any addiction, the high soon fades and we crash. Then we go back to what gave us pleasure before, trying to achieve more "if onlys," even though it gets harder to reach them, and the highs become less enjoyable. After a while, we might realize that commercial success won't bring us lasting happiness. Still, we keep chasing after it because it's what we've learned to do.[3]

The myth that commercial success brings happiness is so pervasive, so thoroughly reinforced by our culture, and so deeply programmed into us from a young age that it's almost impossible to dispel. Which is why, rather than struggling against it, we might want to alter how we think about success so that it serves us better.

For starters, let's make "success" into something healthy and attainable.

---

[3] Even well-meaning friends and family members can reinforce toxic success myths. For example, several writers I know have had family members say to them variations of, "When are you going to write a best seller?" Although such comments might be said with the intent of being supportive, the underlying message is that, for a creative practice to have value, it must result in commercial success.

A Better Notion of Success

You most likely already have goals that you're trying to achieve, and this can be good. Goals point you in a direction and help you be more focused and effective. However, judging yourself by whether you achieve your goals (especially if your goals are ambitious) can be counterproductive.

There's a simple equation for why this is so: The greater the goal, the harder it is to reach, and the bigger the next goal will need to be to have the same payoff. Even if you achieve a goal, you probably won't feel successful for long. You'll just come up with new goals because that's the way you've learned to go through life. As was discussed, when you stake your sense of success and happiness on achieving goals, lasting success and happiness will remain perpetually out of reach.

You can motivate yourself this way, but it's not much fun and it's easy to burn yourself out. This is especially true for creative endeavors, because it's hard to stay highly creative and productive for long when you're constantly dissatisfied. Eventually, like Monet, you might end up feeling like your whole life is "nothing but a failure."

Instead of constantly chasing after goals to be happy, recognize goals for what they are: **tools that are useful for direction, but not for self-judgment. They're coordinates to set off in, not destinations**.

What does success look like then, if not achieving goals or attaining fame, fortune, and recognition?

Here's a good working definition: **Success is being happy on the deepest, most fulfilling level you can conceive of.**

Notice what that definition does?

Since people frequently get led astray by chasing after success only to find it doesn't make them happy, redefining success as *being happy on the deepest, most fulfilling level you can conceive of* will help you chart a better course for your life. Every time you start thinking about how you want to be more successful, remind yourself that real success is *being happy*—and not just shallow, temporary, reactive happiness, but deep, fulfilling, lasting happiness.[4]

Maybe what makes you deeply happy and fulfilled is creating things (that's the case for many writers and artists). If this describes you, then you might want to add this to your definition of success: **Creative success is doing what you love and loving what you do.**

That's the sort of success this book is primarily concerned with. For most of us, it's a better notion of success to seek than fame, fortune, or recognition. After all, would you rather be rich

---

[4] I used to think of happiness as a superficial, unimportant pursuit. I'd tell myself that it was better to live a "good" life than to be happy. What I didn't realize was that the reason *why* I wanted to live a "good" life and contribute to the world in positive ways was because it made me feel happy to do so. Essentially, I was driven by a desire for happiness, even while I eschewed happiness. Absurd, right? If you consider your motivations deeply enough, I bet you'll find that the reason why you do almost anything is because deep down you think it will make you happy.

and famous but miserable, or deeply happy doing what you love and loving what you do?

If you want to look at this a different way, the change in how you define success that I'm suggesting shifts your focus from **conditional happiness** ("I'll be happy *when*... I get a book published, make a bunch of money, finish this project, get a movie deal...") to **unconditional happiness** ("I'm happy *being*").

Conditional happiness is the way many of us learn to motivate ourselves, thinking that if we allow ourselves to be unconditionally happy, we'll stop doing things. But this isn't true. We can be far more productive and creative when we're happy than when we're miserable and suffering. The question is, how do you shift your perspective from the conditional happiness approach that's widely reinforced, to unconditional happiness? We'll explore several ways to do this in Parts II and III, but it all starts with changing how you think of success to prioritize unconditional happiness rather than constantly creating to get things.

The beautiful thing is that if you focus on doing what you love and loving what you do (unconditional happiness), you'll be far more likely to achieve other notions of success as well. Dolly Parton (someone who's managed to stay amazingly creative throughout her life with over 60 albums, 47 Grammy nominations, and dozens of film roles) effectively summed up this approach in a recent interview when she said, "I don't work for awards or rewards. I just work because I love what I do."

On the other hand, if you focus on achieving fortune and fame, chances are you'll be disappointed. Even if you do beat the odds and become rich and famous, you probably won't feel satisfied for long since there will always be others who are wealthier and more famous than you, and there will always be more "if onlys." Your happiness, and your sense of success, will remain at a distance thanks to the comparison game and the "if onlys."

Why Changing Your Notion of Success Isn't the Whole Answer

Changing your notion of success can help you chart a more effective and enjoyable course for your life, but it probably won't solve everything for you.

Take a look at that question my wife asked me again. Why did I want to be successful?

Because I feared not being able to continue creating.

But if success is being happy doing what you love and loving what you do, by that measure, I should have felt successful (or at least partly successful, since I got to write stories—doing what I loved—almost every day).

The trouble was, I didn't feel successful, and I wasn't happy. I was too addicted to the notion of success as achievement to let it go. It was a cycle of struggle, achievement, and reward that I'd learned early in life—struggling to get good grades, praise, and accolades. I couldn't shake it. Not only that, I was too addicted to playing the comparison game to give it up. It was the only way I knew to motivate myself. I feared that if I stopped, I'd be a lazy slacker. I had to keep pushing myself with more "if onlys," or I wouldn't achieve anything worthwhile. I had to constantly struggle to create more—that's what suffering artists do.

On some level I knew that such thinking was wearing me down and eroding my ability to create. Still, I kept motivating myself by making comparisons and coming up with "if onlys." The more miserable I felt, the more I returned to my addiction. After all, I knew so many writers who were doing great things. I needed to do great things, too.

The comparison game kept winning. Even after I changed my notion of success so that living a happy, fulfilling life became my priority, I couldn't stop playing the comparison game and feeling inadequate. Try harder to achieve more or give up were the only two options I saw.

But there's a third way—a way that leads to both greater creativity and greater happiness. To find this way, I first had to exhaust all the other options I could see. This took me many years. I'd like to save you some of that time and frustration.

So here it is: what doesn't work, and then what does, for beating the comparison game.

Four Common Ways to Beat the Comparison Game (and Why They Don't Work)

1) Using Positive Self-Affirmations

Over time, playing the comparison game causes us to feel lesser than others and discouraged. This is usually perceived as a lack of self-confidence. One remedy for this that's frequently espoused is to increase belief in one's self through positive affirmations. For instance, saying statements like, "I'm creative," "I'm a talented writer," "I'm a great artist," and "I will be successful" several times a day.

Why this doesn't work as a long-term solution:

Positive self-affirmations might seem like a magical fix, and at certain stages they can be useful. If you find them helpful, great! However, it's important to construct your affirmations carefully (see "Some Mantras" in Part III for tips and examples) and be aware of how affirmations can backfire.

A recent study published in *Psychological Science* found that, for people who are struggling with self-confidence, affirmations usually don't work and can even cause people to feel worse about themselves. One theory on why this happens is that subconsciously, we feel the affirmations aren't true, so we start to distrust them and ourselves.

In addition, affirmations that focus on what we want to have happen ("I will be successful") lead to unhealthy mental habits by focusing our attention on the future rather than the present, and by making our happiness contingent on certain outcomes. Often this leads to disappointment when what we tell ourselves will happen doesn't occur.

Even if you do get a boost in self-confidence from positive affirmations, this won't stop the comparison game. No matter how self-confident you feel, you'll always be able to make comparisons to people who seem better or more successful. You'll keep chasing after something that remains out of reach, and the comparison game will keep tearing you down. No amount of positive affirmations will beat it.

The main reason why statements like "I'm a talented writer" and "I'm a great artist" won't eliminate the comparison game is because they feed your ego. Although people often confuse having a big ego with self-confidence, they're actually very different things. **Having self-confidence means being aware of your potential to adapt, learn, and grow. Having a big ego, on the other hand, means fixating on how great you *think* you are.** For reasons we'll explore in coming chapters, the bigger your ego gets, the more it demands, and the more it gets in the way. Becoming ego-bound leads to becoming disconnected from others, unable to access creativity, and blocked from achieving your full potential. For creators, the demands of the ego can be immensely limiting to both creativity and happiness.

There are dozens of motivational books out there about the importance of "thinking big" and "believing in yourself." These are great qualities to have, but there are better ways to develop such qualities than repeating self-affirmations that ring untrue and lead to becoming ego bound. The way to really think big is to recognize that you're connected to something much greater than yourself—that infinite source of creativity. That's as big as you can get because you're part of creativity and the creative energy of the universe flows through you.

So, believe in yourself, but don't get trapped in yourself. You're bigger than you think.

2) Picking Your Comparisons Carefully

I used to think "if I only choose the right folks to compare myself to, I can beat the comparison game." I picked James Patterson and Harper Lee. Why these two authors?

Let's start with James Patterson. He's one of the most commercially successful authors of all time. His books have sold over 300 million copies, and he's done wonderful philanthropic work to promote literacy and help book stores. He's also a clever story teller who understands audiences and markets exceptionally well. But, let's be honest, his prose isn't very intimidating. His writing has been generously described by critics as "unfussy" and "basic" (Stephen King even called Patterson "a terrible writer" in a 2009 interview).

For years, I kept a couple James Patterson books by my writing desk. Whenever I felt like I couldn't put together a decent sentence, I cracked open one of his books to reassure myself that my sentences were fine.

The prose I found in these books was a good reminder that writing doesn't need to be fancy to be effective. Often, it's better to step out of the way and let the story unfold as clearly and directly as possible. I'm grateful to Patterson's books for helping me see past my prose paranoia.

And why Harper Lee? *To Kill a Mockingbird* is one of my favorite novels. It's also a Pulitzer-Prize winning best seller that millions of people still read and discuss. Until the recently published *Go Set a Watchman* (released less than a year before her death), it was Harper Lee's only published book.

For me, Harper Lee served as a constant reminder that quality matters more than quantity. Writing (along with other creative endeavors) isn't a race. It's easy to get caught up with how many books some writers have published, but Harper Lee shows that one book can have a more lasting impact than dozens of flash-in-the-pan novels.

Why strategically picking your comparisons doesn't work as a long-term solution:

Getting past prose paranoia and realizing that writing isn't a race are both helpful steps to take, but comparing yourself to other authors or creators (even if they're strategic comparisons) won't end the comparison game.

Instead, this only pulled me deeper into the comparison game. Inevitably, other comparisons snuck in through the door I'd opened and started to tear me down. After all, why weren't my books selling like James Patterson's? And where was my *To Kill a Mockingbird*? Essentially, this coping strategy was like an alcoholic telling himself to only drink rum and gin. You can't beat the comparison game by playing it more.

3) Comparing Fully and Widely

Often what's missing in playing the comparison game is comparing fully and widely. Instead, we cherry pick who we compare ourselves to and what aspects of their lives we focus on. For instance, we might overlook that many of the creators we admire and want to emulate suffered terribly in their lives (indeed, two of the writers I used to want to emulate, Hemingway and David Foster Wallace, died by suicide).[5] Or we might

---

[5] When DFW died, it felt like the North Star fell from my sky. He was my earliest and most significant writing inspiration (my fondness for

only look up for comparisons and fail to recognize that many people have it worse than ourselves.

To address such obvious distortions and the feelings of inadequacy that they cause, we might think that if we compare more fully and widely, we'll be able to beat the comparison game.

Why this doesn't work as a long-term solution:

Although comparing fully and widely seems a better way to play the comparison game, you're still playing the game, and still judging yourself in terms of others.

Also, since it's hard to know what it's like to be someone else, your comparisons will inevitably be incomplete and inaccurate. Not to mention that obsessively comparing yourself to others will distract you from your own artistic path.

4) Quitting Cold Turkey

Just stop playing the comparison game. Makes sense, right? If you can do this, hats off to you.

Why this doesn't work as a long-term solution:

It's funny, but the more you tell yourself not to think about something, the more you'll probably think about it. The mind is tricky this way. Forbidding yourself to play the comparison game often results in giving it more power over you. As the Zen saying goes, "**What we resist persists.**"[6]

Once you start playing the comparison game, it will keep finding you. It even found me today when I read an article writ-

---

footnotes probably comes from him). His loss left me adrift. The challenges of the creative path and the toll it can take are why I think it's vital to find healthy, joyful, sustainable ways to create—not just for ourselves, but for all those we're connected to.

[6] Psychiatrist Carl Jung also spoke about resistance, and he's sometimes given credit for this pithy phrase. The concept was around long before him.

ten by a guy who claims to write 5,000-10,000 words a day. Immediately after reading this, I compared myself to him and felt inadequate (perhaps you did, too, when you considered that 10,000 words is around 40 pages). But, after a brief moment of discomfort, the comparison left me and I found it amusing that my mind wanted to go down that path.

Rather than resisting the comparison game, accept that you're going to compare yourself to other writers or creators from time to time. That's okay. It's part of who you are, and maybe even part of the creative process.

Fortunately, there's a way to shift your perspective so when the comparison game (with its incessant "if onlys") finds you, it no longer has power over you.

How to Really Beat the Comparison Game

Start by asking yourself three questions:

1) Is there something else you feel called to do besides writing or creating things?

If the answer is "yes," then go do that other thing. Creating is flippin' hard.

But if the answer is "no," and you feel called to create, then keep creating and don't worry about whether you're as "good" as others. This is what, for whatever mysterious reasons, you're called to do. Congratulations on finding your passion and having such a wondrous calling! Now enjoy the journey and focus on loving the process as you create.

2) Are there things you want to create that currently don't exist?

If the book you want to read already exists, go read it and ask yourself this question again when you're done. Likewise, if the song you want to hear exists, go listen to it. If the painting you want to see exists, go admire it...

But if what you want to create doesn't exist, then it's up to you to bring what you're called to create into existence. That's both the burden and blessing of being called to create. There's no sense wondering if you're up to the task. You have work to do and a purpose that's calling you. Get started and focus on loving the process as you create.

3) Is someone else going to create what you want to create?
I know this is a fear that many people have, but no one will ever create exactly what you can create. Others might paint a similar scene or tell a similar story. Still, out of the nearly eight billion people in the world, **there are stories that only you can tell and things that only you can create. If you don't find ways to bring them into existence, they won't exist.** It's as simple as that.

Forget whether some critic out there might say one story is better than another. Your stories are needed. At the very least you need them (and if you need them, chances are other people need them, too). The things you can create will add to the richness of existence. Many voices make up a choir. Many instruments form an orchestra. Many colors are needed to make a painting. You get the picture. If you don't find the courage to create what you're called to create, existence will be poorer as a result. Don't waste any more energy worrying about how you compare. Instead, allow yourself to do what only you can do, and focus on loving the process as you do.

See the pattern?
The way out of the comparison game is to recognize that you create things because this is what you're called to do.

There are things you can create that only you can create. I don't know why this is who you are, or why this is what you're called to do. Just accept it and focus on loving the process.[7]

Whether you see this from a Buddhist perspective (accept what is), a Hindu perspective (live your dharma), a Christian perspective (this is God's will), a determinist perspective (a series of causes beyond your control led to you being this way), a classical perspective (this is your destiny), or some other belief structure—there's a shared wisdom here that will lead you to similar results. It's the wisdom of becoming aware of something greater than yourself and aligning yourself with it.

If you can accept that being creative is who you are and what you're called to do, you can stop struggling against the universe and learn to work with it to actualize your immense potential.[8] You can channel the creative energy of something greater than yourself and become aware of how you're more than you think you are. You can stop *worrying* about what you're doing and focus on *enjoying* what you're doing.

After all, if this is who you are and creating things is what you're called to do, don't you want to enjoy it, too?

---

[7] Calls that get ignored sometimes grow silent, leaving one to feel abandoned and alone. But creativity that gets ignored is often like a stream that's blocked from flowing. The water doesn't go away. It simply finds other, sometimes destructive directions to flow. Which is one more reason why, if you feel called to create things, it's important to heed that call.

[8] I use the term "universe" in this book because it's an open, inclusive term for the wholeness of existence, but if you want to replace this with your own notion of a greater whole or higher power (God, Allah, Brahman, Yahweh, Waheguru, Wakan Tanka, Nature, Being, Infinite Consciousness, Truth, Awareness, the Force, etc.) go for it.

Okay, But…

It's hard to stop playing the comparison game. I get it. It's a habit we form early on, and our ego relies on making comparisons. Comparing ourselves to others is how we define ourselves, and making comparisons is often what we think we need to do to motivate ourselves. Whenever the comparison game and its endless "if onlys" find you, remind yourself of these three things until they become your new mental habit:

I'm a creator—I need to create.
There are things I can create that no one else can create.
This is what I'm called to do.

It might help to post these three things on a note that you place near where you work so when doubt, anxiety, procrastination, and distraction (the four horsemen of not getting shit done) turn up, you have a quick response to give them. Then, instead of worrying about what you're doing, you can accept your creative calling and focus on loving the process.

"That sounds great," you might say. "But what does it mean to love the process? And how do I learn to do it?"

As we explore these questions, know that the more significant, transformational steps that will enable you to fully leave behind the comparison game and access greater creativity are ahead, but accepting that being creative is what you're called to do is the start of the journey. It's how you board the ship and embark.

Once you're on the journey, the next steps will make more sense. However, you can't see these steps from the shore. You need to leave the land you know to find them.

Part II

"No vision is real until it is enacted
upon the earth for the people to see."

—Black Elk

What Does it Mean to Love the Process?

To embrace every stage of the creative process because in every stage there are things to discover and learn—that's what it means to love the process. It sounds simple, but it's hard to do, and it's incredibly important.

The key to loving the process starts with recognizing what the creative process actually involves. Black Elk, the Lakota Sioux medicine man, once said, "No vision is real until it's enacted upon the earth for the people to see." Writing, along with other creative endeavors, involves enacting visions. You have a vision of something you want to exist, then you set about bringing it into existence in a form that others can see and experience. But wrestling down visions and enacting them for others to see is a tricky, counterintuitive process. As you write the story, the story changes. "No vision is real" means that it's not real for the reader *or* the writer—not until it's all there on the page.

You might think you know what your vision is about, just as you might think you know what will happen in a story you're starting to write. However, it's not until you fully portray the story on the page for others to see that you actually know it. And even then, once the vision is enacted for others to see, you probably don't understand it—not fully. In this way, creating things is a lot like traveling to a new place. Although you can envision how to get to a place from looking at a map, the map is not the journey. You don't know what you'll encounter on the way, who you'll meet, what will happen, where you'll end up, or how the journey will impact you until you experience it.

Likewise, when writing fiction, you might envision what a story will be before writing it, but often the story and characters will change as you write the story and discover who your characters actually are, what the story is really about, and how it needs to be told. Along the way, you discover problems to be worked out, new insights, and unexpected images, details, and lines that surprise you. Hence, the creative process is a journey of discovery and learning.

Such learning can take place at any stage of the journey. A beginner can learn as much as an expert. A wise expert knows there's still much to learn. The beginning of a journey can teach you as much as the end of it. The only true end of a journey is when the learning stops. First drafts, revisions, final drafts, rejections, doubts, failures, re-writes, hopes, frustrations, accomplishments—they're all important parts of the journey.

To love the process means that you see every step in the journey—regardless of whether it's easy or difficult, pleasurable or painful—as something to appreciate and learn from.

Loving the process doesn't just lead to greater satisfaction with what you're doing, it's critical to establishing a healthy and sustainable relationship with creativity. Ultimately, loving the process can radically transform your life (more on this in Part

III). It's how you step out of your own way and stop holding yourself back.

Creators who've learned to love the *whole* process are extremely rare. They persevere in a seemingly effortless, blissful way by embracing every challenge and gaining the most from each experience. Like jujitsu masters, they turn failure, rejection, and doubt into experiences that enrich their art and further their growth. Rather than getting weighed down by frustrations and fears, they channel the energy of resistance into greater awareness and openness, allowing creativity to flow through them more effectively.

All this might sound "out there" (it would have sounded that way to me once), but loving the process isn't some idealistic, unreachable goal. In coming chapters we'll explore several practical, concrete steps you can take to profoundly shift your relationship with creativity and learn to love the process.

For now, all you need to accept is that learning to love the process is how you actualize your creative potential. You won't get there by rejecting or resisting parts of the process. Reaching a place where you're able to love the whole process genuinely and consistently takes work. And it's work that your ego doesn't want you to do.

Your Ego is Holding You Back

Wait, what? Can't having a big ego be a good thing? Don't many highly successful people have big egos? Isn't that what gives them the courage to boldly create new things?

Having a big ego might seem like an asset in the short term as it fills you with confidence and a sense of superiority, but it's a false confidence (or worse, arrogance). Eventually, an inflated ego will get in the way and hold you back.[9]

---

[9] Remember, self-confidence is different from having a big ego. To understand the difference, consider how people with big egos project an illusion of confidence while constantly needing praise because they lack real self-confidence and are actually insecure. Confident people don't need external validation, can admit when they're wrong, don't feel threatened by others, and frequently help others thrive and succeed. Conversely, people with big egos constantly need to be praised, always claim they're right, feel threatened by others, and frequently put others down to protect their illusory sense of being "the best."

We'll dig into what exactly I mean by "ego" in the next section. In general, though, the ego is the part of your psyche that swells when you feel proud ("Look how great I am!") and it makes you suffer when you don't live up to your expectations. That may seem like an okay trade off at first, but the ego always wants to be fed, and it's insatiable. The more you feed your ego, the more it wants to eat. **No one's ego ever gets satisfied through accomplishments**. This is one of the reasons why many highly accomplished people are unhappy—when you reach the top and find that your ego still isn't satisfied (it's only grown bigger and hungrier) then what? You're left feeling isolated and miserable with nowhere left to go.

For artists, a big ego can be particularly vexing because the more you're beholden to your ego, addicted to praise and validation, the harder it becomes to take artistic risks. It's a common story. Think of all those writers, artists, and musicians who did their best work *before* they gained popularity and became servants to their egos.

Of course, not all famous artists become ego bound. Consider some of the extremely successful creators who've managed to continue creating new work long after becoming famous. In such artists, you'll find a fundamental creative humility that allows them to transcend their egos and stay open to new discoveries. Pablo Picasso, for instance, once said that he'd spent a lifetime learning to "paint like a child."

Or consider Paul McCartney, one of the most successful and prolific musicians of the last century. In a 2016 NPR interview for *All Songs Considered* he expressed the sort of creative humility I'm referring to when he said of songwriting, "I don't know how to do this. You would think I do, but it's not one of those things you ever know how to do."[10]

---

[10] I'm not claiming that Picasso and McCartney were humble saints. It's possible to dissolve the ego's limiting influence in one area only to build it up in others. In regards to creativity, though, they both demonstrated creative humility. Nothing shuts one off

The ego likes to control things, and it likes to claim it's an expert that knows what it's doing. Notice how learning to "paint like a child" and approaching song-writing from the perspective of "I don't know how to do this" represent the opposite of such thinking? It's no wonder that Picasso and McCartney were not only able to stay highly creative, they each explored a wide variety of subjects, styles, and artistic disciplines throughout their careers.

On the other hand, artists who become servants to the praise their egos demand often struggle to create new work. Instead, they imitate their earlier work, chasing after what fed their egos in the past. Although this might appease the ego for a short while, they'll eventually become ego-bound—stuck in very limited notions of who they think they are.

New things can only be discovered and created by escaping the limiting grasp of the ego.

---

from discovering new possibilities more than claiming "I know exactly what I'm doing."

What is the Ego Anyway?

The collection of thoughts, memories, beliefs, emotions, and reactive patterns that you identify with and often *think* is who you are—that's your ego.[11]

If this seems a bit broad and abstract, let's break it down.

The word "ego" comes from the Latin word for "I." Freud wrote about the ego (or "das Ich" in German, which translates to "the I") as being the part of the psyche that mediates between the unrealistic id and the external world. According to Freud, the primal id is like the horse, and the ego is its rider. The ego is the "I" that loves to think of itself as being the decision maker—the identity in control of the self (even though, in reality, the horse and forces beyond the horse are actually in control and may or may not listen to the rider).

---

[11] If you imagine all of existence as an infinite ocean, the ego is the invisible line that you attempt to draw around a tiny, constantly shifting cluster of molecules by saying, "This is me! This is what I identify with and want to preserve and protect."

Another way to think about Freud's notion of the psyche is with *Star Trek*. (If you're not a Trekkie, bear with me—this will hopefully still be useful). Dr. McCoy is the passionate, instinctive doctor on the ship. He represents the id. The id hungers, fears, and desires, but doesn't think about how to rationally get what it wants. Then there's Spock, the superego, who serves as the moral conscience working to keep the reactive, emotional id in check (think of all the times Spock criticized Dr. McCoy for being "illogical"). And then there's Captain Kirk, who represents the ego, because the ego loves to see itself as the decision maker—the "I" in total control of the ship. To Kirk, it's "his" ship.

Carl Jung further refined Freud's theory of the ego by describing the ego as being the notion of ourselves that we're *consciously* aware of. Although the ego is "the I" who we think we are and see ourselves as being, Jung pointed out that the ego "knows only its own contents" and not the unconscious or the collective unconscious. Therefore, knowing the ego is different from knowing one's self, because the self is actually far bigger than the ego.

To illustrate this with the *Star Trek* metaphor, at the very least the self is the ship, not the captain. The captain is only a small part of a ship that includes hundreds of other crew members. Although the captain often takes credit for what the ship does ("*I* made the ship go there"), it's the hundreds of other crew members who cause the ship to function the way it does (in addition to the influence of countless forces beyond the ship). These crew members are constantly doing important tasks that the captain isn't in control of and doesn't even know about.

Just as the captain is only a small part of the ship, the ego is only a small part of the self. Hence, we might consider the ego to be a limited, incomplete, false notion of the self. Or, to be more precise, **in this book I'm using the term "ego" to refer**

to the mental construct of a separate self we identify with and often *think* is who we are.[12]

Here are some qualities of the ego to further clarify what the ego is and what it does:

- The ego exists by perceiving the self as being separate from other people and other aspects of existence. It constantly manipulates the way you think to bolster this illusion of separateness.
- The ego believes it's in control, and it constantly seeks to bolster this illusion of control.
- The ego doesn't want you to see what it is, what it's doing, or how it limits you. It survives through deception (which is why recognizing the ego can be so challenging).[13]
- To perpetuate itself, the ego needs you to identify with a collection of thoughts, forms, beliefs, and emotions. It's the voice in your head chanting *I*, *me*, *my*, and *mine* statements.

---

[12] It's important to note that as a "mental construct" the ego is something we build in our minds. When we're born, we're pretty much egoless. We construct an ego by identifying with certain forms, thoughts, memories, beliefs, and emotional patterns that we perceive as our self and work to protect and perpetuate. Although this is a necessary step in consciousness development, the more rigidly attached we become to our ego, thinking that it's what we are, the more isolated and detached we become from the rest of existence.

[13] Because the ego doesn't want you to realize that it isn't your true self (it's just a tiny fragment of what you are) it makes becoming aware of the ego and its limiting influence difficult. If you're noticing resistance to the concepts in this chapter, or if discussing the ego seems boring and confusing, that's the work of your ego. Keep going. Becoming conscious of the ego and how it's limiting you is difficult, but worthwhile. Doing so will not only help you access creativity more effectively, it's the key to liberating yourself from the suffering the ego causes.

- The ego likes to take credit for all that you do and all that you create.
- The ego sometimes makes you feel big or powerful, even while it confines you to a small, limited notion of the self.
- The ego is rigidly attached to what it believes it is.
- The ego clings to what it knows and fears what it doesn't know.
- The ego, by keeping you focused on protecting the construct of a separate self that you identify with, is fundamentally selfish.
- The ego always wants you to do what it sees as being good for the ego.
- The ego believes that the self is finite, and it fears the loss of this finite self (or death).
- The ego constantly judges everyone and everything, labeling things as good or bad based on what it wants and what it fears. It defines itself through judgments and comparisons ("I'm this, not that." "This is good. That's bad.")
- The ego reacts strongly against anything it sees as threatening to itself and its self-interests. It craves praise and hates to be questioned, challenged, or criticized. When it feels attacked or diminished, it strikes back to protect and inflate itself.
- The ego's primary concern is preserving and protecting itself—that self that you identify with and *think* you are.

Take another look at that last point. See the dilemma here?

This is why your ego is holding you back. **By constantly trying to get you to fixate on preserving and protecting what you *think* you are, the ego keeps you from growing, transforming, and transcending the ego to become aware of how you're more than this small, limited, incomplete notion of yourself.**

Why the Ego Makes You Feel Bad (And Why Making it Your Enemy Won't Help)

Sometimes, when we feel bad, we think we need an ego boost, but the ego is the thing that's making us feel bad.

The ego has high expectations and it's constantly hungry. When you fail to satisfy the ego (which is almost always the case), the ego lashes out. It loves to tell you that you aren't good enough, because then you'll stay focused on yourself. And that's the ego's goal—to keep you fixated on yourself and preserving what you think you are no matter what happens.

Consider this: Whenever you get an ego boost and start thinking "I'm awesome" or "I'm the best!" what happens next?

The triumphant feeling might last a short while, but sooner or later you'll notice that someone else is doing something better than you. You'll play the comparison game, and you'll feel threatened by others. Then you might attempt to make yourself achieve more so you can reclaim that feeling of being the best. And, just like that, you're caught in an ego trap—doing everything you can to satisfy your ego.

No one can stay the best for long. The ego rush always runs out. When it does, the ego resorts to negativity. Instead of keeping you focused on yourself through pride, it keeps you focused on yourself through shame and misery.

"You suck," it might say. "You need to try harder. What's wrong with you?"

Either way, the ego wins by keeping you focused on yourself and what you think you are.

People frequently bounce back and forth between positive and negative ego-centric thinking. You can try to feed your ego through accomplishments, but when this fails to satisfy the ego's relentless appetite, your ego will switch to negative thinking. You might tell yourself that you're terrible. Your work is awful. You have no artistic ability at all.

Because we often think of people with "big egos" as being arrogant, narcissistic jerks who see themselves as superior, we might make the mistake of thinking that exhibiting the opposite characteristics—seeing one's self as being lesser, unworthy, or inferior—are ways of becoming egoless. But that's not the case. The narcissistic person and the self-loathing person are two paths to the same destination for the ego. In both cases, the ego gains power by keeping you focused on who you think you are. The more negative you feel about yourself, or the more self-critical you are, the more you'll focus on *your* inadequacies, *your* blunders, and *your* pain. Ego-centric negativity is just another way to become ego bound.[14]

---

[14] In Jungian psychology this is often referred to as ego-inflation, which can happen in both positive and negative ways. Positive inflation refers to identifying with positive archetypes (such as hero, god, or savior) that result in seeing one's self as being superior, while negative inflation refers to identifying with negative archetypes (such as scapegoat, loser, pariah, or perpetual victim)

So, what do you do? Feeding your ego makes you more ego bound, and seeing the ego as your enemy and attacking it won't free you from your ego either. The ego is part of you. The more you fight it, the more power you give it. What you resist persists.

It's probably a good thing that the ego is part of you, too. You might not be here otherwise. The ego has a very important purpose. Since its primary concern is self-preservation (the preservation of what you think you are), it constantly directs your focus to your individual needs for survival, which helps keep you alive. In a competitive system with limited resources, the ego's relentless emphasis on identifying threats and preserving itself kept your ancestors from getting eaten by a tiger, and it keeps you feeding, clothing, and caring for yourself.

The ego can, when consciously understood and tamed, serve us.[15] However, the challenge we're presented with is that the ego distorts our perception of reality to get us to serve *its* interests. In our hyper ego-driven, ego-reinforcing consumer culture, it's easy to lose perspective and think that the ego is all that we are. When this happens, we become trapped in the ego mind, incessantly working to satisfy our ego's demands. Such egos readily become overbearing masters that torment us even when our self-survival needs are met. If you're feeling anxious, isolated, fearful, frustrated, scorned, depressed, disappointed, embarrassed, unsuccessful, dismayed, inadequate, angry, or miserable, that's due to your ego. Ego-centric thinking is the root cause of most of our societal problems as well. The origin of many of our biggest problems, including war, income inequality, bigotry, and environmental destruction, can be traced back to the ego's influence (more on this in "Tyrants, Artists, and the Ego").

---

and seeing one's self as being inferior. Either way, the ego is inflated.

[15] To quote healer and counselor Jon Mcintosh, "The ego is here to serve the unfoldment of the mystery of life."

Nevertheless, the solution isn't to feed the ego *or* to fight it. Instead, acknowledge the ego as part of you—the part of your psyche that's focused on preserving and protecting what you identify with and think you are. Strive to recognize and become conscious of the ego's influence. Recognize that it will keep demanding things and clamoring for what it wants. Accept that it's doing its job, then calmly step past it.

Of course, it can be difficult to step past the ego, which is why we're going to explore techniques to reduce the ego's influence and become conscious of what's beyond the ego (especially during the creative process). The more you free yourself from the ego's limiting grasp, the more your creativity, resiliency, awareness, and happiness will increase.[16]

For writers, artists, and creators, reducing the ego's power over you means that it's crucial to be skeptical of praise that causes you to fixate on how great you are, and be wary of criticism that causes you to fixate on how terrible you are. Both are simply opinions that don't change the *reality* of who you are or what you've created. Although this might seem obvious, the ego often tries to get us to forget this, so it's worth repeating: **praise doesn't make something better and criticism doesn't make something worse**. If someone criticizes you or your work (and people are going to do this for their own ego-driven reasons—believing that the more they tear down others, the greater they'll seem), it doesn't change who you are or what you've done. Not one bit.

Both praise and criticism can keep you stuck in a limited notion of yourself. If you find yourself creating to get praise, or altering your work to avoid criticism, then your ego is strangling

---

[16] Although the ego causes much suffering, it's important not to vilify the ego. Before one can transcend the ego, one must first develop and understand the ego (developing an "I" you accept and embrace). As philosopher and author Ken Wilber put it, "'Transcending the ego' thus actually means to transcend but include the ego in a deeper and higher embrace."

your creativity. Pride and shame are two sides of the same coin, and they can both be damaging to creators.

There's a short graphic essay by author and cartoonist Lynda Barry on creativity called "Two Questions" that illustrates this last point well. In it, Barry explores how the two questions "Is this good?" and "Does this suck?" caused  her to focus on creating in order to win praise and avoid criticism. The two questions, represented in her essay as two little ghosts, promise to help Barry make "only good drawings" in exchange for a magic cephalopod that represents the wonderful "floating feeling" of creativity.

After the two questions take away the magic cephalopod of creativity, Barry feels that something is missing from her work. She chases after "only good drawings" for 30 years, but the process is no longer enjoyable ("While I drew, my main feelings were doubt and worry, and when I finished my only feelings were relief and regret.") Eventually, she reaches a place where she can't create at all.

Barry tries to find a logical way to get her creativity back, focusing on "technical ability" and "story structure," but nothing works. In one panel the little ghosts representing the two ques-

tions think that she's about to find a way to regain the magic cephalopod of creativity, so they "man the torpedoes!" to stop her. There are four torpedoes, drawn at the bottom of the page, labeled "Stupid," "Brilliant," "Moron," and "Genius"—illustrating how criticism and praise can be equally destructive.

The solution to regaining the magic cephalopod of creativity depicted in this fabulous graphic essay? "It turns out the answer was unthinkable," writes Barry in the essay. However, an answer is still hinted at in the image of the magic cephalopod on the final pages, whose body contains the words "don't know." This "don't know" suggests that the way to regain a connection with creativity (the way that seems "unthinkable" to the ego mind which always wants to know things) is to stop judging whether something is good or bad, and to simply create without knowing what something is. Then, as Barry puts it, "that strange floating feeling of being there and not being there came back. One line led to another and a story slowly formed under my hands. To be able to stand not knowing long enough to let something alive take shape! Without the two questions so much is possible. To all the kids who quit drawing… come back!"

The ego is a judgment machine, constantly striving to win

praise and avoid criticism. It's what compels you to ask the two questions "Is this good?" and "Does this suck?" At times, asking them might seem necessary and even helpful. However, the more one creates to win praise and avoid criticism, the more the ego blocks the creative process. To understand why the ego does this, let's delve deeper into what creativity itself involves.

Want to take things a step further?

Ask yourself the following questions:
- How have the two questions "Is this good?" and "Does this suck?" entered my life?
- How have they changed my creative process?
- How might I return to a state of creating without knowing (or even asking) whether something is good or bad?

Try spending fifteen minutes a day creating something without regard to whether it's good or bad. Simply let your wild mind run free. Doing this every day for a month is a wonderful way to open yourself up to greater creativity.

"To be an artist you have to give up everything, including the desire to be a good artist." —Jasper Johns

What is Creativity?

One generally accepted definition of creativity is that it's the ability to create something new and "somehow valuable"—whether it's a work of art, a way to solve a problem, an unusual idea, or even a new use for something that's existed before.

People often think of creativity as a fixed trait. How many times have you heard someone say, "I'm not very creative"? Such claims reflect a profound misunderstanding of what creativity actually is.

A growing body of research shows that, rather than being a fixed trait that you're either born with or not, creativity is a skill you can get better at. People who work on their creativity can become more creative, and these increases in creativity can be measured by creativity tests (yup, there are such things).

Psychologists frequently talk about creativity as a process that involves both divergent and convergent thinking. Divergent thinking means thinking big and coming up with many possible solutions. It's often the first step in solving a problem or developing something new. Those who are good at divergent thinking have great creative potential. However, creative potential doesn't always result in creative achievements. That's where convergent thinking comes in.

Convergent thinking involves selecting an idea or solution and taking the necessary steps to enact it. As you try to create something (or creatively solve a problem), you often switch back and forth between divergent and convergent thinking, seeing possibilities then determining which ones will be most effective and attempting to enact them. Therefore, creating new and "somehow valuable" things requires coming up with new ideas (divergent thinking) *and* selecting ones to enact (convergent thinking).

Let's take a closer look at the first part of creativity—divergent thinking. Or as it's commonly referred to, coming up with ideas. Have you ever wondered where new ideas come from? What's their source? And where do potential ideas exist?

Maybe you think that all your new ideas come from somewhere inside you. This is the way the ego likes to think about creativity, because the ego wants to take credit for everything you do ("*I* did that"). We can see this notion of creativity reinforced by some of the common ways we talk about creativity. For instance, we'll say, "I *have* an idea." Or we might be afraid that someone will "steal *my* idea."

But if we "have" ideas, where are they kept? Is there some place in our brains where all of our ideas are stored, waiting to be used? And if so—if everything we can create is already stored somewhere inside us—then does that mean we could "run out" of ideas, or that all of our ideas could be stolen?

Hopefully, you see why this ego-driven way of visualizing creativity is problematic. It leads to thinking of creativity as a fixed trait (something you have or don't have). And it puts limits on creativity that lead to creative stinginess and anxiety because you might run out of good ideas or lose them all.

One thing I'm sure of is that you'll never run out of ideas. Creativity doesn't work like that. There isn't a limit on your creativity or a chance of using up all your ideas, because new ideas don't come *from* you. They come *through* you.

To understand how this works, a better way of visualizing creativity is necessary.

What Creativity Really Is

Have you ever had an idea come to you completely unbidden when you're mowing the lawn, taking a shower, picking dog hairs off a sweater, or doing some other activity that's entirely unrelated to the idea that arrives? Perhaps you've had stories, songs, images, or the solution to problems come to you in dreams or daydreams.

Artists often talk about entering a trance-like state where new images and ideas simply appear. Writers sometimes say, "I heard the character speaking to me," or "This story just came to me." I've heard poets say, "I don't know where those lines came from, but I liked them." Musicians often express a similar sentiment when they say, "The song seemed to write itself."

The greatest creative leaps are rarely intended. Instead, they're discovered. They come in unpredictable realizations

and visions.[17]

I often know that I'm creating something good when I'm surprised by it. For me, much of my daily writing practice revolves around reaching a trance-like state where I'm able to let words flow through me with as little resistance as possible. The best writing happens when I'm writing to discover what a character might say or do. It happens when I'm not sure why the next sentence appears, or why the character does what she does, but it feels right. The lines I consciously intend land dead on the page, but those unexpected lines are gold.

The process of reaching this creative trance is, for many artists, a process of losing conscious control without becoming completely detached. Sometimes this is done through a rigorous attention to craft that distracts the conscious mind enough to let something else slip through. Or it's done by entering a dreamlike state where creativity flows through the creator. **But where do the words, ideas, or creative visions flow from?**

Consider Robert Louis Stevenson—the prolific author of classics such as *Treasure Island* and *The Strange Case of Dr. Jekyll and Mr. Hyde*. He describes in "A Chapter on Dreams" how his stories came to him in dreams from "the little people of his theatre" who would perform in their entirety the stories he'd later write. Or consider more recent best-selling authors like Stephenie Meyer and J.K. Rowling. Both described characters and storylines for their books coming to them in dreams and daydreams.

In all of these examples, the stories that made these writers famous arrived *without* conscious control, and receiving these stories was described as being similar to watching a play or a movie. If the author is receiving the story without consciously inventing it, then the question remains, where do such ideas come from? Who really is the author?

---

[17] Leonard Coen alluded to the mysterious unpredictability of creativity in a speech he delivered in 2011 when he said, "If I knew where the good songs came from, I'd go there more often."

Ancient Greeks personified the notion of a creative source beyond the author with the Muses. There were nine Muses, and they each specialized in different creative endeavors including poetry, history, myth, music, song, tragedy, dance, comedy, and science. According to Hesiod's *Theogony,* the Muses were the daughters of Zeus and Mnemosyne, the Titan goddess of memory. Hence, not only did the Greeks see creativity as coming from something beyond one's self, the sources of creative inspiration were seen as divine.

Whether the creative source really is something beyond ourselves or whether it's something so deep within us that it's inaccessible to our conscious ego minds is a question I'll leave to philosophers. What's clear is that **creativity comes from stepping past the ego that clings to what it knows and connecting with a source beyond what's consciously known.**

This creative source is a wellspring of the undiscovered. It holds not what is, but what could be. Before things come into existence they're unmanifested. As such, they come from what Buddhists refer to as the "great void." It's the infinitely abundant unknown—a bountiful sea of formlessness from which all new creations, ideas, forms, and possibilities emerge.[18] As writer and teacher Eckhart Tolle put it, "All true artists, whether they know it or not, create from a place of no-mind."

Although describing creativity this way may sound abstract and paradoxical, it's crucial to recognize that rather than painstakingly constructing things from what the ego mind already knows, creativity involves **opening yourself up to the unknown** (the magic cephalopod of "not knowing" that Lynda Barry depicted). Therefore, the creative process involves letting go of what the mind *thinks* it knows, connecting with the creative energy of the universe, and channeling unknown possibilities into existence. To me, this is divine work that can

---

[18] If you want to explore this notion of emptiness/formlessness (or sunyata), check out commentaries on the ancient Buddhist *Heart Sutra* which states "Form is emptiness. Emptiness is form."

only be accomplished by transcending the limited ego mind of the small self.[19]

Some people are so proficient at connecting with this creative source that it may seem like they're inherently more creative. But what highly creative people get good at is simply the practice of opening themselves up to creativity and allowing it to flow through them with little resistance.

Everyone has immense creative potential. To say "I'm not creative" is like saying "I can't be visited by the Muses." The Muses can visit anyone. The question is, will you be home when they do, and will you be listening? Will you respect the Muses? Will you let them in? And when they call on you, will you be bold enough to embark on the creative journeys they offer you by attempting to enact the visions they give you?

It takes practice (often a great deal of it) to transcend the ego mind and connect with the creative source day after day. You can't just watch squirrel videos while waiting for a Muse to

---

[19] The term "small self" is often used as a synonym for the ego, but it's a slightly more inclusive concept because the ego is only part of the "small self." To use the *Star Trek* metaphor, "small self" could refer to the ship (not just the captain). If you're thinking dualistically, then you might think that the opposite of the small self is a "large self," but **any notion of the self as a separate, limited entity is the "small self."** This means that you can have increasingly larger notions of the small self. For instance, you might see the "small self" as the captain, the ship, or the Federation as your notion of "self" expands. But anything that brings you back to a separate, limited self is still the "small self."

To take this a step further, sometimes the small self is called the "false self" because it's based on an ego-driven illusion of being separate from the rest of existence. Transcending the false self requires recognizing that all notions of a separate self are ultimately delusions. Consequently, the opposite of the small self or false self is "no self," "all self," or "true *Self*" (in nondual traditions, these are essentially the same thing). To transcend the false self and become aware of the *Self* that's one with everything is to be enlightened.

come by. The Muses visit those who are standing outside, waving them in. You wave the Muses in by practicing being open and available to the Muses. Often this means reaching out with your craft—filling a blank page with story notes, sketching, or strumming cords on your guitar until one of the Muses sees you waving and comes closer.

Even though making yourself available to the Muses involves practice and dedication, it's vital to remember that, deep down, creativity isn't about what *you* do. That's the small self talking. Instead, creativity is about being open to what's beyond the small self. **In such a process of transcending the small self, the ego, with its constant "me me me" focus on preserving what it thinks it is and what it thinks it knows, often gets in the way.**[20]

---

[20] To further understand how being creative involves an essential "not doing," consider this quote from Rupert Spira, "The Ego is not an entity. It is an activity. It is an optional activity of identifying itself with a fragment that Consciousness is free to make or not, from moment to moment." Just as the stillness and "not doing" of meditation takes practice, transcending the ego to connect with creativity involves the sustained practice of relaxing the limits we ordinarily place on ourselves. We are naturally creative when we allow ourselves to be so.

When You Create, You're Not Alone

People sometimes ask me how I can spend hours alone in my basement, writing each day.

I tell them that I'm an introvert. I tell them that I have a nice basement. I tell them that as much as I love people, it feels like I don't get to sit alone in a quiet room to write enough. But I rarely tell them the truth because the truth makes me sound crazy.

The truth is, when I'm writing by myself, I'm not alone at all.

If I don't have a good writing session for a day or two, I get cranky. This crankiness comes from being stuck in my small self, unable to connect with the creative source—that wellspring of undiscovered ideas and visions that thrills me.

A day of only writing what I know doesn't feel like writing at all. It's typing. Real creativity is about exploring and being surprised. It's writing to discover. When the things I create are different from what I thought they'd be, that's both exhilarating and satisfying. That's when I become smarter than my limited, small self. And that's when I don't feel alone in the basement.

Instead, I'm connecting with the creative source beyond the ego mind, and the creative source is an infinitely entertaining presence. It's no wonder the ancient Greeks personified it as nine divine Muses. It's hard to imagine better company than the Muses.

In fact, if I stay apart from the Muses for too long, *that's* when I feel empty and alone.

On Visualizing Creativity

Whether you picture nine divine Muses, a magic cephalopod with eight encompassing arms, or some other creative source, how you visualize creativity can influence how you connect with it and channel new things into existence.

One extremely prolific writer friend of mine told me that she sees creativity as a spring bubbling up in a forest. There are places in the forest where the spring water rises to the surface and collects, making it easier to drink from. Although such springs may seem precious and small, the aquifer deep underground is unimaginably vast. It's just a matter of finding ways to access it.

Another way to think about creativity is to picture it as a sphere of ideas and possibilities that surrounds us, much like the atmosphere surrounds our planet. The French philosopher Pierre Teilhard de Chardin called such a sphere of thoughts, ideas, and consciousness the "noosphere" in his 1922 book, *Cosmogenesis*. He postulated that the noosphere evolves from the collective consciousness of humanity, and influences how people think, just as the biosphere evolves from the collective network of living organisms, and influences how organisms grow.

More recent philosophers have referred to this concept of an evolving transpersonal realm of thoughts, ideas, and possibilities as the "ideosphere." As evidence of such an ideosphere, people often point to instances of simultaneous invention, where radically new ideas have entered society at nearly the same time from distant sources. For instance, Isaac Newton and Gottfried Leibniz both independently developed calculus around the same time, and Charles Darwin and Alfred Wallace each separately devised and wrote about the theory of evolution by natural selection during the same years. Such instances make it seem as if ideas evolve on a level beyond individual minds, and there they roam until someone takes notice and describes them.

Sometimes, I envision creativity as being akin to standing in a stadium full of whispers, and it's my job to listen closely and tease out what threads I can, then weave them into a story.

Other times I picture creativity (especially when it comes to discovering new books to write) as a playground full of ghostly children eager to exist. At first, it's hard to see them. I might only catch glimpses out of the corner of my eye. Every now and then, though, one will linger. It might even talk with me if I give it enough attention. And the more attention I pay to this unformed spirit, the more it will materialize. Then, if it trusts me, I can take the spirit's hand and coax it into the light of day for others to see.

Such a process of helping spirits gain form takes time. I've learned to only focus on the ones I want to be with for years, day after day. I never know how long it might take for a story or book to become solid enough to wander the world on its own. One spirit has been visiting me for fourteen years, and I'm still working on bringing it into existence.

There are countless ways to visualize creativity and the process of enacting visions. It can be an endless river flowing through you. A wind surrounding you. Cosmic radio waves you tune into. Energy that can be conducted into stories, songs, and pictures, bringing them to life... The important thing is to see creativity as something vast and limitless (so you don't get stingy with it), while seeing it as wondrous and divine (so you don't take it for granted and disregard it).

Above all, it's critical to visualize the creative source as something beyond yourself that cannot be completely understood, controlled, contained, or owned by you. Stay humble and open to creativity. After all, it was there long before you, and it created you—not the other way around.

Want to take things a step further?

Consider closely the story you tell yourself about how to engage in the creative process. To do this, ask yourself the following questions:

- How do I visualize creativity?
- Is this notion of creativity limitless and beyond myself, or am I subconsciously limiting creativity?

If you have a limiting notion of creativity, see what happens when you visualize the creative source as something beyond you, limitless, and life-giving.

Before you sit down to create something (and anytime you feel creatively blocked) take a moment to envision the limitless, sublime creative source. Recall how wondrous it feels to connect with creativity. Thank the creative source for the times it's helped you create things in the past, then invite it to flow through you again so you can create what you're called to create with as little resistance as possible.

You might be surprised by how shifting the way you perceive creativity enhances your ability to receive new ideas and channel creative energy.

The Paradox of Creativity, Control, and Intention

Having an intention, or a compelling ambition to create something, is often necessary to set off on the creative journey and stick with it day after day. And some degree of control might seem necessary to effectively shape, revise, and enact a vision. But intentions that are too controlling crush creativity.

When you try to control creativity, the ego gets in the way. The more you attempt to make something be exactly what *you* want it to be, the more you limit it and yourself. Forcing creativity rarely goes well. Tell yourself to write something "good" ("Is this good? Does this suck?") and your writing will suffer. Pressure someone to "be creative," and they'll become less creative. Pressure yourself to solve a problem, and your chances of solving it go down. Pull the reigns too tight and you choke the horse.

Instead, the way to become more creative is to let go of controlling intentions that come from the ego. This can be done in little ways and big. For instance, instead of telling someone to "be creative" (which often makes folks less creative by causing them to limit themselves to what the ego mind *thinks* a creative response should be), say "let your mind go wild." Instead of telling someone to "make something good" (which puts heaps of ego-driven pressure on the process), say "let it be whatever it wants to be." Shifting the way you approach creativity can help you move past ego blocks and start creating.

Some writers and poets I know escape their controlling intentions by focusing the parts of their minds that want to control things on other tasks. For instance, they might use poetic forms or procedures (like starting each new line in a poem with the antonym of a word used in the line before) to occupy the more rigid, controlling aspects of their minds. With the mental gatekeepers thus distracted, surprising new things can slip in.

A process I often use to escape my ego's controlling intentions involves shifting my focus from telling something what to be to asking something what it wants to be. For instance, when I'm writing a story I'll keep asking the story and characters questions such as, *What am I missing? Why did you do that? What are you afraid of? What do you want to do?* and so forth until something responds and I write a passage I didn't expect. (We'll explore this process further in the chapter on "Revision and the Hero's Return.")

Escaping the ego's limitations and controlling intentions enables us to make surprising creative leaps. That's when we become smarter than our small selves. And that's when the creative process becomes a process of discovery that teaches us.

One interesting quality of transcending the ego mind like this is that it's common to lose track of time and self-awareness. Psychologist Mihály Csíkszentmihályi referred to such an experience as a flow state. In an interview, Csíkszentmihályi described the mental state of flow as "being completely involved in an activity for its own sake. The ego falls away. Time flies. Every action, movement, and thought follows inevitably from the previous one, like playing jazz. Your whole being is involved, and you're using your skills to the utmost."

The more you focus on the ego's desire to control things and make things be what you think they should be, the harder it becomes to enter a flow state. To get there you need to reach a place where "the ego falls away." When you feel your ego start to limit the creative process with its desires and demands, focus on things beyond yourself (experiencing the present moment, what the story or characters want, what the song demands, etc.). Trust that not only will you enjoy creativity more this way, you'll be more effective, too.

Despite this, maybe part of you still thinks (like the ego prefers to think) that this whole "creativity comes from beyond the ego" stuff is overblown or flighty nonsense. The ego wants to be involved. It doesn't want to fall away. It's the captain who thinks it's in charge of the ship. It has to intentionally shape and control things for anything good to get created, right?

If your ego is raising objections like these, try this: For one minute sit back and stop thinking. Intentionally try to make all of your thoughts become silent. It sounds simple, right? If you're in control of your thoughts, then stopping your thoughts from happening for one minute should be easy.

Go ahead, try it. I'll wait.

What did you notice? Could you do it? Could you even do it for thirty seconds? (Note: thinking "don't think" is still thinking, and not all thoughts are verbal. Abstract, non-verbal thoughts count too.[21]) If you're aware of your thoughts, then I bet you

---

[21] It wasn't until I was doing research for this book that I learned that some people think almost exclusively in words (hearing an internal "voice"), some people think in a combination of words and images,

couldn't stop your thoughts from happening for very long at all.[22]

Thoughts, like ideas, frequently arise involuntarily. They emerge, then we decide what to do with them (or at least we think we decide what to do with them, but that's another matter).

Now see if you can predict exactly what your next thought will be. Granted, you can tell yourself to think of a turtle, and then imagine a turtle. But if you think this is intentional control, ask yourself why you picked a turtle.

Now try to predict what your next new creative idea will be.

Obviously, for an idea to be new to you, you can't know what it will be. New ideas can only come from beyond the ego mind that knows things.

Here's the tricky paradox of creativity: **the more you *try* to create something new, the more your ego gets involved and the harder it becomes to connect with the creative source beyond your ego mind.** Focus too much on the ego's controlling intentions and you'll become ego bound and cut off from the wondrous, unknowable creative source.

So, how do you keep the ego's desire to control things from interfering with the creative process? The answer to this conundrum, and the secret to lifelong creativity, is wonderfully simple: **Stop *trying* to create things and focus on *being* creative.**[23]

---

and some people rarely hear internal voices at all and think primarily in images and abstract, non-verbal impressions.

[22] This is not to say that it's impossible to consciously stop thinking. By expanding awareness beyond one's ego mind to a state of "no mind," one can experience the thoughtless bliss of being. However, most people are stuck on a level of consciousness where thoughts are uncontrollably and incessantly arising. The more people identify with their thoughts and believe that they control them, the more stuck they become.

[23] Ray Bradbury put it this way: "Don't think. Thinking is the enemy of creativity. It's self-conscious, and anything self-conscious is lousy. You can't try to do things. You simply must do things."

The difference between "trying" and "being" in the above sentence may seem merely semantic, but it actually describes a profound paradigm shift that's essential for effective creativity. Trying involves the ego—it's something *you* do. Being is effortless—it's something you inherently are that encompasses you.

Since creativity requires transcending the ego to connect with the creative source, "being creative" means being open and letting creativity flow through you with as little ego resistance as possible. By focusing on being rather than trying, you can get past the ego in *both* the divergent (coming up with ideas) and convergent (selecting, developing, and revising) stages of the creative process. The less your ego gets involved overall, the better.[24]

Although this might sound like a simple mindset shift, making the change from *trying* to *being* can be challenging—especially if you've spent most of your life *trying* to do things to earn rewards and gain approval. If reaching a state of effortless, blissful creativity seems elusive, don't sweat it. There are many ways to get there, and failure (as we'll soon see) can help.

---

[24] Ram Dass described this egoless approach to creativity when he wrote, "If I am a potter, I make pots. But who is making the pots? I am not under the illusion that I am making the pots. Pots are. The potter is. I am hollow bamboo."

A Brief Excursion into the Difference Between Trying and Being

Years ago, when my life had become particularly hectic and I felt exhausted from trying to do things all the time, I said to a friend of mine, "I feel like I never get to live my life. It's always out of reach."

My friend, a writer, yoga instructor, and the most agreeable guy I know, seemed puzzled by this. "That's not good," he said.

I shrugged. I thought everyone lived like that—constantly chasing after something that was always out of reach. Sometimes where I wanted to be seemed far away. Sometimes it felt close, but I could never get there because then I'd do nothing (or so I feared). I always had to try harder to achieve more. That's how I kept myself going.

In retrospect, I now see my exhaustion and discontentment as warning signs about the path I was on. Constantly trying to achieve more to be happy not only didn't work, it was counterproductive. However, back then I was too focused on my achievement addiction to recognize that there were other ways to succeed. Try harder or give up were the only two options I saw, and giving up seemed intolerable.

Essentially, I'd forgotten how to *be*. I only knew how to *try*. This disconnection from being was destroying my creativity, my health, and my happiness.

If recognizing the difference between trying and being in your own life seems esoteric, that's okay. That's how it seemed to me for years. Logically, I understood the words and the concept, but I didn't "get it" because getting it required letting go of everything I thought I knew about myself and existence.

Still, I bet you can easily recognize the difference between trying and being in other situations. For instance, imagine someone who's trying hard to be funny. Are they funny?

Usually the more someone *tries* to be funny, the less funny they are, and the more annoying and obnoxious they become.

Conversely, someone who *is* funny might not act funny at all. Rather than behaving in ridiculous, silly, or intentionally comical ways, they might do the opposite and deliver jokes in a deadpan, somber voice. Think of comedians like Stephen Wright, Tig Notaru, and Bill Murray whose deadpan deliveries made them famous.

Of course, comedians don't have to *try* to be deadpan (that would be trying instead of being). Some comedians laugh at their own jokes, and this can be wonderfully funny (think of Tom and Ray Magliozzi, the *Car Talk* guys, who became famous for their infectious laughter). The point is, those who are often most effective at getting laughs aren't *trying* to act funny. They're *being* funny.

Now imagine singers who are trying to sound great. Do they sound great? Or do they sound like over-the-top showoffs aggressively belting out notes?

It's counterintuitive, but truly great singers allow themselves to be imperfect and vulnerable. It's the imperfections in voice and delivery that make performances by singers like Billie

Holiday, Tom Waits, and Janis Joplin extraordinary. To be great at something is to be able to risk sincerity, intimacy, and imperfection. As the legendary dancer and choreographer Mikhail Baryshnikov put it, "…communicating with an art form means being vulnerable. Being imperfect. And most of the time this is much more interesting. Trust me."[25]

You might notice the same difference between trying and being in other artistic endeavors like acting, art, and writing. Writers who "try" to write a great story often compose thesaurus-riddled lines, formulaic characters, and contrived plots. Such writing is about as much fun to read as wading through a mound of dead beetles. Great writers, by boldly stepping out of the way and letting the story be what it wants to be, are able to risk raw, imperfect lines that have power in their sincerity.

Trying is all about appearance and imitation. It involves trying to make something fit a pre-existing idea of what the ego thinks something should be, and it's precisely this forceful imitation of what one *thinks* will impress others and win praise that causes trying to become derivative, insincere, and annoying.

Being, on the other hand, doesn't have anything to prove. Which, counterintuitively, means that when you create from a place of being rather than trying, you're able to do more. You're free to take risks, make discoveries, and be vulnerable, imperfect, and inventive.

Recognizing the difference between trying and being in your own life is vital. However, the real benefits come from put-

---

[25] "Imperfect" and "perfect" are tricky words. They're almost conceptual contranyms (words that mean themselves and their opposites). On the one hand, *trying* to be perfect is something that holds creativity back. On the other hand, when you create from a place of being, then so-called "imperfections" are part of what make a work "perfect." Just as the flaws in a diamond make it sparkle, it's the crack in a singer's voice, the missed note, or broken line that can make a work exquisite, memorable, and perfect. In being, all things belong. Imperfections are part of the perfection of being.

ting this difference into practice by consistently creating from a place of being rather than trying. If you're struggling to do this in your own life, have no fear. We're going to explore several ways to become more aware of being, starting with failure. Although it might sound strange, trying to do something and failing is one of the best ways to learn how to truly be—because failing is something almost no one *tries* to do.

Want to take things a step further?

To get a visceral sense of the difference between trying and being, imagine a time when you weren't trying to do anything. You were simply being. This doesn't mean you were inactive. You might have been climbing El Capitan, skiing a powder-covered slope, or singing your heart out, but rather than *trying* to make things become a certain way, you were caught up in the moment, purely *being*. Put yourself in that state again. As you breathe, let yourself simply be. There's nothing to change. Everything is perfect as is. How does it feel to be?

Now imagine a time when you were struggling to do something, *trying* to make things become what you thought they should be. Put yourself in this state again. What does your body feel like when you're trying? What is your mind doing? Do you have expectations? Anxieties? Frustrations? Does your body tighten? Jaw clench? Brow furrow?

Can you feel the difference? Notice how *being* is open, effortless, flexible, accepting, and energizing, while *trying* is tense, rigid, controlling, judgmental, and exhausting. Next time you start to feel tense or controlling, see what happens if you let go of *trying* to make something become what you think it should be. Instead, allow yourself to align with *being* by appreciating what is. To do this, it might help to take a deep breath and focus on staying open, present, and aware while enjoying the experiences you get to have.

The Gift of Failure

You know you've reached rock bottom when your wife tells you, "You could write a book on failure."

She wasn't being mean. She was right. Before I started writing this book, I'd had many failures. On the exterior I might have appeared somewhat successful with a good career and several publications, degrees, and awards, but my sense of failure—of not accomplishing what I believed I needed to accomplish, letting myself and others down, and failing to make a positive difference in the world—became overwhelming. The more I tried to achieve, the bigger my failures seemed.

This can be challenging to talk about. As we discussed in Part I, our ego-centric society encourages people to perpetuate success myths and shun failure. But this obsession with success and rejection of failure often keeps us ego-bound and miserable.

The truth is, failure isn't something to fear. I had to fail in many ways before I was able to recognize that how I'd been going through life wasn't working. It wasn't sustainable or enjoyable. I was missing something crucial, and I needed a dramatic reset to find it.

If I'd had more superficial success, I might have missed out on the chance to learn what failure taught me. I might have kept ignoring my anxiety and despair while desperately trying to achieve enough to be happy. That's how I'd kept going for decades—fighting, clawing, striving, struggling, and trying every inch of the way. Fortunately, my sense of failure finally got too big to ignore.

I'm deeply grateful now for the failures I've experienced because the things I've learned from failure have led to some of the greatest realizations and changes in my life.

Success may feel good, but it feeds your ego and can make ego blocks worse. Failure is difficult, but it offers critical lessons and insights. It's failure that put me in the perfect position to discover a better way to be. And it's failure that enabled me to expand my awareness and gain the understanding needed to write this book.

Failure's greatest gift, though, is this: **it provides a way out of the ego's limiting grasp**.

How I Failed

All failures are perceived failures. Selling 1,000 books could feel like a tremendous success to one author, and a failure to another. There's nothing about any event that makes it objectively a success or a failure. Instead, the experience of failure is created by a person's expectations. Essentially, failure is when the ego wants something to happen that it perceives as good, and reality does something else that the ego perceives as bad.

If you want to know what the failures were that caused me to let go of my old way of living and find a better way to be, please understand that from other perspectives, they might not seem like failures at all. Nevertheless, in the interest of honest sharing, here's a brief outline of how failure finally got through to me.

After years of writing professionally, I wrote a novel that I thought was well-crafted and important. My agent and editor both thought it was great, too. Although previously I'd published three other novels with major publishers, I still hadn't had a huge commercial success. I decided that this was my all-or-nothing book. If I didn't get my new book to sell well, then I was finished. My life-long dreams of being an author would be shattered. No publisher would want to publish me again (whether this was true or not I don't know, but this was the story I told myself). Everything rested on the success of my new book.

As a result, I went all out to promote my new novel. I spent months planning and putting promotional pieces into place. When the book came out, I did everything a writer of modest means could do to promote a novel—readings, book signings, conference presentations, radio and TV interviews, newspaper articles, magazine articles, online interviews, guest blogs, massive giveaways, and dozens of author visits to schools. I spoke with thousands of people. The book got great reviews. It garnered attention in all the right ways and even won a couple awards. Yet, despite all my efforts, it didn't sell nearly as much as I wanted it to.

Those who found the book seemed to appreciate it, but not enough people found it. For over a year I exhausted myself trying to change this outcome, except nothing worked. The irony was that I did more to promote this novel than I had for any other book I'd written, and it ended up selling less than some of my previous novels. After many months of promoting my heart out, I had to recognize that I'd put it all on the table, and I'd failed.

Not only had I failed professionally, I felt like I'd failed at my life's purpose. You see, the book that I'd made my "all-or-nothing novel" wasn't just any book. It was one I'd written with my ten-year-old daughter to address issues that both she and I cared a great deal about. It was a profoundly personal story that I felt, down to the marrow of my bones, needed to be told. And it was my lifelong hope to plant a seedling of positive change in the world by writing a book like this.

Instead of making a difference, though, I felt that I'd failed there as well. During the years I worked to complete and promote my new novel, I watched several of the things I valued most—democracy, justice, truth-seeking, science, art, education, and the environment—come under a greater assault than any I'd experienced in my lifetime. And I watched places that I loved, like forests and coral reefs, go from being vibrant ecosystems, to being almost entirely dead within a couple of years.

Sadly, I saw these devastating losses happen firsthand to coral reefs in the Caribbean and the Pacific that died in record-setting heat waves, and to forests near my home that turned to ash in record-setting droughts and wildfires. It was heartbreaking to watch places I loved become burnt-out graveyards. The more I tried to protect these places, the less effect I seemed to have, and no amount of will or effort on my part seemed able to change that. Everything appeared to be heading in the wrong direction.

To make matters worse, I put so much energy and attention into having some sort of positive impact on the world that I started to grow distant from my wife and kids. I became frustrated and stressed out. I stopped sleeping well and started grinding my teeth (I even chipped a tooth one night). I experienced back problems, shoulder problems and foot problems that landed me on crutches for months. My body fell apart and gave me constant pain. I felt disconnected from everything I valued. Eventually, I fell into a deep depression and didn't know how to go on.

I'd been given the gift of an important purpose and the education and ability to achieve it. I did all that I could think of to succeed but, from my perspective, I failed.

It took this cumulative experience of failure in multiple realms (personal, professional, environmental, and global) to get through to me. When it did—when I hit rock bottom and my sense of self broke open—I was finally able to see past the ego-driven illusions that had been causing me to suffer for most of my life.

How Failure Can Be Your Friend

Perhaps nothing holds creators back more than the fear of failure. This fear comes from the ego, which is terrified of experiencing failure. To understand why, first let's clarify what failure is and isn't.

Failure isn't giving up or not starting something in the first place. Those two habits are the work of the ego as it tries to protect itself from failure. The ego uses doubt and procrastination to stop you from attempting things. If you don't start a project, you can't fail at it. And if you give up on something before it's done, then you haven't really failed because it was your "choice" to give up and abandon the project. Giving up reinforces the illusion that the ego is in control (more on how to overcome ego blocks like doubt and procrastination in the next chapter).

Experiencing failure is different, though. **A perceived failure happens when you do everything you can to succeed and the world doesn't respond the way you want it to. This is the thing the ego fears most.**

Why?

Because failure is the ego's kryptonite. By enabling you to see that you're not in control of the things your ego claims to be in control of, failure gives you the awareness needed to dissolve the ego's limiting, isolating grasp.

I still prefer experiencing success to failure, but I don't fear experiencing failure anymore or throw myself off-balance trying to avoid it (which has made me both more resilient and more creative). When you free yourself from the fear of failure, you become pretty unstoppable. Therefore, with the hope of balancing things out and fearing failure less, let's take a closer look at some of the ways failure can serve us:

1) Failure provides valuable learning opportunities

Consider two scenarios. In scenario A, you're playing a game of chess against a beginner, and because you're much better than him at chess, you barely need to think about the moves you make. Instead, you rely on sequences you've developed in the past. You win easily, making it clear that you're the superior player.

In scenario B, you're playing against someone who's a better player than you. First, you try strategies that worked in the past, but she easily predicts and counters these. Then you struggle to come up with new strategies. Your brain races to devise ways to beat your opponent, but she employs moves you never considered, and ultimately you lose.

Which scenario would you choose for yourself?

Your ego probably prefers scenario A. Winning is temporarily pleasurable, and failing to win, especially when you're doing your best, is difficult. But what did you gain from scenario A? Did you develop much as a player? Probably not. Did you learn new moves or strategies? Not likely. The main thing you accomplished was to feed your ego which, although temporarily pleasurable, can lead to problems as your ego gains power and demands to be fed more (making it even harder to take risks and learn).

If what you're interested in is discovering new moves and developing as a player, then scenario B is more beneficial.

Stanford Psychologist Carol Dweck conducted several studies that show how, when people attempt difficult tasks with a growth mindset that involves embracing risk, struggle, and failure, they learn more. Conversely, when people stay in their comfort zones (only playing the easier player), they reinforce a fixed mindset that makes learning harder and less productive. Other researchers, like Michigan State University Psychology Researcher Hans Schroder, have demonstrated how, when you make an error and fail, your brain becomes measurably more active (an indication of learning). For productive learning to take place, though, it's imperative to develop a growth mindset where you see failure as a helpful experience rather than something to avoid.

2) Failure helps us break free of ego traps

Ego traps come in many flavors, but the impacts are usually similar: they make us self-absorbed, stuck, and miserable.

For creators, ego traps frequently happen when you become addicted to achievement as a way to feel good about yourself. The more you turn to accomplishments and external validation to placate the ego, the more power the ego gains over you. In bad cases, you'll become trapped—unable to see beyond your desperate need to satisfy your ego.

It's a trap because there's no way to ever fully satisfy the ego. Instead, the way out of ego traps is the thing the ego fears most—failure.

When you fail, the ego switches from pride to frustration, anger, shame, and disappointment. Although these feelings can be unpleasant, they give you an opportunity to recognize exactly how the ego is causing you to suffer. Remember, failure isn't objectively bad. Your ego simply causes you to *perceive* it as bad. It wanted something to happen and it didn't get what it wanted, so it's punishing you.

People often need to experience a bit of failure before they're able to recognize how their ego is causing them to suffer. Once you become conscious of the ego and what it's doing, it will no longer have the same sway. Consciousness itself dissolves the ego's grasp, enabling you to become more aware of what's beyond it.

In addition, experiencing failure can lead to becoming more compassionate and connected to others. When people only experience success, they tend to see themselves as superior to others. But failure shatters such egotistical, isolating delusions and helps us become more empathetic toward other's struggles and failures.

That's ultimately the way to avoid ego traps: **the less you fixate on your small self, and the more aware you become of your connection to the rest of existence, the less power the ego will have over you.** When an ego trap creeps up and makes you feel desperate to control things with a "this needs to happen the way I want it to" mentality, failure might swoop in and help you escape such egoic thinking.

Welcome your failures and the opportunity they give you to tame your ego. Because, if you don't tame your ego, whatever success you experience might feel temporarily satisfying, but it will ultimately lead to dissatisfaction and isolation as your ego grows.

You may intuitively know this already. On some level, you might even be holding yourself back from actualizing your potential because you haven't dealt with your ego yet, and you're wise enough to be wary of what will happen if your ego grows. **Just as it's common to fear failure, people sometimes fear success.**

There's no need to fear either experience. Both can be beneficial, as long as you realize that what you perceive as failure and success are simply experiences to appreciate—the thrill of success and the surprise of failure. Try not to let either one go to your head.

3) There is no absolute failure

The wonderful paradox of failure is that there's nothing to fear about failure because nothing is ever truly a failure. Every failure teaches you something, and simply being able to exist and experience failure is an incredible success. When you're able to fully understand this *and* feel this way about failure, then you're able to create without fear of failure.

One way to attain this fearless perspective is to **celebrate failure**. This doesn't mean that you try to fail (that would be giving up, which is different from failure). Instead, recognize that failure requires risk, and having the courage to risk failure can be an accomplishment in itself.

Here's an example of what I'm talking about: in 2020 a friend of mine, the fabulous writer Nicole Vanderlinden, started a Facebook group for writers called 30 Rejections in 2020. The goal was to see who could get 30 rejections the quickest. Celebrating rejections became a way to encourage each other to take risks and send things out more, which made it easier to keep writing and submitting. In this way, failure became something we celebrated. (And when members of the group got a piece accepted instead of rejected, we celebrated that too.)

Although celebrating failure might sound like a crazy strategy for success, many revolutionary developments have come *because* of failure. Alexander Fleming, for instance, famously discovered penicillin when he accidentally left out a contaminated petri dish, then noticed that no bacteria were growing around the mold on his "failed" experiment. As Jeff Bezos, one of the most commercially successful businessmen of all time, put it, "failure comes part and parcel with invention. It's not optional." By celebrating failure, you can make it easier to take the bold risks and unconventional leaps needed to make radical new discoveries and innovations.

To further shift your perspective of failure, every time you experience a setback or a perceived failure, ask yourself, "**In what ways might this failure serve me?**" What insight, awareness, or new idea can you gain through the experience? How might this trigger a positive transformation?

Sometimes the gifts failure brings are so great that you might even feel excited about the possibility of failure. You might wonder, every time you experience a perceived failure, what unexpected breakthrough is lurking around the corner? When this happens, failure stops feeling like failure at all and becomes an opportunity for discovery and growth.

Want to take things a step further?

Think about past failures you've had. For each one, ask yourself:

- In what ways did that perceived failure serve me?
- What new insights or awareness did I gain from it?
- How did it present me with new possibilities?

Anytime you feel like you failed or are failing at something, ask yourself these same questions. See if you can embrace the perceived failure as a valuable learning experience.

Once you've recognized what can be learned through a difficult experience, try putting this awareness into a positive reframe statement. For example, if a story gets rejected, you might say to yourself, "I used to be afraid of rejection, but now I know that it's part of how I learn and grow."

Taking a growth perspective on failure liberates your creative process from fear.

Twelve Practical Ways to Get Past Doubt, Procrastination, and Other Ego Blocks

Some days, picking up the dog poop in the yard seems more appealing to me than sitting down to write. Once I get into a writing trance where I'm open to the creative energy of the universe and am surprising myself with what's being created, I enjoy it. There's nothing more gratifying than the thrill of transcending the small self and connecting with the creative source. Nevertheless, my ego continues to attempt to block me from the thrill of creating.

It's important to recognize why the ego does this. Because it's the ego's job to preserve and protect what you think you are, the ego constantly wants to keep you from transcending your small self, expanding awareness, and experiencing criticism, failure, or other things beyond its control.

Doubt, fear, and procrastination are common ways that the

ego tries to accomplish its job. As was mentioned in the previous chapter, with doubt and fear, the ego can get you to abandon a project before you fail. And with procrastination, the ego can prevent you from working to create something because you can't fail if you don't try. Either way, the ego maintains its illusion of control.[26]

Fighting against ego blocks like doubt, fear, and procrastination rarely works. Anyone who struggles with procrastination knows that telling yourself not to procrastinate, or getting angry at yourself for procrastinating, just becomes another way to procrastinate. Likewise, focusing on your doubts and fears often makes them grow. Because these creative blocks come from the ego, the more the ego gets you to focus on yourself (*your* doubts, *your* fears, *your* procrastination, *your* inadequacies...) the more power it has over you.

The solution is to accept doubt, fear, and procrastination as parts of the creative process and continue on.

Of course, saying this is akin to a football commentator saying that all the trailing team needs to do to win is score more touchdowns. Although the solution might be simple, *how* to do it is rarely easy. In the interest of making the "how" more attainable, here are twelve practical techniques for getting past doubt, fear, procrastination, and other common ego blocks:

1) Get yourself excited to start creating by reminding yourself of the benefits of creating.

By focusing on the joy of creating—the thrill of connecting with the creative source and discovering new possibilities—

---

[26] Often, simply recognizing that doubt, fear, and procrastination are manifestations of your ego trying to hold you back from creative work will lessen the ego's limiting grasp. However, even when you're aware of the ego and what it's doing, it still might get in the way—which is why it's helpful to learn techniques to make accessing creativity easier.

you can psyche yourself up for the day's creative adventure.[27]

2) Start small. Procrastination is usually most debilitating with large tasks.

Having big goals can make it easy to feel overwhelmed. Instead of thinking of the big things you want to accomplish (like write a novel), focus on taking small steps (like writing a sentence). All you need to do is get started. Just write one sentence, draw one line, play one phrase of a song, dip the paintbrush into one color, etc. You can do that, right?

Once you write a sentence, write another, and another. Count by ones. Doing a hundred pushups is daunting, but doing one is manageable. Rather than telling yourself that you need to do a hundred, do one, and one, and one. The mind will travel down the path of least resistance, so when the path is challenging, focus on taking one easy step at a time.

3) Start anywhere you like.

Don't worry about writing or creating what you think you "should" create. All you need to do is start somewhere (in whatever part that calls to you). Starting is often the hardest part. Once you get going, you can see where the Muse takes you. Keep your creative momentum up and trust that the Muse will lead you somewhere interesting.

4) Take the pressure off.

Don't worry about creating something "good." That's the ego talking. Instead, view any creation as a success. After all,

---

[27] If you struggle with setting aside time for creative work, it might help to remind yourself of three essential things from Part I: "I'm a creator—I need to create. There are things I can create that no one else can create. This is what I'm called to do." To make time for your calling, make a list of things that take up time each day, and see if you can put off 2-3 things on your list until after you attend to your calling.

you're bringing something into existence that wasn't there before.

With writing, I often think of the first draft as merely giving myself a lump of clay to work with. When I feel blocked, I let myself write terrible sentences to provide more clay. Only when I have all the clay I need to construct a story do I focus on shaping the clay into what it wants to be. That's when I allow myself to question what's working and what needs to be revised or cut.

During the early revision process, try not to let the clay dry out and harden. It's better to stay open to new possibilities and discoveries. Once you've found the shape that works best, then you can smooth things out and focus on the polishing, glazing, and finishing stages of revision.

5) Create a daily work habit so the decision to start is out of your hands.

Every day, you simply need to show up and start creating at a certain time, just as you have to show up for a job (even when you don't feel like it). It might help to make a schedule for yourself, with a clock where you punch in. Close the door to your workplace and tell yourself that you're at your job (or, more importantly, your calling). You've been called to do this, and you need to honor that calling by showing up for the time you promised. It's out of your hands, so the ego can go sit in a corner for a while. You've got work to do.

6) Minimize distractions—these are the ego's allies that help it slip back in to keep you from creating.

Turn off your phone. Use an app to shut yourself out of the internet (I use SelfControl for this). Toss the TV remote under the couch. Because the mind will travel down the path of least resistance, the harder distractions are to access, the less tempting they'll be.

If you still keep getting distracted during creative work, try noticing when this happens. For instance, if you can't think of the word you want, do you search the internet and end up spending hours watching Twiggy the waterskiing squirrel videos? Figure out what your distraction triggers are and accept that they'll probably happen again. Then put plans into place (like using an app to block you from visiting social media sites and YouTube) to create a different outcome. In this age of aggressive technological distractions, technological measures are needed to keep them at bay.

7) Maximize productivity by using optimal work habits.

Personally, I've found that I'm most productive when I write in 30-minute focused sessions, with 5-minute breaks between them (this is similar to the Pomodoro Technique). I use a timer to make sure I don't stop working (no matter how hard it becomes) until I've completed my 30 minutes of focused writing. Often, I enter my most creative stage after 10-20 minutes of flailing around. If I can do four 30-minute sessions a day, I'll usually accomplish more than if I sat in front of the computer trying to work for eight hours.

8) Your brain needs oxygen to function effectively, so increase your blood flow.

Work until you're stuck or your efficiency lags, then exercise (or exercise between 30-minute sessions). It might sound ridiculous, but try this: As soon as you get stuck, do 50 jumping jacks, pushups, burpees, or whatever gets your heart pumping (burpees are the single best way I know to get my blood flowing. Try doing 30 of them—you'll see). Taking exercise breaks will also help you get new ideas. Plus, if you don't enjoy exercise, the threat of exercise can give you extra incentive to keep creating (it's that or burpees).

If aerobic exercise doesn't work for you, there are other physical activities that can be beneficial. A counselor I know recommends tensing and relaxing different muscle groups as a way to lessen stress and heighten focus. Simply pick a muscle group and tighten it. As you do this you might think, "These are my hands clenched." After five seconds, focus on relaxing the muscles in that area ("These are my hands relaxed"). Continue with various muscle groups—toes, legs, arms, chest—until you feel blood circulating more freely through you.

Toward the end of a long writing day, my brain will feel fuzzy and I won't make much progress. However, after writing for a couple hours (doing four or five 30-minute writing sessions), my mind will be submerged deep within the story I'm working on. To take advantage of this immersive perspective, I'll do a body/mind workout.

Basically, I'll do my regular 70-minute workout, but between every few sets, when my heart is beating vigorously, I'll sit before my computer and write whatever calls to me. Sometimes I'll just outline things for the next day. Sometimes I'll jot down dialogues as my characters tell me what I didn't get right about them. Or I might explore alternatives to the scene I've been struggling with. The point is to stay open to new possibilities and see what comes up after spending the day immersed in a piece.

Try a body/mind workout. You can even do this while walking or jogging by taking a digital recorder with you (most phones have a voice memo app). As you walk, record whatever pops into your head so you don't have to worry about remembering it. Then your mind will be free to discover more.

9) Give yourself notes for the next day to make starting easier.

Nothing is more intimidating than a blank page. To make starting easier, try leaving things in the middle of a scene, or even stop mid-sentence with ideas listed below for how to continue. That way you have a thread to pick up and begin with the next day.

10) Accept that doubt will keep coming back. Nearly every writer doubts. There's never a moment when I don't have doubts. Hell, I'm even having doubts right now as I write *this* sentence. Part of me fears that you'll think this is stupid and doesn't need to be said. If writers listened to such doubts, few books would get written.

Rather than resisting doubt or waiting for a doubt-free moment that might never arrive, recognize doubt for what it is—a manifestation of the ego, coating creations with its fear that if you put something out there, it will be criticized and rejected. So be it. You can't control what others think. Things still need to come into existence, and most will emerge through a primordial pond of doubt.

11) Think of creativity as coming from beyond you, so there's no point in doubting it.

Michelangelo described it this way: "Every block of stone has a statue inside it, and it is the task of the sculptor to discover it." Seeing creativity as a process of discovery in which you uncover what wants to exist gives you a way around doubt. After all, *you* didn't come up with the ideas. That's just your ego talking (remember, you don't even know what your next idea will be). Creativity isn't something you "have." It's something that flows through you, and the source of creativity is beyond your ego mind. Doubting it would be like doubting the wind.

If you must doubt, doubt the things that *you* think must be a certain way, but don't doubt the Muse—that's how you offend the gods.

12) Practice creative gratitude.

The ego loves to tell you that you suck and aren't accomplishing enough. To lessen resistance to creativity, develop the habit of noticing and feeling grateful for even small creative acts. The more you notice and focus on the pleasures and benefits of creativity, the easier it will be to start creating the next day when new doubts, fears, and ego blocks arise. (See the first technique—things come full circle).

Techniques like these can help you develop a foundation of healthy creative habits to work from, but all this is just the tip of the iceberg. The radical life-changing stuff is yet to come.

> ### Want to take things a step further?
>
> Try keeping a gratitude journal. It only takes a few minutes a day. Before you go to bed, simply list in a journal five things from the day that you're grateful for. Include at least one or two aspects of the creative process, no matter how small. For instance, you might write, "I'm grateful that I wrote a paragraph," or "I'm grateful that a new insight into my character came to me," or "I'm grateful that I got to sketch a squirrel during the department meeting." Building a habit of gratitude, even for small things, is a powerful way to both increase enjoyment and reduce ego blocks.
>
> It's hard to overstate the beneficial impacts of gratitude. Sadhguru, a well-known yogi, brought up the importance of gratitude in an interview when asked what's the one thing people should do to increase awareness, perception, and thoughtfulness. He replied, "Just do this much—before you go to bed today... every hour remind yourself 'Wow! I'm still alive.'" The audience chuckled, but Sadhguru went on to explain, "So many people who go to bed today will not wake up tomorrow morning. More than a million people on the planet will not wake up... Tomorrow morning, if you *do* wake up, first check 'Am I really awake? Alive? I'm still alive. Wow!' You don't have to do anything... 'Okay, I'm still alive. Over a million people didn't wake up this morning, but here I am, alive.'"

Tyrants, Artists, and the Ego

Let's step back and look at the big picture for a moment. In addition to making us suffer, giving us doubts, fears, procrastination, and other barriers to connecting with the creative source, the ego (or more specifically ego-centric thinking) spawns most of the societal problems we face—from internecine partisanship, to war, bigotry, economic inequality, and environmental destruction. Although many philosophers and spiritual leaders have pointed out the perils of ego-centric thinking, it's hard to escape this destructive cycle.

One reason why has to do with the fact that, instead of helping people step past their egos, our society often does the opposite. Those in control usually want to maintain their power and control. Such ego-centric leaders often encourage people to become more ego bound—more fixated on their individual selves and threats to their self-interests—since ego-bound people (for reasons we'll explore in a moment) are easier to manipulate and control.

In addition, ego-bound people make great consumers. That's why consumer culture surrounds us with messages designed to encourage us to constantly serve our egos. Think about it—the ego is never satisfied and it always wants more. Whether it's the desire for possessions, power, fame, achievement, or other forms of temporary pleasure, the "me, me, me" and "more, more, more" focus of the ego readily leads to obsessive, addicted consumers. And addicts, as the tobacco, alcohol, and drug industries know, are the most profitable consumers.

Sadly, ego-driven consumerism never satisfies people. But in a society that equates being happy with having more, the more unhappy people become, the more they often turn to consumerism to try to feel better. For an example of how this ego-driven feedback loop works, just look at how many advertisements use variations of the message "you need more" and "you deserve better." Such direct appeals to the ego's self-serving desires work to keep people stuck in addictive cycles of consumerism.

Appealing to the ego's innate selfishness is one powerful way to influence people. Another powerful tool is fear. The ego is terrified of losing what it has.

Promise people they'll get more if they do what you say, and stoke people's fears that others are going to take away what they have if they don't follow you—that's how cult leaders and far too many political leaders assert control over groups. These days, there are entire media outlets dedicated to stoking greed and fear in viewers to keep them ego bound and easy to manipulate for political and commercial gain.

Artists, writers, musicians, and other creators have always been harder to control. Perhaps this is because, through their creative practice, artists have experienced what it's like to momentarily transcend their egos and be unbound.

In their art, creators often try to communicate this boundless perspective. When we read a compelling story, for instance, we might forget our own ego-driven concerns for a time and experience other lives and perspectives. By doing so, we develop the empathy, compassion, and connection that enables us to see past our own egos.

Great music, poetry, art, and drama does something similar, helping us peer beyond our small selves to connect with something greater. Think of the transcendent feeling you get when you experience an amazing concert or theatre production. For a time, your heart may swell with a sense of wonder, awe, and a joyful awareness of your connection to others.

This is why, throughout history, tyrants have feared artists, writers, and other creators who have challenged their attempts to control people. Hitler began his rise to power by attacking "degenerate" art, and he quickly sought to oppress artists for his own ego-driven purposes (forcing them to create Nazi propaganda). Stalin did something similar during his rise to power, enforcing censorship and strict controls over what sort of art could be produced, and executing those who refused to conform.[28]

The fundamental way the ego causes problems for us on a societal level is well-illustrated by an old parable about heaven and hell. An elderly man, afraid of dying, asks a wise sage what hell is like. The sage tells the man to picture several starving people sitting around a big stone table. In the center of the table is a steaming pot of soup. Each person has a spoon that's ten feet long. With their spoons they can reach the pot, but every time they try to feed themselves, they cannot reach their own mouths.

"That's terrible," says the elderly man. "To be hungry and have plenty of food in reach, but to never be able to eat it would indeed be a hellish torment. What does heaven look like?"

"It looks exactly the same," replies the sage. "Except in heaven, people feed each other."

---

[28] Stalin also shot several portrait artists for painting unflattering portraits of him—that's how ego-driven he was.

The ego makes hell hellish by keeping us separate and focused on ourselves. A tyrant controls people by keeping them separate and focused on how they need more and must fear each other, even while there's a pot of plenty sitting in the middle of the table. When we reduce the hold the ego has over us, we can escape these methods of control. Through openness, awareness, and connection, we can turn hell into heaven.

Enough About the Ego and Long Spoons, I Want to Publish

Go for it! Publishing is a great goal to have. The challenge of connecting with an audience beyond one's self, and the cycle of rejection, feedback, and revision that often accompanies the publishing journey, can be vital to developing as a writer and creator.

I can't tell you how many times folks have asked me "how do I get published?" There are several steps I could go into here (work with a writing group, get critical feedback, revise constantly, research markets, go to writing conferences, develop connections with editors and agents, etc.) but if that's what you want, the internet already has plenty of articles for you.[29]

---

[29] You can find one nifty post on publishing titled "Get Published in Ten (easy) Steps" at ToddMitchellBooks.com.

The thing that usually gets overlooked in such posts, though, is the essential thread that runs beneath all the other steps: sticking with it. If you find the courage to write the stories you most want to read, keep sending things out, don't give up, and keep developing your skills, eventually you'll get published. I know hundreds of writers, and the ones who published are the ones who stuck with it. The ones who gave up didn't.

So, if publishing is your goal (or if you've already published and want to continue publishing and connect with a broader audience) nothing matters more than perseverance.

What About Talent and Intelligence?

Maybe you think talent and intelligence have more to do with getting published or succeeding creatively than perseverance. If that's the case, I'll refer you to our 30th President, Calvin Coolidge, who put it this way:

> Nothing in this world can take the place of persistence. Talent will not: nothing is more common than unsuccessful men with talent. Genius will not; unrewarded genius is almost a proverb. Education will not: the world is full of educated derelicts. Persistence and determination alone are omnipotent.

You don't need to be a genius, or extremely talented, to create something new and significant. If you can tell a story that keeps you interested, you can interest others. If you can create a work of art that surprises and intrigues you, you can surprise and intrigue others. Deep down we're more alike than we think. **Write the book you most want to read (or create the art you most want to exist) and there's a good chance others will want it too.**

Genius might even hinder your chances of writing a book or creating a work that others connect with. The smarter you are, the harder it can be to relate to those who don't share your intellectual gifts. Create something genuine, revise it until it becomes what it needs to be, keep sending it out, and eventually it will find a home.

As for talent, that's a nice thing to have but it's not worth worrying about since it's not in your control. It also doesn't matter nearly as much as people seem to think. I mentioned earlier that I'm dyslexic. Not only has this increased the challenges of writing for me, it's made me an unusually slow reader. However, my struggles with writing and reading caused me to spend more time exploring how stories are put together. And dyslexia has made me more aware of how others might struggle with literacy, which helps me be a better teacher. **A lack of natural talent in some areas can lead to developing strengths in other areas.**

Music might seem an exception to these claims about talent, since music is an area where natural talent makes an obvious and pronounced difference. Some musicians, for instance, are gifted with beautiful voices from a young age, and they quickly gain attention. But does this mean that if you don't have such natural gifts, you can't become a great musician?

Hell no!

Several of the greatest singer songwriters of the last century weren't gifted with impressive singing voices. Rather than relying on vocal magnificence, they learned to excel in other ways, developing raw expression and lyricism. By writing songs that worked for their limited vocal ranges, they created music that more people could sing (which might have helped their songs become popular).

Follow your bliss and don't worry about talent or genius. They're overrated, and you can't change such things anyway. What you can change is whether you stick with it or not.

Why Perseverance Matters More Than You Think

There's an old joke about a religious man who encounters financial trouble. He prays to God to let him win the lottery so he can keep his home, but sadly, he's not a winner. The next night he prays again for God to let him win, this time climbing to the top of a hill and shouting at the sky. Still, he doesn't win the lottery. On the third night he climbs to the top of the hill and prays until his voice is raw. Tears stream down his face. "Please! I beseech you! Let me win the lottery so I may keep my home!"

Finally, a thunderous voice replies from the heavens, "Meet me halfway. Buy a ticket."

The dirty secret to achieving commercial success—the thing that most "success" books don't mention—is that commercial success is largely due to luck. You can't make yourself win the lottery. You could do everything right and still not win, and it won't be your fault (no matter how much your ego tries to blame you for it). **But, if you want to raise your chances of winning the lottery, buy more tickets.**

Perseverance is how you buy tickets. The more you create, and the more you send out into the world, the greater your chances will be of creating something that finds its audience and takes off.

Even if you logically accept this reasoning, I bet that you're still underestimating the role luck plays in commercial success. The ego loves the idea that it's the master of its own destiny (despite the fact that this contradicts the meaning of "destiny").

Because the ego needs to believe it's in control, it downplays the role of luck and other factors outside of its control, and it perpetuates the myth that you can will yourself into attaining commercial success if you only want it enough and take the right steps. If that's the story your ego keeps feeding you, here's some research you need to see.

The Study That Will Forever Change How You Look at Commercial Success

One of the ego-driven myths that pervades our society and shapes the way we think about books, movies, art, and music is that the artistic works that become hits are the ones that are "the best." For instance, how often do we think that because a book is a best seller, it's better than others? Or conversely, that if a book isn't as successful as others, it's because it's not as "good" as others?

If these claims are true—if the works that become hits are qualitatively better than those that don't—then those qualities should be measurable, and what will become popular should be relatively predictable. But that's not the case.

In reality, experts frequently fail to predict what will become popular. Think of all the producers who've put millions into movies that flopped. Or think of the numerous books that got rejected by scores of editors before becoming huge hits. In the publishing industry, it's said that on average around seven out of ten titles will not earn back their advance. Of the other three titles, two might break even, and one might become a hit. Producers and publishers are surprisingly bad at predicting what will or won't take off.

In 2005, social scientists at Columbia University set out to explore why predicting "hits" is notoriously difficult. One of the challenges of testing this is that we live in only one reality. As a result, when something becomes a "hit" we tend to think it must have become a hit due to special qualities the work possesses, and we use those qualities to justify why the work took off.

We might think, for example, that *The Hunger Games* became popular because it had a strong female protagonist, it was written in a gripping present tense voice, and it tapped into anxieties over economic inequality during an economic crisis. All this is true, but it overlooks the fact that several other well-written books also had these qualities and did not take off. And there may have even been "better" books that didn't get published. In order to effectively test *why* a work becomes popular, what's needed are multiple duplicate realities that all start from the same place.

Princeton Professor Matthew Salganik, one of the lead researchers in the study, explained it this way, "To see the role of chance you need to see multiple realizations of the same process. But we only get to see one outcome. So we see the world where the Mona Lisa is one of the most famous paintings, and it's hard to imagine that something different could have happened." Fortunately, Salganik and his fellow researchers came up with an ingenious way to use multiple virtual worlds to explore why some works become hits and others don't.

The experiment went like this: researchers gathered 48 contemporary songs from 48 randomly selected bands that were determined to be unknown by the study participants. The 14,000 study participants (recruited voluntarily from a popular website) were then divided into nine different online "worlds" that operated completely separate from each other.

In each of these nine virtual worlds, the participants could listen to, rate, and download any of the 48 songs they liked for free. In eight of the virtual worlds, study participants could see how many times a song had been downloaded in that world (a measure of the popularity of that song in that world). In one control world, participants couldn't see how many times a song had been downloaded, and simply had to go off their own preferences.

Now, if songs that are qualitatively "the best" rise to the top and become the most popular, then one would expect that the songs that become popular in all nine virtual worlds would be the same or similar. Except that didn't happen—not by a long shot.

Instead, the top songs in every world were vastly different. Overall, songs that were generally seen as being "high quality" productions tended to do better in each world than ones that generally ranked lower, but not always. And in no two worlds were the top ten most successful songs close to being the same. For instance, one song, "Lockdown" by *52Metro*, ranked 1st in one world and 40th (out of 48) in another.

Think about that for a moment. Nine different virtual worlds, and nine completely different results for which songs became popular. If you lived in the world where "Lockdown" became a number one hit, you'd likely think, "Of course 'Lockdown' is a hit. It's a great song. How could it be otherwise?" But in another world "Lockdown" was a complete flop, barely noticed by the hundreds of study participants in that world. If you lived in that world, you'd think, "Clearly, this song is missing something people want," and you'd see other songs as obvious hits.

What can we learn from this?

One conclusion the researchers gave is that, to a surprising degree, blockbusters are random. Songs with higher production qualities tend to outperform poorly produced songs, but once a song reaches a high level of production quality, whether it becomes popular or not is largely unpredictable. And more than something intrinsic to the work, social factors and social influences often determine how popular a work becomes. The study also found that the more social influences are involved, the more unpredictable popularity becomes.

For writers this means that, beyond writing a well-crafted, well-revised book, producing it in a high-quality way (working with a professional editor), and letting others know about it, you can't control whether your book becomes a hit. Whether or not a book (or song, or work of art) becomes a hit is mostly a matter of chance and social factors that may be impossible to predict and are largely beyond your control. You could put hundreds of thousands of dollars into promoting a work, but that still won't guarantee that it will take off, and most of us can't afford to do that. In short, **once your work has reached a high level of production quality, whether or not it becomes a hit has surprisingly little to do with the work itself.**

Recognizing this is essential. As Salganik put it, "if you believe that there's a large role for chance in the outcomes that people have and the kinds of success that people have and also the kinds of failures that people have, it changes how you treat other people."

Does that mean there's nothing you can do to influence your own success?

No way. We're going to explore several things you can do that make a tremendous difference. But knowing that commercial success is largely due to chance will hopefully help you become more compassionate when considering the successes and failures of others *and* yourself.

Your ego wants you to believe that it's all in your control. Research shows that's not how reality works. Don't shame yourself when a well-crafted work fails to take off. And don't let it go to your head when a work does. Realizing that commercial success is largely due to chance and social factors beyond your control is crucial to persevering effectively and staying creative.

Take Away Two: Undiscovered Van Goghs

It's important not to misunderstand the findings of that study I described in the previous chapter. Just because chance plays a big role in commercial success doesn't mean you should give up or use "being unlucky" as an excuse not to attempt something. It's the opposite. The fact that chance plays a significant role in commercial success makes perseverance even more critical. After all, raising your odds by continuing to create is the part you can change.

I'm also not saying that the works that become hits *only* rise in popularity due to luck. Although this might be true for a few, most works of art, music, or literature that become popular deserve the attention they get. And most of the time the creators of these works have dramatically increased their chances of getting discovered by persevering, developing their craft, and seizing the opportunities that came along. Take Suzanne Collins, the author of *The Hunger Games*. She was a television writer for over a decade, and she published seven books *before* her wildly popular *Hunger Games* series became a blockbuster hit. That's how you increase your odds.

Just as it's important to recognize the role of chance in achieving commercial success, it's also important to recognize that there are many great, high-quality works that don't become hits due to chance.

Consider Vincent van Gogh. He only officially sold one painting, "The Red Vineyard at Arles," during his lifetime. The rest of his 2,000 works remained unsold and largely unappreciated while he lived, despite the fact that his brother, Theo, was a renowned art dealer who tried for years to promote Vincent's work. Vincent van Gogh could very easily have faded into obscurity and been forgotten. Instead, his sister-in-law, Johanna van Gogh-Bonger, inherited his paintings after both he and his brother Theo (her husband) died only a few months apart.

Suddenly in possession of hundreds of Vincent van Gogh oil paintings, Johanna did as her late husband had done and tried to sell them. She published Vincent's letters to Theo and organized exhibitions of his works, until gradually his popularity spread and he became one of the most famous and valued artists of all time.

Although the incredible popularity of Van Gogh's art is great for his legacy, he never got to experience such notoriety during this lifetime. The only reason most of the world knows Van Gogh now is due to the brilliant efforts of Johanna van Gogh-Bonger (and a bit of belated luck). For every painter like Van Gogh who gets resurrected from obscurity, how many other extraordinary artists are there who don't get discovered? Whose works are never lifted up for others to appreciate?

For every *Zen and the Art of Motorcycle Maintenance* (rejected an astonishing 121 times before selling over 5 million copies), or *A Wrinkle in Time* (rejected 26 times before winning a Newbery Medal and becoming one of the most read children's books of all time) or *The Help* (rejected around 60 times before selling over 7 million copies) how many other great books are there that don't gain attention?

We'll never know all those creations and creators who remain overlooked. We live in only one reality. We only know the works that are lucky enough to be held up and praised in our reality. Undoubtedly, there are numerous amazing artists who work in obscurity, and numerous brilliant works that end up gathering dust in an attic somewhere until they're thrown away. Other works might get published but don't receive the attention they deserve (some of my favorite books, as well as my favorite bands, have come and gone with barely anyone noticing).[30]

The way to increase your chances of having something take off is to persevere and keep creating. Keep growing as a writer or artist, stay open to new possibilities, keep sending things out, and embrace the opportunities you encounter. That's what you can do.

To do this over many years—to keep functioning at your creative best—it's essential to approach creative endeavors in a way that enables you to love the process. **Not only does loving the process make it easier to persevere while staying highly creative, it's how you create new opportunities for yourself.** If you don't love what you're doing, it's going to be hard to get others to love it. But if you love what you're doing, you increase your chances that others will love it too. Even if commercial success doesn't come your way, you'll still have spent your precious mortal hours doing what you love, which is what a truly successful life is all about.

---

[30] Case in point, a couple days ago I asked an editor who used to work for one of the big five publishing houses why she thought some books rose in popularity and others didn't. "If I knew, I'd be a millionaire," she replied. Then she told me that the "best" book she'd edited—the one she was certain would be a huge hit due to its beautiful prose, engaging story, and unforgettable characters—barely sold any copies at all.

But Perseverance Isn't Fun

You've probably noticed that we keep coming back to the fundamental importance of perseverance. Maybe you think that perseverance—constantly persisting despite the ups and downs—sounds like a drag. Or worse, an exhausting struggle against the currents. This is how I used to see perseverance, and I prided myself on being able to do it despite how hard it got or how terrible it felt. It took me decades to learn that persevering this way isn't very effective. It just wears you down and crushes your creativity.

Perseverance doesn't need to be a struggle. Remember, it's far more enjoyable and sustainable to persevere by loving the process and enjoying the experiences you get to have. Falling down seven times and getting up eight becomes significantly easier when you're able to appreciate falling and appreciate getting up. Persevering this way is similar to what Joseph Campbell was referring to with his famous advice, "Follow your bliss."

Following your bliss doesn't mean that you chase after every shallow, temporary pleasure that crosses your path. Bliss runs deeper than that. We feel bliss when we do what we're called to do on the deepest level we're aware of.

To follow your bliss, seek out your inner purpose by becoming aware of what gives you long-term fulfillment, then follow it to see where it leads. As Campbell eloquently put it, when you follow your bliss you "put yourself on a kind of track that has been there all the while waiting for you, and the life you ought to be living is the one you are living. When you see that, you begin to meet people who are in the field of your bliss, and they open the doors to you... If you follow your bliss, doors will open for you that wouldn't have opened for anyone else."

"Great," you might think, "following my bliss, loving the process, appreciating the experiences I get to have no matter how difficult they are—that all sounds nice, but *how* do you do that? Creating things is flippin' hard. Doubt and rejection are hard. How do you keep the challenging aspects of the creative process from weighing you down and making it difficult to continue creating?"

To help put some of the concepts we've discussed into practice, think about what makes persevering a struggle. Often, it's the sense that what you're doing isn't good enough and where you are right now isn't where you want to be. It's comparing yourself to others and feeling inadequate. Or it's feeling that you're not living up to your (or other's) expectations. **Essentially, it's wanting things to be different than they are—that's what causes suffering. And that's what makes persevering a struggle.**

The solution is to change your perspective so that you fully accept what is. Although this sounds simple, doing this requires a radical paradigm shift (we'll explore more specific ways to make this shift in Part III). Even if fully accepting what is sounds abstract or unrealistic to you, I bet you already know what creating things from this perspective feels like. To reconnect with this feeling, see if you can recall what it was like to create something when you were a child. Remember how you approached drawing, painting, or making things before the pressure to make something "good" got in the way?

Sometimes I watch my two young daughters write stories, draw pictures, and make videos. They don't tell themselves that they don't know enough or aren't good enough to create something, and they don't build up expectations and want things to be different than they are. Instead, they dive in, start exploring, and become wholly absorbed in the unfolding present. They discover what things are as they create them while reveling in the process of creating.

Similarly, when I go to schools and teach creative writing, I'm often amazed by how quickly ten-year-olds can fill pages with fresh, stunning lines. True—they still have much to learn about craft, revision, and how to enact visions for others to see, but their ability to access wild, playful creativity is astounding. Picasso had good reason to praise the creative abilities of children.[31]

Return to that child mind openness. Before you face the page, get yourself excited to create. Remind yourself that you're doing this because you're called to do it. Remind yourself that where you are is exactly where you need to be. Then immerse yourself in the unfolding present by allowing yourself to create without judgment, expectation, or resistance. Create for the pure joy of creating and appreciate all the twists and turns as they

---

[31] This doesn't mean that the child artist and mature artist are the same. The pre-judgmental "child" mind is only similar to the trans-judgmental "actualized" mind in that both are able to freely connect with creativity and create without resistance. To think that they're the same (that adult Picasso was just a large toddler with a paintbrush) is to make what Ken Wilber called the pre/trans fallacy. If he were talking about creativity, he might explain it this way: the trans-judgmental creative mind *includes* and *transcends* judgment, so people who create from this level of consciousness are able to make judgments about their work to revise, develop, and improve it, *and* they can transcend those judgments to connect with the creative source without resistance.

arise. *That's* how you persevere—by embracing your creative impulses and accepting what is.

This subtle shift in perspective makes a profound difference. When you accept what is, you can stop struggling against existence and move with the creative energy of life. Let go of the grasping, striving, constantly-trying-to-make-things-be-what-you-want-them-to-be illusion of control. Trust that when you accept what is, you'll be more effective. Creating new things and actualizing your creative potential will become easier.

Initially, this might seem paradoxical—how can accepting what is make you more effective at bringing *new* things into existence?

To wrap your mind around how this works (and to see how perseverance can be fun), let's take a look at the difference between surfing and swimming.

To Surf or to Swim?

Here's a counterintuitive axiom about control: **The more you cling to the illusion of control, the less control you'll actually have and the more frustrated you'll become.**[32]

If this seems confusing, consider surfing as an example. I love to surf ocean waves. It took me a long time to get good at

---

[32] The phrase "illusion of control" is also used in psychology to refer to a form of cognitive bias. In this book, I'm using the phrase to refer to something much more fundamental. On the surface level of consciousness, we experience control and often think our small self is in control. When our consciousness expands, we become aware of how the small self we think is in control is actually not in control. Another way to think of this is as "the illusion of *separate* control" because the separate self you think has control is an egoic delusion. Hence, the illusion of control goes hand-in-hand with the illusion of a separate self. It's a problematic illusion because, as nice as control sounds to the ego, it's one of the most powerful ways the ego keeps us separate and unaware of our connection to being. Simply put: as long as your ego is trying to control things, you're resisting being.

it, though, because I kept fighting against the waves and the waves always won.

Effective surfers know that it doesn't work to fight against waves. The waves are stronger than you'll ever be. The more you struggle against them, the more you'll exhaust yourself. However, if you accept and understand the waves, you can ride them and become skillful at this.

When a surfer rides a big wave and travels toward the beach, the surfer doesn't say, "What a great person I am for pushing myself here." It was the wave that did the work, so a wise surfer will say, "That was a great wave."

And when a wave breaks on top of you and causes you to struggle, there's no point in blaming yourself. Again, it's the wave. It's simply what is. Observe what it is, learn from it, and move on so that you can experience the next wave and the next.

To get really good at surfing, you need to let go of the illusion of control and become part of the wave. Instead of thinking that you can control the ocean, accept the wave as it is, work with it, and ride it. Few people do this perfectly. The ego often intrudes and gets in the way. It might cause you to fight against the wave in big or subtle ways. It might even cause you to want the wave to be different from what it is. But you cannot ride a wave you don't accept. **If you try to change the wave, or if you try to ride it as you want it to be and not as it is, you're going to wipe out.**

Skillful surfers become so absorbed in their awareness of the wave that they forget their small selves. Essentially, they enter a flow state where they transcend their egos and their sense of separateness from the wave, if only for a little bit. By becoming part of the wave and the ocean that forms it, they're able to ride the wave and do amazing things. They're able to align themselves with the ocean's power and energy, letting it become their power and energy, which is what makes surfing so transcendent and thrilling.

Of course, you don't have to surf the waves. There are times when you might duck under them, entering a different current. And there are times when you might try to swim against the waves and the currents because you want to head in a different direction. You might think that you're stronger than the waves and the ocean that forms them. You might even convince yourself that you're making progress this way. Regardless, the ocean will always be stronger. It's what you're swimming in, and the more you resist the waves, try to change them, or try to swim against the currents, the more you're going to exhaust yourself.

The bliss of surfing waves far outweighs the struggle of swimming against them, and you'll go further this way, too. Clinging to the illusion that you have control over the ocean and can make the waves be what you want them to be doesn't work—not in the ocean or in life. You'll just end up making yourself miserable.

Now imagine what you'll be able to do when you let go of the illusion of control and work with the waves, aligning yourself with the ocean's power and energy so that you can surf in wondrous directions. In Part III we'll explore exactly how to do this in life.

Part III

"When I run after what I think I want
My days are a furnace of distress and anxiety;
If I sit in my own place of patience,
What I need flows to me,
And without any pain."

—Rumi

A Tale of Two Paths: Struggle vs. Surrender

Most of us are programmed from a young age to struggle against the currents to get what we think we want. For artists, writers, and creators, this programming often leads to the "suffering artist" paradigm of creative living.

The suffering artist is never satisfied. The suffering artist constantly struggles to achieve more. The suffering artist often feels disappointed, misunderstood, jealous, and overlooked. The suffering artist seeks to control everything. The suffering artist is a harsh judge of themselves and others. The suffering artist believes that to create great art they must sacrifice everything, always do more, and suffer to create.[33]

---

[33] I don't know when or where this suffering artist notion of creative living first emerged, but it's become so deeply ingrained in our culture that there's now a Wikipedia page on the "suffering artist" or "tortured artist" as a stock character and "real life stereotype."

Growing up, this was the main model of creative living that I saw in our culture at large. It's no wonder that I thought to create anything good, I had to struggle and suffer. But this isn't true—not even close. You can be much more effective and prolific creating from a place of bliss.

To accept this, it might help to consider two different paths and where they might take you. First, there's the ego-driven path of struggle, control, and resistance (fighting the wave). It's easy to see how fighting against the wave isn't effective in surfing, but what does this look like in life?

For most folks, it looks something like this (I know this path well, since I followed it for many years):

Work hard every day to get good grades, win awards, and accomplish things. Get into a good college so that you can get the finest education, and more importantly, a prestigious degree. Go to graduate school to earn more degrees. Why do all this? So you can finally do what you want to do when you graduate.

Get a job (or a couple) and start climbing your way up the professional ladder. Try to achieve things. If you're lucky, you might win some awards and gain some recognition (but most of the time, you won't). Still, keep going after your "if onlys." Fight to make yourself stand out.

Spend years chasing after bigger "if onlys." Exhaust yourself. Keep struggling, because it's what you've been taught to do and it's the only path you know. If you could just achieve more (you think) your growing sense of discontentment will go away. Maybe you get lucky and experience a big hit. Fame and fortune might come your way. Are you happy? Does it fulfill you? Not for long.

Now what?

You could step back onto the hedonic treadmill and go another round, chasing after bigger "if onlys" with the hope that *this* time your achievements will give you the lasting happiness you seek. Perhaps that's what you do. Addictions are hard to stop. Maybe you keep going until you have a breakdown—one that's finally big enough to cause you to step back and assess what truly makes you happy. At last, you're ready to end your ego-driven achievement addiction and discover a better way to be.

You might have spent decades getting to this point, but at least you've reached a place where you're ready to focus on living in a truly fulfilling way. The fact that you reached this moment of awareness at all is a blessing. Most people never step off the treadmill. You have. Congratulations on becoming ready to find a more authentic, connected, blissful way to be.

Or, there's another path. A short cut. Instead of chasing after things to make yourself happy (only to discover that this leads to misery and doesn't bring lasting happiness), why not focus on *being* happy on the deepest, most fulfilling level you can conceive of? Why not embrace what is and follow your bliss? Not only is this more enjoyable, **you'll most likely accomplish more by embracing what is and following your bliss than you will by struggling against the currents.**

Taking this path might look like this: You still might go to college, and maybe even graduate school. You still study hard and work hard. But you do all of this for entirely different, intrinsic reasons. You do it because you enjoy learning and because you're aware that where you are is exactly where you need to be.

The same goes for creativity. You still might write books, paint paintings, create music, and make things, but you do it because it's what you feel called to do and you enjoy doing it. You're too focused on the present and appreciating the experiences you get to have to be distracted by endless "if onlys." You might do many of the same things on this path as you would on the first path because that's where the currents take you, but instead of constantly struggling against the currents, you're working with them and appreciating the ride.

As a result, you're more aware and better able to surf the wave. Being aware makes it easier to notice opportunities. And creating from a place of bliss instead of struggling like a suffering artist makes it easier to persevere and stay creative. By persevering blissfully, you increase your odds of having something take off. If something does take off, you can have that experience, but it won't change your creative vision or your creative voice because your creativity, and your well-being, aren't dependent on achieving lofty outcomes. All you're doing is embracing what is and enjoying the experiences you get to have (loving the process).

You don't need to become a millionaire to learn that many millionaires aren't as happy as monks who only own a bowl and a blanket. You know that already. In fact, when you take the blissful path, you already have what millionaires wish they could buy: unconditional happiness.

From the outside, these two paths might appear similar, but the experience of taking them is radically different, and ultimately the difference in the experience will lead to different reactions and different results. On the first path, you live a life of struggle, frustration, and exhaustion (sprinkled with some temporary pleasure) as you chase after an achievement-based notion of success and often end up disappointed. It's no wonder that many artists, writers, and creators who take this path become frustrated and burn out. On the second path, you live a truly successful life—a life that's shaped by loving the process rather than outcomes, and is full of love, openness, discovery, connection, creativity, and appreciation.

Perhaps I make taking the second path sound too easy. When you look at it objectively, taking the second path seems like a no-brainer (or a "no-minder" if you want to get Zen about it). And taking the second path *is* simple, in the same way that becoming enlightened need not be complicated. All it takes, as sages have explained for hundreds of years, is to stop seeking enlightenment—stop wanting things to be different than what they are—and become aware of how you are enlightened.[34]

Likewise, the way to reach the second path is to step off the path of egoic illusions and become aware of the greater reality the ego has kept you from seeing. This reality has been there all along, but it's not visible from the first path. Only by stepping off the first path will you be able to discover another way to be—a way to stop struggling and exist more consciously and blissfully.

The trouble is, we live in a culture that's constantly funneling us onto the first path by pushing us to chase after material rewards, achievements, and other "if onlys" to attain temporary, conditional happiness. In this culture we're frequently told that the first path is the only path, and whenever we stray we're prodded back onto it. Add to this the fact that your ego desperately doesn't want you to step off the first path, and you can see why most people never consider other paths until the suffering caused by the first path drives them to a point of exhaustion. Breakdown can then become breakthrough. That's why reaching the second path, although simple, is rarely easy.

Don't be afraid to step off the first path. Know that there's another way to be. Let go of all attachment to the struggling, suffering artist paradigm and trust that it will be okay. It may take some work to find the second path and work to stay on it, but don't let that scare you. The hard part is dissolving your ego's grasp enough so you can become conscious of what's beyond it. When you're aware of how you're much more than

---

[34] As Eckhart Tolle recently put it, "You get there by realizing you already are there."

what your ego thinks, the work will feel effortless because you're no longer standing in your own way. You're *being* rather than trying.

Take another look at the Rumi quote included at the beginning of Part III: "When I run after what I think I want, my days are a furnace of distress and anxiety; if I sit in my own place of patience, what I need flows to me, and without any pain." Running after what I think I want is the first, ego-driven path that makes the days "a furnace of distress and anxiety." Sitting in a "place of patience" describes transcending the ego and connecting with being. By being instead of trying, "what I need flows to me, and without any pain."

This is the second path, and you have everything you need to reach it. All that's required now is a radical change in how you see yourself and what you're doing. Fortunately, this change is exactly the sort of transformation that creating things can lead you to experience.

The Transformative Journey

There's hidden wisdom in the structure of stories that can help us navigate the creative process.

To uncover this wisdom, first let's look at plot. In the simplest sense, the purpose of plot is to get the reader to turn the page and keep reading. But plot can be much more than this.

Writers know that problems are needed to make a plot interesting. A plot where everything goes well for the characters is both unrealistic and boring. Problems are necessary in stories (and in life)—to bring about change. If you want to make the plot more compelling, make the problems more perilous. Then find all the nefarious ways you can to raise the stakes, turn up the conflict, and challenge your characters.

Developing a great plot is rarely easy. Although critics sometimes dismiss "plot-driven" stories for being the low-brow territory of pulp fiction while praising "character driven" stories for being literary and sophisticated, the most effective stories have *both* compelling plots and engaging characters. **It's the successful marriage of plot *and* character that creates a**

great narrative.

Rather than simply seeing plot as a way to keep a reader reading, I like to think of plot as simultaneously emerging from the characters (as what happens externally in the story reflects the characters' internal conflicts), while challenging the characters to be more than they currently are (as the plot pushes characters to new realizations and actions). In this way, plot is both how you reveal who characters are *and* how you bring about transformative moments.

Now let's talk about stories. Ever wonder what makes something a story, and why we enjoy them?

One thing most stories have in common is the depiction of transformation in the face of adversity. In a story, a character faces some problem or adversity, and in response, the character needs to transform (or at least have a possibility of transforming) to deal with that problem.

Characters don't always transform in time. Sometimes they fail to change enough, or sometimes the problem wins and destroys them—in which case the story is probably a tragedy. But in almost all stories, there's a problem the character faces, and because this problem is related to their character—to what they desire, think, and fear—the character must change to address the problem. Hence, **stories can be broadly described as narratives that depict character transformation in the face of adversity.**

Seeing things change is entertaining. Witnessing character transformation in the face of adversity is more than simply entertaining, though. It's enlightening.

Consider, for instance, how the adversity that Luke Skywalker faces in *Star Wars* helps him transform from a whiny farm boy constrained by narrow self-interests to a Jedi who's willing to take on the Empire and risk his life for a greater cause. Or how Katniss Everdeen goes through a similar transformation in *The Hunger Games* series, becoming not just a survivor, but a revolutionary leader who inspires others to create a more just society. Adversity isn't only about physical threats, though. The greatest challenges are often psychological. One of my favorite characters is Scout Finch from *To Kill a Mockingbird*. For the most part, Scout isn't physically fighting for her life. Still, her understanding of herself, her family, and her community change dramatically in response to the adversity she experiences.

Change is hard. Significant changes, or transformations, don't come easily. The more we're able to change to adapt to new challenges, the more likely we are to thrive socially, psychologically, and even biologically. Transform in response to adversity or perish is what evolution is all about. Therefore, it makes sense that narratives that depict transformation in the face of adversity interest us. We want to know *how* others change to deal with adversity so we can discover how we might change to deal with the problems and challenges we face.

Now, here's the wonderful thing about *writing* stories: **when we write stories, we're not only engaged in a process of transforming our characters through adversity, we're transforming ourselves.** The steps that characters take as they transform often mirror the steps we take as creators recreating ourselves.

To successfully navigate this transformative process, both in stories and in life, it helps to understand narrative structure and the common steps through which transformations unfold.

Transform Your Characters, Transform Yourself

Characters in different stories often experience a remarkably similar process as they transform in the face of adversity. Writers might use various terms for the steps in this process, but the commonalities are pretty astounding. Joseph Campbell wrote about these narrative patterns in *The Hero with a Thousand Faces*. Most writers are at least partially familiar with the steps of the hero's journey and the three-act story structure of departure, adventure, and return that Campbell discussed (if you're not familiar with the hero's journey, there are plenty of depictions of versions of it online.)[35]

---

[35] Campbell originally called the three acts "departure," "initiation," and "return," but most folks now refer to the middle act as "adventure." However, this is just one way to think about narrative structure. Personally, I prefer to think of the first act as "thesis" because it's where the big question of the story is posed.

As you engage in a big creative project, you might notice how the process of bringing something new and significant into existence also sets *you* on a transformative journey, and the steps in this journey parallel those in the hero's journey. Consequently, the hero's journey provides a useful roadmap for understanding how personal creative transformations occur.

For instance, at the beginning of a creative endeavor, there's often a "call to adventure"—a story you feel you must write, or something you feel called to create. And there may be a "refusal of the call"—a sense that you're not up to the task, or good enough to do the thing you feel called to do. There may be a "meeting with a mentor"—someone who influences you and gives you the courage and ability to move forward. And there may be a "first threshold" that you pass through—that moment when you realize the call to adventure you've received can't be ignored and you say, "Fine! I'll attempt this!" Then you embark on the creative journey.

That's the first act.

The second act involves the journey away from the known "ordinary world" into the unknown "special world." I often think of Act II as taking place in bizarro world, because to effectively challenge the main character it helps to have things swing as far as possible in Act II from the ordinary world depicted in Act I. For example, if in Act I a character is living the life of a lonely bachelor in his perfectly organized and meticulously clean, monotone apartment, in Act II he'll be surrounded by people and bright, bombastic chaos.

For the writer or creator, there's also a "special world" you enter into. At this point, you might get so absorbed in a project

---

The second act is "antithesis" because it's where the main character is challenged, and their situation is often the opposite (or anti) where things were in the first act. And the third act is "synthesis" because it involves the integration (or synthesis) of what was learned from the journey with a transformed self that's able to bring some degree of change back to the ordinary world.

that you become obsessed. You might start to think from within the project and lose perspective about where you're heading or what you're creating. During this stage, it's typical to feel out of your depth, lost, and separated from your ordinary life.

A large part of Act II involves what Campbell referred to as the "road of trials." There are tests, allies, and enemies at this stage. For creators, doubt is one of those trials ("I can't do this"). The comparison game may become your enemy and seek to cripple you ("This isn't good enough"). Some people may become your enemy at this point as well, and they'll say or do things to hold you back and keep you from completing your transformative journey ("Why are you wasting your time on this nonsense?"). Fortunately, you might also discover allies at this stage who will assist you and give you the encouragement and support you need to continue.

Temptation is another big part of Act II. You might feel tempted away from your creative work by distractions, temporary pleasures, and an endlessly hungry internet that wants to devour your attention. If a project requires research, this research might become relentless and confounding at this stage. In narratives, Act II is where the hero gets swallowed up by the "belly of the whale" as Campbell described it. For creators, it's where you might become consumed by what you're creating, lost in your research, or shipwrecked in a sea of doubt and uncertainty.

Then, usually toward the end of Act II, there's "the ordeal"—the biggest challenge yet. This is the part of the transformative journey that interests me most, because this is where persevering gets particularly hard.

Facing the Ordeal

The ordeal can come in many forms for writers and creators—rejection, feeling like a failure, thinking that what you've created sucks, feeling inadequate, worthless, or foolish for believing you could be an author, artist, or creator.

When you reach this stage, embrace it. Tell yourself it's part of the process. Tell yourself all is as it should be, and where you are is exactly where you need to be. This is what the transformative journey is about. You've made it this far—through the questioning, distractions, and struggle. Well done! The ordeal has good things to teach you.

For guidance through this tricky stage, think again of the hero's journey. There's a moment in the ordeal that's sometimes called "the dark night of the soul." Usually this happens after a big conflict when the character is alone and mortality becomes a prevalent theme. The character may contemplate their death, or the death of another (a friend, loved one, pet…).

For writers and creatives, *this* is the moment where many give up. It can be the death of the project, or the death of a dream. We might expect to face difficulties before we begin a creative project, but in the ordeal, things become far more difficult than we imagined. This, too, is as it should be.

In stories there's a concept that some, like screenwriter Robert McKee, refer to as taking the story to the end of the line. To do this effectively, the writer needs to make the ordeal one step worse than what the character (and the reader) expect it to be. It's not just rock bottom. It's a level beyond what the character thought would be rock bottom.

Often, taking a story to the end of the line involves bringing the external conflict back to an internal realization. For instance, when a character in a romantic comedy is actively despised by the one he loves, that might seem like rock bottom. But the story isn't taken to the end of the line until the character realizes he deserves to be despised because he doesn't even like himself.

For writers and creators, this part of the ordeal could be when you go from having a project be rejected to thinking that the creative project you've been working on deserves to be rejected and you were an idiot to think you could ever create what you felt called to create. You have no business attempting this. You're not smart enough, talented enough, or dedicated enough to do what you set out to do. You're making a mockery of the art you love. Everything you've done is just a waste of time, and every word you wrote is a stain on existence. (These are all things I've thought at this stage in the journey). The ego often becomes brutally negative during the dark night of the soul as it attempts to hold you back and keep you from transforming. This is also a normal, important step in the process.

"Hold up," you might say. "I thought this book was about overcoming doubt and struggle and enjoying creativity more. Going through an ordeal like this sounds terrible."

You're right—facing the ordeal is hard. Creating something significant and new will be hard *every time* in ways you can't foresee. That's the process. That's how the transformative journey goes.

To love the process, it's imperative to recognize that unexpected challenges are not only part of the process—they're useful. You don't need to fear the ordeal. You can accept the ordeal as a necessary step in the transformative journey. You can even embrace the ordeal and turn it into something exciting and rewarding *because* of the difficulty. Before we get there, though, it's important to fully recognize what the process involves. There's no sugar-coating it—creating things will challenge you more than you expect, and in ways you can't anticipate.

So, why the ordeal? Why are unexpected challenges part of the process? Why the dark night of the soul where a profound sense of loss, mortality, and maybe even death seep in?

It's because real, significant changes—real transformations—involve the death of the old self (the old ways of thinking and acting) and the birth of a new self. It's death and rebirth, and the old self doesn't want to die.

Change is never easy, and significant transformations are especially difficult. That's what most stories are about. And that's what attempting to create something new can bring about in you.

Fortunately, you're not alone in doing this. For instance, think of all the times great artists like Frida Khalo, Georgia O'Keeffe, Claude Monet, and Pablo Picasso transformed and discovered new ways of perceiving and painting. They didn't simply *decide* to perceive and paint things in new ways. They had to face ordeals and fail enough to let go of their old ways of perceiving so that new ways could be discovered and brought into existence.

If you're lucky enough to keep growing as a writer, artist, or creator, then you'll probably experience the death of what you think you know and the birth of new ways of perceiving several times during your creative life. That's what makes the creative path so challenging, and so magnificent.[36]

---

[36] The 13th century Persian poet and Sufi mystic Rumi depicted the transformative power of death when he wrote: "I lived for thousands of years as a mineral, and then died and became a plant. I lived for thousands of years as a plant, and then died and became an animal. I lived for thousands of years as an animal, and then died and became human. Tell me, what have I ever lost by dying?"

The Dark Night of the Soul

There's a reason why the dark night of the soul—that part of the ordeal where a character contemplates loss, mortality, and death—often happens when the main character is alone. This is the stage in the story where the main character turns inward and frequently realizes "I'm the problem." Although this might seem negative, it's actually empowering. As the writer David Gerrold elegantly put it, "The moment in which the hero recognizes, 'I'm the problem—' he also recognizes the corollary: *'therefore I'm the solution!'*"[37]

The character in the romantic comedy who realizes that the one he desires rejects him because he hates himself, and that's why he's been behaving in such self-destructive, contemptible ways, now has the perspective he needs to transform himself.

---

[37] This quote comes from Gerrold's book on writing science fiction and fantasy, *Worlds of Wonder,* in which Gerrold states, "Transformation is the reinvention of the self by the *Self*" (emphasis mine).

Instead of trying to impress the one he loves by making superficial changes, he recognizes that real change must come from within. He might begin to reconnect with himself and his deepest values. He might start to become the person he's called to be. The selfish womanizer he was before has died, enabling him to finally develop relationships with others as a genuine, compassionate person.

Maybe in the end he'll get back together with the one he loves because he's started to become a person who can truly give and receive love. Or maybe the person he desired to be with was just a catalyst for the real growth and transformation the character needed to experience. The details differ with every story, but the essential steps in the transformative journey are often similar.

The dark night of the soul reveals one of the greatest insights stories give us: **when characters realize how they're causing their own problems (taking responsibility for what they're experiencing), they're able to discover the solution. The transformation is tied to the realization.**

Likewise, when a writer, artist, or other creator descends into the dark night of the soul—when we feel lost, exhausted, doubtful, and ready to throw in the towel—we have a potent opportunity to recognize how we're causing our own suffering. With such a recognition, we might also discover a solution—a glimpse into how we hold the keys to our transformation.

Perhaps it's the ego's never-ending demands for approval that's causing us to suffer. Perhaps it's the way the ego drives us to judgments and criticisms that inevitably become self-judgments (the more harshly you criticize others, the more you hold yourself back with those same criticisms). Perhaps it's the ego's fear of failure that's limiting the self. Or maybe it's the comparison game, and the unending string of "if onlys" that's fueling a breakdown. The ways we suffer might differ every time we reach the dark night of the soul, and every time we'll be given an opportunity to see how we're causing our suffering.

This step in the creative process presents us with a valuable chance to let go of the old self we're clinging to so that a new, more aware self can be born.

That's the beauty of the creative process. It provides those who are willing to embark on creative journeys with a powerful practice for learning, growth, and transformation. **Through our creative work, we recreate ourselves**.

Which is why it's important to embrace the ordeal! Embrace the dark night of the soul. You probably won't be challenged in the ways you expect, and that's a good thing. Such unexpected challenges give you a chance to grow beyond your perceived limitations. Let go of the suffering self you're clinging to and let a new self be born. Because, as those who study and understand narrative structure know, once the hero passes through the ordeal, there's a reward.

This reward might not be what your old self thought it would be. It might not be the commercial success you once desired, or the fame and fortune your ego sought, but ultimately it will make you happier than such things ever could.

Apotheosis and Reward

In the Joseph Campbell way of thinking about story structure, Act III generally focuses on the return to the ordinary world as a changed person who's better able to help others. Campbell described the final stages of the hero's journey as "apotheosis," "the ultimate boon," "refusal of return," "the crossing of the return threshold," "master of two worlds," and "freedom to live." Of these steps, the one people frequently seem the least familiar with is apotheosis. However, this is precisely the step in the journey that's most helpful for writers and creators to explore.[38]

---

[38] In *The Hero With a Thousand Faces* Campbell also included "the magic flight" and "rescue from without" as steps in the return, but I left these out since they're not as common in contemporary stories. Also, Campbell put "apotheosis" and "the ultimate boon" at the end of Act II, Initiation. However, in many books on narrative structure, these steps (or ones like them) are usually grouped in Act III. I'm using Campbell's terms loosely here to refer to com-

Apotheosis comes from the Greek *apotheoun* meaning "to deify." In theology, it's used to refer to an individual being raised to a god-like status. In stories, apotheosis refers to how the death of the small self (the ego-bound self) enables the character to expand their consciousness and move beyond suffering to a state of divine knowledge, love, compassion, and bliss.

For writers and creators, there's also a state of apotheosis that can be achieved through transcending the ego. Dissolving the ego's grasp can lead to a state of open, compassionate, blissful creativity. But, as we explored in Part II, the ego doesn't want to be transcended. It wants to preserve its sense of being a separate self in control of things. Consequently, the path to apotheosis requires setbacks, suffering, and failure. Often, it's only after hardship and failure enable us to recognize how the ego-driven way isn't working that we're able to transcend the ego and reach apotheosis.

Reaching apotheosis is a reward in itself, but in myths and stories apotheosis also gives the hero the ability to attain "the ultimate boon"—a gift that requires an expanded "god-like" consciousness to receive. Indiana Jones, for instance, is only fit to take possession of the Ark of the Covenant after going through many ordeals (snakes!), temptations ("Don't look at it, no matter what happens…"), and facing his own mortality as he's chained to a post surrounded by flesh-melting spirits. Indiana emerges from this harrowing experience a changed person who's able to take the Ark and not be ruined by it. Powerful gifts, when bestowed on someone without the expanded consciousness that's attained through apotheosis, will eventually destroy the bearer.

Similarly, powerful gifts like fame and fortune, when given to someone who hasn't tamed their ego by developing humility, awareness, and a deep sense of connection to others, can become isolating and destructive. You don't have to look far to see

---

mon stages in narrative structure that writers might be familiar with, and that most stories include.

this reflected in the world around us. Give the fire of the gods to someone who hasn't expanded their consciousness enough to handle the fire of the gods, and they'll burn themselves up.

How I Died and Found a Better Way to Be

I've avoided telling you the specifics of my own transformative journey until now for a few reasons:

1) I'm not all that interested in my past these days. My old self feels like a different life that's about as relevant to who I am as clothes that no longer fit. I'm far more interested in being present, experiencing life, and bringing new things into existence.

2) This book isn't about me. It's an 'effing self-help book, not a memoir, and talking about my own journey might be a distraction for you. The specific ways that breakdown became breakthrough for me probably won't be the same for you.

That said, it might help to see the transformative process illustrated more specifically. If you want to know how breakdown became breakthrough for me, read on (and if you're sick of hearing about me, skip the next few chapters and meet me at "The Ego Mind is a Box" chapter).

Earlier, in the "How I Failed" chapter, I described how my experience of struggle, exhaustion, and despair built up over many years. This was a decades long process that culminated when I went all in to fulfill what I saw as my life purpose and failed on multiple fronts. In short, I did everything I could imagine doing, and I didn't get the outcomes I wanted.

This ended up being a very good thing for me, but I didn't see it that way at the time. Instead, I felt like I'd reached the end of my rope and I didn't know how to go on.

Prior to this, I'd struggled with anxiety and bouts of depression throughout my life, and I'd learned the importance of getting help when I got stuck in a dark place. I'd talked with many counselors over the years. Some were helpful. Others weren't. But this time, when I hit rock bottom and couldn't see a way out, I knew that I needed more than ordinary counseling.

I found a psychiatrist. He was a holistic guy (into making changes with diet and exercise) who also had the necessary medical degrees to prescribe the manufactured stuff. Since my diet was already pretty good and I exercised frequently, there wasn't much room for improvement there. We decided it was time to try out supplements and other approaches to adjust my brain chemistry.

One of the useful things I gained from this doctor involved recognizing the difference between anxiety and depression. Anxiety is essentially excitement that turns against you due to a low mood (mind racing to find things to be worried and stressed about). Depression (mind numb, sluggish, and finding little to care about) is a lack of drive and liveliness that energetically can be the opposite of anxiety.

Or, as I came to know them, anxiety is what caused me to check my book sales numbers ten times a day, then look up other books that appeared to be doing better than mine, research the authors of those books to find out what they'd done to promote their novels, draw up plans for similar promotions, launch such promotions, and check my sales numbers again only to find that nothing had changed.

Depression was what I felt when, after spinning my wheels like this for several hours a day and not making a whip of difference, I didn't have enough energy left to write a single decent sentence of the new book I wanted to work on.

The two extremes of anxiety and depression (with their energetic ups and downs) often worked together to create a wicked rollercoaster of misery and exhaustion for me. To address this, I tried a variety of supplements that were supposed to even out my brain's swings between anxiety and depression, improve my mood, and increase my overall mental functioning. And the drugs worked. Sort of.

After a few months, my brain seemed to be functioning slightly better. But adjusting my brain chemistry didn't address the underlying problem.

I still felt that I constantly had to do more to succeed and make a positive difference in the world. And I still felt that nothing I did was enough. I was failing at my life purpose. With the supplements, I just felt all this with a more even-keeled, energetic, effective brain. Which, ironically, made the problem worse.

After about a year of doing everything I could with chemicals, exercise, diet (yogurt for happiness!), and other healthy habits, I felt more desperate than before. After all, I'd changed all that I could. What else was there to try? Maybe things would never get better. Maybe there just wasn't a place for me in this life. The world might be better off without me.

Pro tip: If you start having thoughts like these, get help. Such thoughts are the catchphrases of despair, and despair can be dangerous.

On the plus side, messing with my brain chemistry got me to realize that the real problem wasn't my brain. It was me (this was my "I'm the problem" moment). I realized that the way I'd learned to perceive myself and my place in existence was causing me to suffer. I knew that I needed to take drastic action, but I didn't know what that action could be. I searched for counselors again, and this time I decided to try something new: Existential therapy.

I'd never been all that interested in existential questions before because I (secretly) believed that I had all the answers I needed. I'd always had a strong sense of purpose, rooted in a belief that living a good life meant giving back more than I took away, and if I failed it was because I wasn't trying hard enough or doing enough. I simply needed to use my willpower, grit, and determination to do more to make a positive difference in the world.

I believed so strongly in having a meaningful, purpose-driven life that I'd frequently gotten into heated debates with friends and colleagues who were philosophy professors. Several of the philosophers I knew were determinists—meaning that (in an over-simplification they'd probably abhor) they didn't believe in individual free will. Instead, they thought that everything was the result of cause-and-effect relationships. Although we might think we make choices and control our lives, to a determinist, the decisions we make are actually the result of prior causes determining what we'll do. For instance, even though I deliberated over which words to use in this sentence and believe that I chose them, a determinist would point out that the choices I made were entirely determined by things set in motion long ago with the Big Bang and the endless chain of cause-and-effect that happened afterward, leading to the formation of my body, brain, experiences, memories, and the thoughts that caused me to put these words down in precisely this order.

The determinist perspective had always depressed me. I saw it as anathema to my identity. Everything I did revolved around choosing to have a purpose and create positive meaning out of my life. But if everything is determined by what happened before—it's all just cosmic clockwork and there is no free will—

then what's the point of it all? How could meaning exist? Determinism didn't just seem empty and depressing to me, it seemed destructive to all that I cared about. Which is why I had a long history of arguing with friends, colleagues, and sometimes even strangers to battle back the faintest whiff of determinism.

At this point, though, I was so desperate to find a way to change my life that I was willing to try anything. Maybe revisiting some existential questions with a therapist was exactly what I needed. After all, I was having an existential crisis in a ridiculously clichéd form (should I continue to exist or not?). And just because something is existential doesn't mean it's deterministic. Traditionally, existentialism is all about finding meaning and purpose in one's life.

The first time I met with Chris, a therapist I found online who'd included existential therapy in his bio, I explained to him that I kept trying to do more to make my life worthwhile, but it made no difference—my life, and it seemed the world in general, kept heading in the wrong direction. I'd always been on the optimistic side of things, but the facts were all there and I couldn't ignore them any longer. I told Chris about the deep grief I felt for the dying coral reefs I'd seen, the destruction of forests I loved, the worsening climate crisis, and the increasing loss of ecosystems and species that I cared about. I told him that I'd always felt a strong need to give back more than I took away and leave the world a better place, but I was pretty certain that I was failing my children (and everyone else's children) on this front. Although I'd tried to have a positive influence on the world through writing, I couldn't get my most recent book to sell well, and publishers probably wouldn't take another chance on me. Finally, I told him that I felt disconnected from life. It seemed that if I couldn't fulfill my purpose and make the world even slightly better, then what was I doing here? I was just making things worse. There didn't seem to be a place for me anymore, and I had no idea how to keep going.

After I explained all this, I asked, "What else can I do? Nothing I've tried is working."

Chris nodded and his eyes crinkled in what I'd come to know as a smile. Then he said, "There's a solution. Do you want to know what it is?"

"Yes," I replied.

"You need to become a hardline determinist."

I laughed. Loudly.

For a moment, I thought Chris must have a secret file on me. Did he know that I'd argued with one of my philosopher friends about determinism only a couple days before? Did he know how fervently I opposed this way of perceiving things? Was this a prank? To see my life as nothing but a series of cause-and-effect relationships seemed soulless. Meaningless. Awful. I hated it.

But Chris was serious. He encouraged me to adopt a determinist perspective for a while and see what happened. What did I have to lose? I'd said it myself—nothing I tried seemed to be working. Why not try this?

I looked at Chris. He seemed plenty smart, his kids had gone to Harvard, he'd spent years training to be a priest before studying psychology and becoming a counselor, and he radiated compassion. The fact that, out of the blue, he'd brought up determinism (my nemesis) had a curious cosmic symmetry to it that made it hard to dismiss.

If the door we need to walk through is the one we're most afraid to open, then this was that door for me—the one door in the long hallway of myself that I'd always kept firmly shut.

What the hell? I thought. I turned the latch and stepped through.

The Dark Tunnel of Nihilism

I didn't know it then, but that moment in Chris's office when I decided to try out determinism was the moment my transformation began. After 40+ years, I was finally ready to let go of the self I thought I was so I could discover a better way to be.

It didn't happen instantly. There was no magic potion or plump wand-waving godmother who changed me. Things didn't even get better at first. They got worse.

For the next several weeks, the more I took on a determinist perspective (with Chris's guidance and encouragement), the more lost and hopeless I felt—as if I'd fallen into a dark pit of nihilism.

My greatest fear was that perceiving things as all just cause-and-effect relationships would cause nothing to have purpose or meaning for me anymore. Everything would be pointless. And then I wouldn't do anything. I'd just sit on the couch, useless. Worthless. To me, this seemed worse than death.

For a while, that's exactly how things went. My daughters would hug me and I'd think, "They're just atoms set in motion by other atoms, bouncing around."

They'd tell me they loved me, and I'd feel a bit of warmth inside, then I'd think, "That's just chemicals in my brain. It's all meaningless. None of this matters."

To my surprise, though, I didn't just sit on the couch. I still went to work. I still taught. I still sat at my desk in the basement and typed for hours a day. But as I did these things, I realized that I didn't know *why* I did them. *I* was just a bunch of atoms set in motion by other atoms. An ecosystem of cells without a self. A biological robot that thought it was a person.

The thoughts that I'd always believed were mine—products of my own mind and will—simply arose unbidden, and I wasn't in control of *why* I thought them. The feelings that I'd identified with and had given so much importance to were just chemicals in my brain. Even saying "I" or "my" started to sound absurd to me. If everything was merely cause and effect, then where did this "I" who thought it was in control exist?

My sense of self appeared to be a delusion. There was no discrete "me." My whole life had been an insane exercise in fooling myself.

Realizing this often felt like dying, and it was a death of sorts. My old ego-bound self was dying, and it didn't want to die. It fought this death every step of the way.

For instance, I'd make a decision, then I'd realize *I* didn't really make it because there was no "I" in control. I only thought I was in control when, on a deeper level, I could now see that I actually wasn't. My choices were simply determined by pre-existing causes. Still, my egoic self refused to accept this. "Of course I have control," it argued back. "I make decisions and choices all the time."

"Name one," countered the new voice, arguing the perspective I'd learned from Chris.

"I decided to bike to work instead of drive this morning."

"You had the experience of making a decision," corrected the new voice. "But *why* did you decide to bike?"

"Because I like biking. And I don't want to pollute."

"Why do you feel that way?"

"Because I care about creation. I decided to care."

"Really? When did you decide to care?"

"I don't know. It's just who I am."

"Right. And did you make yourself that way?"

"No. But maybe my choices did. They helped shape me."

"And *why* did you make those choices?"

"Because of my experiences. My upbringing. My mind. My nature…"

"Did this 'you' you're talking about choose any of those things? Did you choose your experiences? Your upbringing? Your mind? Your nature?"

"I don't know. Not consciously, but maybe my soul did?"

"And did you choose this soul you think 'you' have?"

"Well… no."

"Exactly. Yet all these things you didn't choose determine the choices you make. It's all cause and effect."

"But it *felt* like a decision."

"Of course it did. That's what experiencing a decision feels like."

These inner debates would go on until I'd end up lost and confused. Groundless. Selfless. Adrift. I'd stubbornly think it was *my* choice to bike because I'd made a choice, while on a deeper level, I knew that the "I" who thought it was in control really wasn't. As the philosopher Arthur Schopenhauer put it over two hundred years ago, **"Man can do what he wills, but he cannot will what he wills."**

I'd always been focused on the first level—doing what I willed, while blindly believing that this meant "I" (that self I thought I was) was in charge. Now I'd started to become aware of the next level—that I didn't will what I willed. Although I could experience choices and control, the "I" who thought it was in control actually wasn't. It just claimed that it was. I felt foolish for not realizing this before because it seemed so obvious to me now. Of course, my ego mind hadn't allowed me to see any of this before because my ego mind was where the delusion came from. I'd spent most of my life fooling myself.

This is a hard realization to have. It was a realization my ego desperately didn't want me to have, so my ego made this process every bit as terrifying and difficult as I'd feared.

Maybe now you can see the third reason why I didn't share the details of how my personal transformation came about earlier. If your ego is at all like mine, it probably doesn't like this story. It's probably urging you to reject the notion that it's not in control, like I rejected it.[39]

However, every now and then as I lost myself in these debates, I'd get a glimpse of something else—a feeling of lightness, warmth, and peace that arrived like a shaft of sunlight through the empty dark.

The more I started to have these moments, the more I realized I wasn't stranded in a pit of nihilism after all. I was in a tunnel. And this tunnel pierced through the barrier that had been holding me back.

As I approached the far side of the tunnel, I discovered that the other side wasn't at all what I'd thought it would be. It wasn't the loss of everything that mattered to me. Instead, it was where all the things I'd been seeking (and had long kept myself separated from) existed.

I started to awaken.

---

[39] Anytime your ego is uncomfortable, that's usually a good sign that you're heading in the right direction to escape the ego's limiting grasp and expand your awareness. Keep going!

The Far Side of the Tunnel

This battle with my achievement-focused, control-obsessed, separate-self clinging ego went on for months. I'd think I was in control, making my own decisions for my own self-initiated reasons, then the voice would pop up and explain to me otherwise. Always my ego mind fought back. However, there were times when my mind grew still, and I began to experience advantages to this new way of perceiving existence.

The first benefit I noticed was that, if it was all just cause-and-effect relationships and I wasn't really in control, then there was no point trying to make things different than what they were. Instead, I could relax and be.

Of course, this was exactly what I'd always feared—that if I didn't have a powerful need to achieve things spurring me on, I wouldn't do anything good (or what my ego believed was "good"). I'd become a complacent, useless waste of life. What I found, though, was that I still did many of the same things as before. I just did them without the heavy burden of trying and struggling.

I went to work, cared for my children, and walked the dog because it was my nature to do so. Realizing this allowed me to do things with greater awareness. Instead of focusing on *trying* to achieve something, I was able to focus on accepting what is and enjoying *being* in the present moment.

I felt lighter. It seems counterintuitive, but by accepting what is, I became more effective at responding to change—which was the second benefit I noticed. When unexpected things came up, I was able to work with them (surfing the wave as it is) more nimbly. I didn't struggle to control what happened or waste energy resisting life and getting frustrated. Instead, I could appreciate whatever happened and react with greater awareness.

For instance, one morning when I was late getting my kids to school and myself to work, I bumped a bowl of blueberries onto the kitchen floor. My old self would have reacted with anger at this inconvenient mess occurring on top of everything else. I might have tried to blame someone else for putting the bowl too close to the counter's edge, and in my frustration, I might have kicked the blueberries, or slammed the bowl down and made an even greater mess. But my new self had an entirely different reaction. As I watched the cascade of blueberries fall, bounce, and roll across the kitchen floor, I laughed at this unexpected turn of events. I felt strangely grateful for how beautiful the falling blueberries looked. Then, without the slightest bit of frustration, anger, or resistance to this new circumstance, I picked up the blueberries, rinsed them off, and took the kids to school.

By accepting what is, I was able to reconnect with the reality I'd been resisting, and this unlocked new possibilities for understanding and (surprisingly) change. Acceptance enabled me to see things clearly and become more energized and resilient. Problems didn't set me back nearly as much as they had before. Rather than persevering by struggling, I persevered by *being*, which not only felt more enjoyable, it made me more nimble and efficient.

The third benefit I noticed was that my sense of separation and loneliness fell away. If, on the deepest level, it was all just cause and effect, then I was part of a wondrously complex system of cause and effect. My fear had been that accepting this would make everything seem purposeless and meaningless. Instead, the opposite happened.

The separation my ego mind had imposed between what I saw as myself and the rest of existence revealed itself to be a delusion I could now see past. Meaning and purpose didn't come from me. I didn't need to consciously create meaning to "have" it. Instead, meaning and purpose, or more accurately what I now think of as consciousness and love, were all around me and I was part of them.

By resisting what is and clinging to my ego (my small-self notion of who I was and what my life was about), I'd created a barrier between who I thought I was and the energy of being. But the more I saw beyond this delusion of a separate self, the more connected to being I felt. Rather than losing purpose and meaning, I began to see purpose, meaning, beauty, and sacredness in everything. I was part of an infinite system of Being (or Consciousness, Awareness, God, Love, the Universe—whatever you want to call it). It was all one.

It's hard to express how incredible this felt and still feels. The more liberated I became from my ego mind, the more I was able to experience the bliss of being. I realized that I'd been addicted to suffering, separation, and struggle as a way of knowing myself, and I began to see how ineffective and limiting this way of going through life was.

Letting go of resistance and consciously *being* enabled me to become more creative, too. Rather than a struggle, creativity began to feel joyful and strangely effortless. Don't get me wrong—a great deal of time and work still went into my creative endeavors, but the effort didn't need to come from me. It came *through* me while I got to observe, experience, and enjoy the process of creating.

One other benefit I noticed was that pride and shame began to fall away. If it was all cause and effect, then there was no point taking pride in things, or in shaming myself (or others). Of course, responsibility still mattered, because that's how a system of cause and effect works (actions have consequences). But on a deeper level of awareness, pride, shame, and hatred no longer made sense. For the first time, the words of spiritual leaders and mystics who talked about unconditional love and compassion for all beings started to make sense to me in a visceral way. The compassion I felt for others and for myself expanded far beyond what my ego had allowed me to experience before.

All this was just the beginning, though. As I passed through the dark tunnel of nihilism, I realized that there's infinitely more on the far side than there could ever be on the limited ego-mind side of the tunnel I'd come from. I began to awaken to a much greater, more connected, aware, creative, and blissful way to be that's free of the fear, resistance, and dissatisfaction that had plagued me.

If you're curious, I don't consider myself a determinist now. Or, more accurately, what I found on the far side of the tunnel isn't what I thought determinism would be, and it's not what many philosophers seem to think it is either. I don't subscribe to any one ideology or philosophy. It's hubris to think my limited mind (or any human mind) could ever encompass what all this is about. Existence is bigger than that. To quote Hamlet, "There are more things in heaven and earth, Horatio, than are dreamt of in your philosophy."

Determinism was simply the door I needed to pass through to sever my attachment to the ego-mind I'd identified with.[40]

---

[40] In retrospect, it makes sense that determinism was the door I needed to pass through. Because I'd always passionately rejected it, adopting it required letting go of who I thought I was and what I thought I knew. Also, the ego mind I identified with was a logical control freak. Determinism presented an effective way to chal-

For you, this doorway might be entirely different. For some, the doorway is letting go of conceptions of the past and future and fully experiencing the present moment. For others, the doorway might involve adopting the Witness perspective (more on this in a couple chapters). Or having transcendental spiritual experiences. Or completely accepting what is. Or developing a profound awareness of holism. Or overcoming an addiction that allows you to see how the illusion of control is deceiving you. Or practicing self-inquiry and meditation until your mind becomes still and you awaken to your true Self. There are countless ways to see past the limited ego mind and develop a greater awareness of being.[41]

Although the door will likely be different for everyone, when you step through the doorway what you find might seem like a dark, scary pit at first. This is because real transformation doesn't come easily. Letting go of the ego you identify with and dissolving egoic perspectives isn't easy. It's a process that requires work. So, if you find yourself in that scary darkness, keep going. It's not a pit. It's a tunnel, and the far side is better than the ego mind can imagine.

Clinging to some notion of being a separate self that's in control isn't worth holding onto. It causes immense suffering.[42]

---

lenge and eventually transcend such a paradigm by confronting my ego mind with the logic of how it ultimately isn't in control.

[41] Even the briefest glimpse beyond the self you think you are can be transformative. As Rumi put it, "If you could get rid of yourself just once, the secret of secrets would open to you. The face of the unknown, hidden beyond the universe would appear on the mirror of your perception." All that's needed for the process of awakening to begin is to become momentarily conscious of the Self beyond the self.

[42] It can take a great deal of suffering before people reach a place where they're ready to let go of attachment to the egoic self that suffers. If you're not ready to do this, that's fine. The suffering we experience as we cling to an egoic notion of the self provides a useful impetus to lessen attachment to the suffering self. Along the way, it might be helpful to remember that, as Leo Gura put it, "The

However, it's hard to let go of attachment to the ego because letting go feels like death. In some ways, it is death. It's the death that needs to happen for a new, more aware, connected, creative, compassionate self to be born. As Zen scholar D. T. Suzuki put it, "Unless we die to ourselves, we can never be alive again."

To understand how this works, look again at narrative structure. For transformation to take place, first you venture into the bizarro world where you explore the opposite of what you thought you were (for me, this involved determinism). Then there's the ordeal with its conflict, turmoil, and the dark night of the soul where the old self dies so a new self can emerge. The transformation process is rarely easy, but it's incredibly worthwhile.

The far side of suffering is transcendence.

---

true self doesn't suffer. The thing that suffers is always the false self."

The Ego Mind is a Box

If the changes in perspective described in that last chapter sound theoretically good, but abstract or unattainable, that's due to approaching them intellectually.

The only way to fully "get" what's being discussed in this book is through direct experience, and direct experience isn't something that can be conveyed through words. At best, words can point you in a useful direction, but they won't get you there. You have to take the steps yourself, and the final steps must be taken without words or thoughts. Here's why:

The ego mind is like a box that only contains and knows things conceptually. However, most of existence lies beyond the box the ego mind creates. For instance, imagine seeing a whale breach off the bow of your kayak. I can describe the bus-sized whale rising out of the water and splashing down just thirty feet from your boat, sending waves your way and filling you with a sense of awe, but the description doesn't give you the experience. The word "awe," which at best conveys a concept, isn't even close to the actual experience of awe because the ego mind cannot adequately contain or communicate what the experience of awe is.

Similarly, the words "whale" and "ocean" convey concepts that don't come close to containing the magnificent and ultimately ineffable reality of what a whale or ocean actually is. One of the ways the ego mind distorts our perception of reality is by claiming that the concept is an adequate substitute for the actual experience of existence, when in truth it's barely a dull shadow of existence.

By constantly trying to know things through words and concepts, the ego mind constructs the box. Almost all the problems we've been discussing come from being stuck in this limited box. **You can't think your way out of the box because your thoughts are what create the box.** The more you believe that you can escape the box by thinking, the more complicated the box becomes, and the more you become stuck in it.

See the dilemma here? This was something that tripped me up for decades because I believed that the intellect was the only way to know things, and I identified strongly with my mind (or more specifically with my ego mind, which is the aspect of the mind that the ego lays claim to as the "thinking self").[43] The

---

[43] By identifying with my mind, I made my mind into the primary aspect of my ego, or what I believed I was, and this created many problems for me. However, it's important to recognize that the mind itself is *not* the problem. The mind is a powerful tool. What's problematic is thinking that the mind is what you are and the only way to know things. That's what makes the ego mind into a box that becomes difficult to transcend. This identification with the ego mind is extremely common and terribly limiting. As Bodhidharma, the 6th Century monk and founder of Kung fu and Chan Buddhism, put it, "If you use your mind to study reality, you won't understand either your mind or reality. If you study reality without using your mind, you'll understand both."

more I thought I was my ego mind, the more stuck in the box I became, unable to see beyond my own ego mind.[44]

When we're stuck in the box, we often feel frustrated, anxious, and isolated. So how do you transcend the box, or become aware of what's beyond it?

We actually do this all the time (but if we're very focused on knowing and understanding things intellectually, we might not consciously realize it). Anytime we allow ourselves to be fully present and experience the bliss of being, or experience a deep connection to another, or a sense of unconditional love or joy, or a transpersonal sense of oneness with something greater than the small self, we're becoming conscious of what's beyond the box. And for many of us, one of the most profound and impactful ways to transcend the box is through creativity.

If you're a writer, artist, or creator, you've probably felt what it's like to become conscious of what's beyond the box because those awesome leaps of creativity—those ideas, insights, and visions that utterly surprise and astound you—come from beyond the box. As we discussed in earlier chapters on creativity, any truly creative act involves momentarily escaping the ego-mind box and connecting with what's beyond it. Alternatively, as long as you're stuck in the box, there's no real

---

[44] Case in point: for years I believed that I understood several of the concepts explored in this book. I'd always been drawn to Buddhist and Zen philosophies, and I thought I "got" things like suffering coming from attachment, the ego getting in the way, and (ironically) what it meant to reach a state of no-mind. However, I only understood these concepts intellectually. I didn't truly grasp them because I hadn't let go of my ego mind enough to experience them (I was too attached to what I thought I was). It wasn't until I reached the end of my rope and passed through the dark tunnel of nihilism that my attachment to my ego mind finally dissolved enough to allow me to become aware of what's beyond the box. Experiencing what's beyond the box changes everything. To paraphrase Zora Neale Hurston, you've got to go there to know there.

surprise or creativity. There's only revisiting what you already think you know.

After we glimpse what's beyond the box, we often retreat back into the box. We might say "this is my idea," laying claim to whatever vision or creative insight we gained. Then our ego mind takes credit for the idea, and we begin to limit it and make it part of the box by trying to understand it conceptually. However, as we attempt to enact a vision, we sometimes escape the ego's limiting influence and become conscious of what's beyond the box again.

Essentially, the practice of being creative involves liberating one's consciousness from the box the ego mind creates long enough to bring something new into existence. Therefore, if you've ever experienced the bliss of creating something that surprises you, you know what it's like to transcend the box.

The more conscious of existence beyond the box you become, the more clearly you'll be able to see the ego mind for what it is—just a box, and a small one at that. But you'll never be able to understand this through thinking because thinking creates the box. This is why consciousness work often involves paradoxes. The mind wants to understand everything conceptually, but cannot understand what transcends the mind. **The box can't contain what's beyond the box.**[45]

An experience of transcending the box, whether it's attained through a creative practice, meditation, a mystical experience, being present, or something else, can't be adequately described using words, because what's beyond the box is beyond the ego mind that understands and communicates things through words (which is what makes writing about this stuff so hard).

---

[45] Anytime you feel stuck in your head, that's the ego mind's doing. You won't be able to think your way out because thinking reinforces the box. The way out is always through the direct experience of things the box cannot contain—experiencing love, connection, presence, being, creativity, or other practices that help you become more aware of existence beyond the box.

Direct experience is the only way to become consciously aware of what's beyond the box. The more you transcend the limitations of the ego mind and experience what's beyond it, the more you'll get the concepts we'll explore in the coming chapters.[46]

As a friend of mine put it, "It's a lot like love songs." Before you ever fall in love, you might understand the words in the songs, but you won't really get what they're talking about until you're in love. Once you have the experience of being in love, songs that may have seemed abstract or even hokey before take on new layers of meaning and become more interesting. But you have to fall in love to get this because the actual experience of love can never be adequately conveyed through words.

Therefore, as we explore more advanced concepts and techniques in the coming chapters, it's important to recognize the limitations of words and thoughts. Words can point to what's out there, but you can't *think* your way there.[47] The things we'll discuss cannot be realized conceptually. They need to be experienced to be grasped and experiencing them requires transcending the ego mind that tries to know things by thinking. You don't have to take my word for this, though. Just look again at the steps in the hero's journey. Transcending the egoic self (the separate self that clings to what it knows and fears death) is what enables the hero to attain "the ultimate boon."

---

[46] Conversely, you don't need to understand these concepts intellectually to actualize them. Experience matters more. Just as great art often defies logical explanation, you can have an experience without being able to understand or explain it.

[47] As Chan Buddhism master Huang Po put it over 1,000 years ago, "Those who seek the truth by means of intellect and learning only get further and further away from it."

To find a better way to be, you first have to reach a state where you're willing to let go of attachment to what you think you are.[48]

---

[48] Try not to get too caught up with understanding all this intellectually. There's no end to the hole the ego mind will dig attempting to figure things out while entrapping itself further. The mind keeps prying up dirt to grasp the bottom, only to toss that dirt aside for a new bottom is now revealed. Thus, the ego mind constantly seeks something it cannot attain while making the hole deeper. Only when you let the mind go quiet and stop digging can you become aware of the hole and the way out. (This is why meditation is helpful—it's how you stop digging holes. See the Addendum for a meditation quick start guide).

Developing Observer Consciousness

One way to transcend the ego and expand awareness is to develop observer consciousness. Here, too, stories provide a useful model.

When we read stories, we probably don't expect everything to go well for the main character. That would be boring. It's the unexpected twists and turns that make stories interesting. For the character, problems and conflicts are full of turmoil, but from the reader's god-like observer perspective, we can see how such challenges are necessary for growth and transformation to occur.

What's hard in a story for the characters is only as hard for us, the readers, as we allow it to be. We may want to feel happy, sad, frightened, or elated with a character, so we allow ourselves to have these emotional experiences when we read. It's interesting to note that in our own lives, we might avoid experiences that cause tension, grief, or fear, but from our reader perspective, experiencing such emotions can be enjoyable. The novels I like best are the ones that put me on the edge of my seat and get me choked-up at least once or twice.

Nevertheless, when bad stuff happens in a story, as readers, we rarely feel devastated by it. Instead, we're able to assume our god-like reader perspective and gain meaning from the ups and downs that characters experience. We can see how difficulties are part of the transformative journey, and part of what makes the story engaging and significant.

Similarly, in our own lives we can adopt this "god's eye" perspective of ourselves. Rather than getting caught up in our everyday struggles and challenges, we can pull back and observe ourselves *as if we were a character in a story.*

When we do this, we're able to see the ups and downs of life as steps in a larger transformative journey, and we become better able to accept these moments and appreciate them—just as we appreciate plot twists and conflicts in a good novel. We can feel sadness, fear, and loss, but we don't have to get caught up in these emotions. **We can learn to love the process, even while we experience the challenges and difficulties of the process.**

Seeing yourself from this "god's eye" observer consciousness perspective can be deeply freeing, and it can help you become more compassionate toward others and yourself. As a reader/observer, your purpose is to experience and enjoy the story. Instead of yelling at the characters and getting frustrated when they don't do what you want them to do, you can focus on accepting and appreciating them. And instead of getting upset when difficulties arise, you can embrace events with interest and awareness.

Not only is this a more enjoyable way to go through life, increasing acceptance and awareness often leads to better outcomes. By perceiving circumstances more fully and clearly, you can react more effectively to what happens, just like the skillful surfer who's aware of the wave, moves with it, and enjoys the ride.

The Benefits of Observer Consciousness

When you start developing observer consciousness, you might notice resistance from your ego. You might think, "I can't observe my life like I'm a reader reading a book. That's ridiculous. I have to do things to create the life I want. Otherwise, I'll become lazy and do nothing."

Contrary to the ego's claims, developing observer consciousness doesn't lead to becoming passive or doing nothing. That's simply not the way your character was written. If you were passive, you wouldn't be reading this book. It isn't your nature to do nothing. It's your nature to do things all the time. You're not, for instance, breathing because you're consciously making yourself breathe. In fact, when you try to breathe, you might even mess up breathing. Instead, release control and let yourself breathe naturally. Observe your breathing. Follow your inhale as air flows deeply into your chest and reverses to exhale. Notice how the switch between inhale and exhale comes without conscious intention, as a wonderful revelation?[49]

Similarly, rather than causing you to become passive or lazy, developing observer consciousness often has the opposite effect. It allows you to become more aware, energized, and effective. Instead of resisting life and constantly struggling against the currents, you can perceive things more accurately and work with the currents. Being, as we explored, is more effective than trying. Learn to appreciate *being* rather than constantly trying to do things. Step out of your own way and see what happens. As the *Tao Te Ching* explains, "By letting it go it all gets done. The world is won by those who let it go. But when you try and try, the world is then beyond the winning."

Chances are, if you develop observer consciousness, you'll still do many of the same things you did before. There's a common Zen saying that reflects this. *Before enlightenment, chop wood, carry water. After enlightenment, chop wood, carry water.* Developing observer consciousness isn't exactly enlightenment, but it's a step in that direction. It's a way of lessening your attachment to your egoic self by shifting your perspective. If you take this step, even though you'll still probably do many of the same things, you'll experience what you do with greater awareness. Over time, if you keep up this practice, you'll become less fearful and more relaxed, open, creative, and skillful in your actions. Sounds nice, right?

The reason your ego keeps telling you that developing observer consciousness will be a disaster—that you'll become a lazy do-nothing and everything in your life will fall apart—is because the ego desperately wants to maintain its illusion of

---

[49] Shunryu Suzuki, the Zen monk and teacher, said of practicing zazen and breathing, "the air comes in and out like someone passing through a swinging door. If you think, 'I breathe,' the 'I' is extra. There is no you to say 'I.' What we call 'I' is just a swinging door which moves when we inhale and when we exhale. It just moves; that is all. When your mind is pure and calm enough to follow this movement, there is nothing: no 'I,' no world, no mind nor body; just a swinging door."

control.[50] It wants you to remain stuck in your small self, constantly struggling to do things. If you let go of the illusion of control, observe and appreciate what is, and see that things are fine (better than fine) then the jig is up.

Which is precisely why it's important to try this out. **For a few minutes each day, see what happens when you adopt an observer consciousness perspective of yourself.** Pull back and observe yourself—your thoughts, feelings, actions, and reactions—as if you were a character in a story. You might even say to yourself, "Now this character is…" so that you can better observe and appreciate what you're doing, just like you would if you were reading a novel about a character who happens to be you.

It can be especially helpful to do this during difficult or challenging experiences. For instance, if you're nervous about giving a public speech, you might say to yourself, "Now this character is nervous about standing in front of an audience and sharing personal experiences. Now this character thinks he's going to say something dumb and embarrass himself." Observe and appreciate the unfolding story. You'll still feel the ups and downs, but they'll no longer consume you. They may even amuse you.

Even if you're only able to adopt an observer perspective for brief moments, you'll still likely experience benefits from it. You might notice and accept more. You might enjoy the experience of your existence more fully while handling difficulties more effectively. Instead of unconsciously reacting to what hap-

---

[50] By the way, if you think doing nothing is easy, see if you can do nothing. To sit and do nothing, not even think, for an hour is nearly impossible to accomplish. It's also the focus of many meditation practices because the ego mind loves to constantly do things to keep you distracted. By attempting to sit and "do nothing," you can dissolve your ego and become more aware of being (this is sometimes referred to as the "goalless goal"). To explore this further, try the "do nothing meditation" in the Addendum.

pens, you might act with greater awareness. Instead of fighting against the universe and becoming anxious and frustrated as you're tossed about by the inevitable waves of life, you might perceive and surf what is.

Once you experience the benefits of such greater awareness and acceptance, the ego's objections will start to seem pretty ridiculous. They may even fade away entirely.[51]

---

[51] As odd as developing observer consciousness might sound, several wisdom traditions focus on practicing variations of observer consciousness (or being the Witness) as a way to develop awareness of the present, transcend the ego, and experience being. Practicing observer consciousness can radically transform how you experience existence. Eckhart Tolle described the change this way; "The beginning of freedom is the realization that you are not the possessing entity—the thinker. Knowing this enables you to observe the entity. The moment you start *watching the thinker*, a higher level of consciousness becomes activated." Later on, Tolle added that becoming the watcher or "Witness" allows you to "realize that all the things that truly matter—beauty, love, creativity, joy, inner peace—arise from beyond the mind." If this still seems abstract and idealistic, read on and the advantages of observer consciousness (and how to develop it) will hopefully become clearer.

On Writing Your Life

Let's pretend that your ego keeps insisting you're more than the observer of your life. You might feel compelled to see yourself as the sole author of your existence (despite the fact that you probably don't recall choosing where you were born, what body you were born into, what brain you think with, or most of the other things that shape your existence). This notion of being in complete control is seductive and difficult to let go of.[52]

---

[52] One reason why this notion of being in complete control and free to do what we will is so seductive is because it's part of our fundamental existence. The true Self (beyond the small separate self) has complete control and freedom to be whatever it wishes. The trouble is that the small separate-self ego likes to claim it's in control, when it actually isn't. As Rupert Spira put it, "Consciousness, that which we are, is freedom itself. We, as Consciousness, have absolute freedom. We *are* absolute freedom. The feeling that we have the freedom to make a choice is a pale and usually misinterpreted reflection of this intuitive knowledge of our own innate

If this is the case for you, then consider how creativity involves escaping the ego's controlling limitations and connecting with something greater than what you already know. Even if you prefer to see yourself as writing your life, who is the "I" that's doing the writing? Where do these writer's thoughts and ideas come from? And *why* are you writing the story that you're writing?

I used to get caught up in the idea that I was the sole author of my life, and that it was up to me to make it a "good story." Although at first this perspective seemed empowering, it ultimately became stressful and exhausting, especially when events in my life didn't go the way I wanted them to.

Now, when I feel pressure to make my life be different from what it is, I remind myself of how great writing happens—that wonderful state of letting creativity flow through me that I experience when I'm deep in a writing trance. Rather than constantly trying to control my story (and blaming myself for not getting it right), I remind myself that I'm discovering my story as it's written.

Recognizing this takes the pressure off, and suddenly everything is okay. I'm able to observe and become more aware of what is, then work with it. I'm able to set my anxious, clutching, frustrated, ego-driven small self aside, and let creativity, including the creative "writing" of my own life, flow through me. By letting my attachment to my over-controlling egoic "author I" go, I'm able to embrace and appreciate the experiences I get to have, aligning myself with life.

This is just one example of how the practice of creating things can help you escape the ego's limiting grasp. In addition, creative activities like writing can help you develop observer consciousness. After all, writers spend countless hours observing and describing others, including imaginary characters. And

---

freedom. As a *reflection* of real freedom it is true, but the *interpretation* that this freedom is the freedom of an individual entity is false."

writers often need to become aware of themselves and their experiences in order to adequately depict experiences. Hence, writing can be a tremendous discipline for practicing observer consciousness and expanding awareness. (Actors and artists who focus on depicting others often have a leg up on developing observer consciousness, too).[53]

If you become really good at adopting the observer perspective of your life, then fear, envy, comparisons, and all the other ways the ego tries to limit you and stifle your creativity will fall away. To the observer, all things belong. The observer doesn't judge. The observer accepts, experiences, and appreciates. The observer can't be hurt and doesn't suffer. The observer self is perfect as it is. When you're the observer, there's nothing you need to *try* to do. Instead you're able to effortlessly *be* as you experience existence.

The observer self is conscious awareness. To experience being the observer is to become conscious of your essential presence as infinite awareness. This awareness is infinitely creative, because it's awareness that brings all things into being.[54]

---

[53] It's important to note that to truly experience observer consciousness one must be able to let go of attachment to the egoic self. Otherwise, rather than developing observer consciousness, you might simply become more self-conscious (more ego-bound and focused on your small self). The two are vastly different states. The self-conscious person fixates on their self as an object to be observed and judged. Conversely, the person who develops observer consciousness knows that, on a fundamental level, their true self isn't the object of the observation, but the observing consciousness beyond the small self. To put it experientially, when we feel self-conscious we shrink in on ourselves and become judgmental, but when we develop observer consciousness, our consciousness expands with awareness and acceptance.

[54] As Rupert Spira reminds us, "It is not possible to have an experience without awareness."

The Practical Power of Observer Consciousness

I often work out while writing—it increases blood flow and frequently helps me discover new ideas. To make this easier, I built an *American Ninja Warrior* inspired obstacle course under my deck, just ten steps from my writing desk. Throughout the day, when I get stuck writing a paragraph or can't figure out how to start a scene, I take a break and do a set of pullups, pushups, or other exercises.

I've done several experiments to see what works best to motivate myself to do more reps of a difficult exercise. The way I originally learned to motivate myself was to get angry. I probably picked this up from coaches in high school who used to yell and call us wimps, pansies, and worse to get us fired up. It wasn't pleasant, but it worked to an extent. By getting myself fired up and angry, I could force myself through a high number of pushups and pullups. But there are problems with this sort of negative motivation. It takes a lot of effort, it's not very enjoyable, and it causes muscles and arteries to clench up. You get exhausted more quickly this way and burn out.

A few years ago I started trying a different motivational strategy. Instead of yelling at myself (internally and externally), I headed in the opposite direction and attempted to motivate myself by operating from a positive, loving mindset. I'd tell myself that I loved doing pullups, and I'd try to convince myself that this was true. I'd think about how much I enjoyed every rep and taking every breath as I worked out.

With this intentionally positive mindset, I was able to do one or two more pullups than I could do out of anger, but it still got exhausting. At some point, my mind would push back and say, "I don't really love pullups," or "this actually isn't very enjoyable." Eventually, I'd realize that I was deceiving myself, and my body would quit. After a few months, it got harder to trick myself into thinking I loved doing pullups. My mind knew what I was up to, and the benefits of this motivational technique diminished (just as the benefits of some self-affirmations tend to diminish and backfire over time).

Fortunately, there's a third way of motivating myself that I've found. Instead of psyching myself up through negative or positive motivation, I take on the observer perspective as I'm doing an exercise. To help situate myself in the observer perspective, I'll internally narrate what I'm doing. For instance, I'll say to myself, "Now this body is doing pullups."

The phrase "now this body is…" helps me situate my awareness in observer consciousness. From there, I simply let energy flow through my body as I witness myself doing pushups, pullups, or whatever exercise my body is doing. When the reps are easy, I observe and appreciate the pleasure of motion. And when my muscles ache and lungs feel like they're going to burst, I observe and appreciate the experience of my body becoming fatigued. From the observer perspective, I can enjoy the whole experience—both the struggle and the pleasure of the activity—and it all feels effortless.

When I'm situated in observer consciousness, I don't have to *try* harder because I don't see myself as the "I" struggling to do pullups. Rather, I'm observing a story unfold that's part of being. I become witness to the energy of the universe flowing through an ecosystem of cells that I often think of as myself. **The less my ego gets involved with its constant resistance to what is, the more freely that energy flows.** As Ram Dass put it, "I am hollow bamboo."

Guess which motivational strategy allows me to do the most pushups and pullups?

And guess which one is the most enjoyable and sustainable?

Trying to do things is hard. It takes effort—whether that effort is provoked by anger or passion, it's still effort. Eventually, it gets exhausting. But being… that's easy. When you develop observer consciousness, you develop your connection to an awareness that's greater than your limited, struggling, ego-driven small self. Adopting an observer consciousness perspective allows you to align yourself with life so that you can act without resistance while appreciating all experiences. It's a powerful way to be. And it's a powerful perspective to live and create from.[55]

---

[55] As long as you see yourself as the one who must do things, you will suffer. This is because there will always be more to do, and what you do will never be enough. Peace comes from realizing that you're not the "doer," but the awareness of doing. The lie the ego tells us to keep us from reaching this peaceful state is that nothing will get done. But this isn't true. Instead, you'll become more effective when you're at peace because you'll be able to let things be done without getting in the way and resisting the doing. As Zen master Dogen put it, "I live by letting things happen." In some traditions, this is referred to as living gracefully.

A Simple Practice for Unlocking Observer Consciousness

Try this: when you wake in the morning, for the first five minutes of your day, carefully observe and narrate to yourself from a third person perspective what you're thinking and doing. For instance, you might say, "Now this body is thinking about what it needs to do today. Now this body is getting up from bed. Now this body is walking to the shower. Now this body is worrying about being on time. Now this body is afraid it won't be able to do what it thinks it should do today. Now this body is thinking about ducks for some odd reason…" (If you prefer to get writerly about it, you might say to yourself, "Now this character is…"). Pick a phrase that helps you lessen attachment to your ego and situate your awareness in an observer consciousness perspective.

Doing this might sound strange, but try it. Since it's only happening in your head, no one will know you're doing it.

As you internally observe and narrate your thoughts, feelings, and actions, you're developing awareness, appreciating existence, and experiencing observer consciousness. You might notice that your consciousness follows your body around like a reader following a character, or a viewer watching a movie. You might also notice that thoughts and feelings often arise on their own without a conscious decision to think or feel them. If you're really good at observing yourself, you might even notice that actions often start to take place *before* you consciously decide to take them, just as you usually breathe without consciously deciding to take a breath.

For instance, you might notice that you start to get out of bed a split second *before* you have the experience of deciding to get out of bed. This awareness reflects something neuroscientists have been able to demonstrate for decades with brain scans. According to studies originally done in the 1980s by Benjamin Libet, and subsequently reconfirmed by researchers using more advanced fMRI machines and intracranial recording techniques, our brains decide to take an action fractions of a second (or even seconds) before we have the experience of consciously deciding to take that action.

The ego makes us think that the "I" is in full control, deciding to do something then doing it, but this isn't how we actually operate. Instead, we often start to do something (or prepare to do something), then our ego convinces us that the "I" decided to do it—that's part of what makes the "illusion of control" an illusion.

Through the observer perspective, we can see more clearly and become more aware of the true nature of our existence. And we can use this perspective to ride the inevitable waves of life more effectively.

Try this technique whenever you're feeling anxious or fearful. Observe what you're feeling and say to yourself, "Now this body is afraid of failing..." or "Now this body is anxious about not doing enough," or "Now this body is experiencing limiting doubts," or whatever it is you observe yourself struggling with.

By becoming aware of what you're feeling through observer consciousness, you'll be able to accept your feelings and turn struggles into valuable parts of your life story. Over time, if you keep doing this, you'll probably start to become more relaxed.[56]

You might find the experience of whatever you're feeling to be interesting and amusing (even while you continue to feel nervous, frightened, or anxious). These days, when I'm able to observe myself becoming anxious or fearful about something, I often laugh and enjoy the way my character keeps revealing himself to me with all his quirks and foibles.

The goal of developing observer consciousness isn't to stop feeling things. It's not a denial of emotion that leads to emotional detachment.[57] On the contrary, developing observer consciousness allows you to become more aware and accepting of what you're feeling—all of it, including the hard stuff. It's all part of your story.

A counselor friend of mine often says, "The universe wants to experience itself through you." Through observer consciousness, you can become more aware of your experience. And the more aware you become, the more alive you'll feel.

---

[56] Psychologists have conducted several studies that show how naming the emotion you're experiencing can have significant beneficial impacts for emotional regulation, overcoming fears, and experiencing less stress. This process is often referred to as "affect labeling." One interesting study that UCLA researchers Michelle Craske, Katherina Kircanski, and Matthew Lieberman did on affect labeling involved getting people who were afraid of spiders to touch and hold tarantulas. Those who could name their emotions were able to do this at a significantly higher rate. Developing observer consciousness involves such affect labeling and takes it several steps further by getting you to develop the habit of observing and naming emotions, thoughts, actions, and reactions without becoming attached to them.

[57] I've experienced emotional detachment, and the numbness and sense of disconnection from myself and others that comes with it. Observer consciousness is the opposite. With observer consciousness, I get all the feels—more than I ever have before. And on a deep level of awareness, I appreciate them all and feel more alive and connected to being.

On Reading Yourself: The Famous Life

Let's return for a moment to the topic of commercial success that we explored in Part I so we can see how developing observer consciousness applies to some of the fundamental challenges many creators face.

Even though you might logically accept that chasing after commercial success isn't a good recipe for lasting happiness, this probably won't stop your ego from wanting things. Maybe you want to be famous, or achieve some form of recognition through your art. Maybe you don't want your life to be "ordinary." Maybe you desperately want to write a best seller, create a hit song, become a well-known artist, or rise to acclaim in other ways. These are common desires because they're things we're taught from a young age to confuse with happiness and having a "good" life.

However, consider this from the observer perspective. As a reader, do you only want to read books about famous people?

Are the only interesting and worthwhile stories about commercially successful people?

Personally, several of the novels I love (*Their Eyes Were Watching God*, *The Catcher in the Rye*, *To Kill a Mockingbird*, *The Color Purple*, and *The Perks of Being a Wallflower* to name a few) are about non-famous people living what might be considered commercially unsuccessful lives. Still, these character's lives are full of exquisite moments of wonder, love, insight, and meaning. In fact, these stories are some of the most read and praised stories of the last century. **From the observer perspective, the story of a non-famous life can be every bit as significant and enjoyable as the story of a famous person's life.**

Perhaps this seems obvious when we think about it in terms of books and movies. Even so, when we think about our own life stories, many of us cling to the notion that if we were commercially successful, achieving fame and fortune, our lives would be better. We cling to this idea because it's what consumer culture teaches us to think by constantly pointing to the rich and famous as models of success to strive for. And we cling to this because it's how the ego perpetuates itself both within us, and throughout our ego-driven society.

Here's a basic truth that it may be helpful to keep reminding yourself of: **publishing a best seller, becoming a famous artist, writing a hit song, having something take off, or achieving whatever "if only" you have in mind won't make you happier in the long run. It will just change the types of challenges that you face.**[58]

---

[58] Some psychological studies have even shown that winning millions of dollars in the lottery doesn't make people happier in the long run. However, this doesn't mean that your level of happiness is set at a certain level and there's nothing you can do about it. It just means that the things we frequently think will make us happy (like fame, luxuries, or excessive amounts of money) don't provide long-term happiness or fulfillment. Nevertheless, there are ways

Becoming famous or commercially successful is neither good nor bad. It's simply an experience. It might not even be as enjoyable of an experience as being non-famous. One writer friend of mine, after having a book sell very well and getting a three-book contract with a major publisher, confessed to me, "When I was most successful in my career, I was also the most miserable."

Another extremely successful Newbery and Caldecott winning author I know (who in addition to winning major awards has had big films made of his books) put it this way when we were talking about his meteoric rise to literary fame; "It's like when you finish the last level of a video game." There's a certain sadness to what he's talking about. A certain lostness as the thing you were working toward is accomplished and you're left vaguely dissatisfied, missing the game you enjoyed, and wondering what to do now.

Despite these examples (and countless other examples of commercial success not bringing long-term happiness or fulfillment) we might still continue to crave commercial success believing that if we had it, our lives would be better. So... what can you do?

Remember that what you resist persists. **Rather than constantly struggling with your desire for commercial success (and trying unsuccessfully to get yourself to stop desiring such things), take an observer perspective of yourself and accept your desires as part of your character and part of the creative process.** For instance, as you observe yourself, you might say to yourself, "This character loves to dream big at the beginning of a project."

As we discussed earlier, if you make your happiness contingent upon achieving something ("I won't be happy until I do this..."), you'll end up disappointed and unhappy most of the time. But if you can see your desire for success as part of your

---

to dramatically change how you experience and enjoy life—that's what this book is about.

character (rather than something you must achieve to be happy), then you can accept your desires as part of the experience you get to have. If a project takes off and becomes popular, great! You can experience that. And if it doesn't, that's great too! You don't have to become rich or famous to have amazing experiences. You still have your wonderful life story, and the desire for success is simply part of that story. Nothing more.

The experience of being non-famous can be filled with just as much meaning, joy, growth, and love as the experience of being famous. And the story of an "ordinary" life can be just as entertaining and important as the story of a commercially successful life.

This is your story. If you can observe and appreciate all aspects of it (just as you might appreciate and enjoy every page in a good book), then you're living life well.

Surfing the River

To help put together complex concepts like the illusion of control and observer consciousness in a way that's easy to envision, let's revisit the surfing metaphor from earlier and take it a step further.

As much as I love ocean surfing, I don't get to do it often in Colorado (where I live now). That's why, a little over twenty years ago, I took up whitewater kayaking (or river surfing as I like to think of it). I'm lucky that a couple amazing Class III and Class IV stretches of whitewater are just thirty minutes from my house.

Part of what I love about kayaking is the many counterintuitive lessons it teaches—things you don't understand until you do them a couple hundred times. Rolling a kayak is one such thing.

When you flip in a kayak, instinct tells you to get your head out of the water as quickly as possible. After all, you can't breathe when you're locked in a boat that's holding you upside down in rushing water. Add to this the fact that, in Colorado, the water is stunningly cold snow-melt and you're barreling toward rocks that could knock you unconscious. It makes sense to want to pull your head out with all of your might.

The trouble is, no amount of strength or thrashing about will get your head out of the water when you're upside down in a kayak. The more you panic and struggle to lift your head, the quicker you'll exhaust yourself and the worse off you'll be. The trick is to stay calm, keep your head underwater, and let it come up last. To roll a kayak, you need to perform a counterintuitive motion that, for most paddlers, makes little sense the first fifty or so times you do it. You just have to trust that the motion will work.

Then, one day, it clicks and rolling becomes intuitive. When that happens, it seems natural to get your head out of the water by letting it stay underwater while calmly performing a sweeping motion that uses the water around you to shift your weight back beneath you.

Similarly, in life there are things our instincts tell us to do that often make a situation worse rather than better. Take failure. As we explored earlier, the more you fear failure and try to avoid it, the harder it becomes to succeed because your fear makes it difficult to attempt new things and take risks. The counterintuitive solution is to embrace failure for what it can teach you. When you do that, success becomes easier—a lot like keeping your head down to bring it up.

Or consider the idea that you cannot change what you do not accept (more on the power of acceptance in a couple chapters). At first, accepting something that you want to change might seem absurd. But as long as you continue to deny something, you'll sabotage your attempts to change it. This is especially apparent with addictions. To change an addiction you first need to accept that you have an addiction, otherwise you'll just end up struggling against yourself. To really grasp how acceptance works, though, you need to practice it (see the "Acceptance meditation" in the Addendum for a great way to do this). Then one day, like rolling a kayak, things click and it all makes sense.

One of the most helpful counterintuitive insights that kayaking illustrates has to do with the paradox of control—the idea that the more you cling to an ego-driven illusion of control, the less control you actually have. Surfing gives us one way to visualize how this works. Kayaking can help us add another dimension to our understanding of this paradox.[59]

For example, picture yourself in a kayak floating down a raging mountain river. There are rocks ahead, and pillows of whitewater, eddies, and holes that are strong enough to suck you under. If you hit a rock the wrong way and breach against it, the force of the river will flip you over and send you swimming. Or worse, the currents might pin you against an underwater ledge until you drown. It's natural to feel a little frightened.

You might want to turn your kayak around and paddle upstream to avoid the rapids. Go ahead—try it. No matter how hard you paddle, you're no match for this current. The river keeps pushing you toward the rapids. The harder you fight the river, the sloppier and less effective your paddle strokes become until you're flailing in the rapids, exhausting yourself while drifting backward toward the rocks.

It's not a lot of fun to struggle against the currents like this. Fortunately, there's an alternative. Paddle with the currents. No one is stronger than the river, so stop fighting against it. Turn your boat around. It only takes one stroke. Feel the currents pushing against the paddle face until you're pointing downstream.

---

[59] You might have noticed that I've mentioned several paradoxes in this book: the paradox of creativity, failure, acceptance, and control. All of these only appear paradoxical from one level of consciousness (when you're stuck in the box). As awareness expands to more holistic perspectives, such "paradoxes" will no longer seem counterintuitive or paradoxical.

Now study the river. See the big picture beyond your small self. There's no need to panic. The water flows *around* the rocks. It pours *through* the rapids. If you're aware of the river, you can use the currents to your advantage.

You're still rushing toward the rapids. Take a deep breath, pull back your perspective, and find the line that will carry you through. Then calmly place your paddle in the currents to direct your descent. You can even eddy out, using the upstream flow on the far side of the rocks to stop right in the middle of the rapids like magic. You can surf the waves and spin on top of them. When you're ready, you can flow with the currents further down the river. By extending awareness beyond your small self *and* accepting the currents, you can navigate the river and enjoy the journey, because rather than fighting against the river you're working with it.

Skillful kayakers understand river currents enough to navigate Class V rapids with a minimum number of paddle strokes. They play in the waves. Less skillful kayakers only see what's right in front of them, and when things look rough they panic and thrash about, causing trouble for themselves (and others). The more aware of the river you become, and the more you learn to work with the currents, the more effective you'll be.

In life, sometimes we become oblivious to the river. Maybe we're focused on what we think we want, or maybe we want the river to be different than it is. We might become so fixated on our separate self that we resist the river entirely. Every now and then, we might get lucky as the river takes us where we want to go, but more often than not, we're fighting against the currents, angry and frustrated that we're not experiencing what we want to experience. We try to paddle upstream, thinking we can control our course with brute strength and effort. When we notice that we're not getting anywhere, or even drifting backward toward the rapids, we fight more desperately, but it doesn't work.

It's exhausting to struggle against the currents this way. Instead, recognize that you're part of the river, and the river is much bigger and stronger than your separate self will ever be. **By becoming aware of the river and embracing what is, you can use the powerful currents of the river to direct your course.**

Not only is this an easier, more effective way to navigate the river, it's more enjoyable and sustainable.

Scouting the River

To be clear, I'm not just saying "go with the flow." That's part of it, but that's an oversimplification that misses several points.

What I'm saying is that fighting against the river is exhausting and ineffective. By letting go of the illusion of control, you can become more aware of the currents that are directing your course. And by expanding your awareness, you can work more effectively with the river to influence your journey.[60]

---

[60] Letting go of the illusion of control is sometimes referred to in spiritual traditions as "surrender." I used to think that "surrender" sounded like giving up, so for years I rejected the concept. Now I know that surrender (in the spiritual sense) refers to surrendering the egoic illusions of separateness and control, accepting what is, and connecting with being so that you're consciously aligned with life. Although it might seem paradoxical to the ego, surrender is actually empowering, just as working with the river's currents instead of fighting against them is empowering. That's why spir-

Every time I feel like I'm struggling too much and getting frustrated (checking my sales numbers six times a day or trying to force a story to be what *I* think it should be), I remind myself of the lessons kayaking has taught me. I surrender the illusion of control that's keeping me focused on my small, separate self and causing me to fight against the river. I open my awareness to the greater currents directing my course, accept the river, and channel the creative energy of the universe. Of course, doing this can seem complicated and counterintuitive, which is why I often simply tell myself to "surf the river."

Surfing the river means that instead of constantly worrying about how a book is doing, I accept that I don't have control over how people respond to creations and move on to the next thing I'm called to create (whether it's a newsletter to let people know about the book, or a completely new project). Then I focus on appreciating the work I'm doing and enjoying the experiences I get to have.

If I'm struggling to write something because I'm trying to force it to be what I think it should be, I pull back my perspective and write whatever calls to me, staying open to what comes up and what it has to teach me. Or I let the character I'm struggling with write me a letter, telling me what I'm not getting about them. Instead of clinging to what *I* want to happen, I accept the river and surf what it presents me.

It can be especially hard to surrender the illusion of control and surf the river when things seem to go wrong and the rapids ahead appear threatening. Before kayakers attempt to navigate difficult sections of a river, they often climb to a high place where they can scout the rapids. Experienced kayakers will observe the river for a long time, looking for hazards and watching how the currents flow. Developing such a big picture perspective enables them to avoid getting caught up in fear and frustration when they're down in the rapids. Rather than panick-

---

itual teachers sometimes call this the "surrender that is no surrender." Let go or be dragged, as the Zen saying goes.

ing, they stay aware of the big picture, work with the currents, and enjoy the experience.

In life, we can't exactly step out of the river to scout the rapids, but we can take on an observer consciousness perspective that allows us to become more aware of the greater currents directing us. When we're stuck in ourselves, we're stuck in the fear and panic we feel, and we're unable to see past the threat that's directly ahead (this is how I was operating when my perceived failures led to a breakdown). Such tunnel-vision often leads to disaster. However, you don't have to experience a breakdown to know the tumult of the river. It's around us all the time. When you're stuck at a red light, panicking and upset because you're late for an appointment, you're paddling against the river. And when you're beating yourself up over something you said earlier, obsessing over something you can't change, or angry that something didn't happen the way you wanted it to, you're paddling against the river.

In fact, if you're feeling fearful, anxious, and upset, inevitably it's because your perspective has become too narrow and you're paddling against the river (resisting what is). To stop fighting against the currents and discover other options, first pull back and expand awareness. Simply observe and accept what you're experiencing without judgment. You might say to yourself, "Now this body is upset about being late for an appointment" or "Now this body feels frustrated about getting rejected." Through observer consciousness, you can see the river and discover ways to work with it.[61]

Consider this: when you're not panicking and struggling against the river, what are you doing? Instead of being focused

---

[61] If accepting the immediate situation seems too hard, take a step back and focus on accepting the *whole situation*. The bigger the perspective you take of a situation (scouting the river), the easier it usually becomes to accept it and work with it. Conversely, resistance and suffering are often caused by taking too narrow of a perspective.

on impending disaster with terrified tunnel-vision, you're free to look around and enjoy the scenery. You're able to notice and appreciate the *whole* experience. By observing the river, you're able to become more aware, and by becoming aware, you're able to navigate the river more effectively.

When you situate yourself in observer consciousness (scouting the river) obstacles and difficulties can become experiences that serve you and enriching opportunities. But this is only one benefit of observer consciousness.

Some teachers, like Rupert Spira, call observer consciousness "the knowing of our own being," and they claim that ultimately all we are is "the knowing." To understand what this means, it helps to consider what you really are.

Want to take things a step further?

The next time you're in an emotionally charged situation (like an argument with someone over the dirty dishes they left in the sink) rather than getting trapped in your egoic concerns and unconsciously reacting in a way that exacerbates the situation, try telling yourself, "This is the experience I get to have." Then pause to observe, accept, and appreciate the experience.

Observe what you're thinking, feeling, and doing. Observe the anger and the frustration that you feel. Observe the tightness in your chest and the sharpness in your voice. Observe what others are doing and everything else that's creating the situation.

It might help to use the "now this body is" phrase to gain perspective on yourself. For instance, you might think "Now this body is frustrated about not being heard. Now this body is speaking louder. Now this body feels bad about yelling."

There's no need to blame others or feel shame about your reactions. In fact, there's no need to judge at all. For now, just observe, accept, and appreciate the *whole situation*. The reactions you're having are part of a system that was set in motion long ago. Your brain is responding the way it was programmed to respond. You're playing a role that was created by countless factors, as are other participants in the situation. Observe, accept, and appreciate it all. From the observer perspective, you might even be amused by the experience, just as you might be amused by a conflict in a book you're reading.

Don't worry about changing things. The effort to control the situation will put you back in your ego, and back in a state of unconsciously reacting. By observing, accepting, and appreciating, you can transcend your ego. And, through acceptance, you can become aware of yourself and others. From this new place of peaceful awareness, new outcomes will naturally emerge because you're no longer unconsciously reacting.

(PS: That voice that says, "No way! I can't just observe, accept, and appreciate tense situations" —that's your ego.)

Wait... Why So Much Existential Stuff? Isn't This Book About Creativity?

I hear you. I didn't think that dealing with doubt, fear, rejection, procrastination, anxiety, depression, and other barriers to creativity would take me on such an existential journey either. But the root cause of all of these barriers to creativity (and to flourishing overall) is the ego, and getting beyond the ego takes a bit of existential work.

Unfortunately, your ego doesn't want you to escape its limiting grasp, so it will do all it can to make transcending the ego and reducing its power over you seem irrelevant and baffling. You might not feel ready to take it on. As was mentioned earlier, people usually need to experience a bit of suffering and failure before they're willing to recognize how their ego is holding them back and change.[62] If you're not into all this existential stuff right now, that's fine. Feel free to skip the next few chapters. However, if achievements fail to bring you lasting joy and satisfaction, you may want to come back to these chapters to address the root cause of what's limiting you and making you suffer.

Fortunately, as someone who's interested in creating things, you've got a head start on understanding all this existential stuff because when you create things, you're engaging in the most existential work of all—bringing new things into existence. Not only that, art itself often enhances people's awareness of the beauty, wonder, and richness of existence. In this way, both experiencing *and* creating art can be consciousness raising practices. This is why one of the greatest things an artist can do is to inspire others to become artists and connect with the creative source beyond their small selves.

When we do this, or when a work of art does this, we're helping others raise their consciousness by engaging in a process that encourages people to become more aware, empathetic, and connected. We're not only creating art, we're creating ourselves and the reality we live in. It doesn't get much more existential than that.

---

[62] The band *Cloud Cult* has a nifty line about this in one of their songs: "Some of us are laughing, some of us are choking. Some of us can't change 'til every bone has been broken."

Who Are You Really?

Let's start on the ground floor. Maybe you think that you are your body. It makes sense since our physical bodily experiences are what we usually identify with most directly. The trouble with this paradigm is that if you are your body, then whenever your body is uncomfortable, tired, or hungry (which can be most of the time), all you are is uncomfortable, tired, or hungry. And if you get a haircut, lose weight, or change part of your body, have you lost or changed yourself? Also, much of what happens in your body—from the digesting of food, to the growing of hair, to the replicating of your cells, to the beating of your own heart—is beyond your conscious awareness and control. If you are your body, then you're down in the rapids of the river (to use the kayaking metaphor), constantly being tossed about by waves and unable to work with the currents to shape your experience.

Maybe you prefer to see yourself as your thoughts. However, if you are your thoughts, then whenever your thoughts turn negative, obsessive, or despairing, all you are is negative, obsessive, or despairing. Also, thoughts come and go like the wind. It's hard (if not impossible) to prevent thoughts from arising while conscious. And if you fight your thoughts, the thoughts almost always win. Therefore, if you are your thoughts, then once again you're stuck in the rapids, clinging to an illusion of control and constantly struggling against the currents while the river jostles you about and takes you where it will.[63]

Perhaps you see yourself as your emotions or moods. However, like thoughts, these rise and fall, and are hard, if not impossible, to completely control. Or perhaps you see yourself as several of your mental experiences woven together—thoughts, emotions, moods, and memories—in something you might call a mind. But what happens when memories are lost (as they constantly are)? Or when your thoughts fall away, or your brain loses its ability to think? What happens when chemicals in your brain alter your emotions and moods, as they frequently do? Are *you* then lost? What a scary notion of the self to have.

Perhaps you see yourself as what you do and the things you accomplish. Or maybe even the impact you have on others and the world around you. With this paradigm, the existence of yourself isn't entirely subject to the whims of your body, brain, thoughts, and moods. But what happens when your actions fail to have the impacts you desire? Or when you fail to achieve something? Does your sense of self crumble? Are *you* then a failure?

All these ways of perceiving yourself keep you stuck in different versions of the small self.

Now, consider what happens when you see yourself as all of these things and more. You are the full integration of body, mind, actions, and a consciousness, awareness, or being that transcends the small self. You're not just your body, mind, and experiences, but the observing of your experiences. You're the

---

[63] If you really want to throw your mind for a loop, consider where a thought exists. If you are your thoughts, then where do *you* exist?

witness or observer consciousness—"the knowing of your being."

To the knowing, any experience is beneficial. The universe wants to experience itself through you, and having any experience, whether difficult or pleasurable, can be seen as an incredible success.

When you're conscious that you're the knowing, then you have the solace of knowing that what you are, on the most essential level, cannot be taken away or lost. The knowing of existence is always there, and there's no need to fear or resist the river. Instead, you can accept what is, become more consciously aware of the river, paddle more gracefully, and enjoy the journey.

Notice, this doesn't mean that you're not a self or that your small self doesn't exist. You still have the experience of being a self. All this means is that you're much more than the small self your ego wants you to fixate on. You're part of something much greater. Becoming aware of this opens up new realms of understanding, and provides liberation from suffering, fear, resistance, and limiting beliefs.

What the Heck Does Being "the Knowing" Mean?

One thing I've noticed since I've started to become more conscious of the transpersonal perspective we've been discussing is that difficulties still happen, my moods still shift, I still occasionally get anxious and depressed (though not nearly as much), and I still have challenging days, but how I perceive these challenges is entirely different, and this leads to different actions and different outcomes. Even when difficulties occur and my body/mind reacts in a negative way, my awareness remains in a peaceful, blissful place. As a result, my body/mind might get depressed, but it doesn't depress *me*. Or I get anxious, but it doesn't make *me* anxious. On a deeper level of awareness, I sometimes even feel grateful for the difficult experience.

Here's one example of how this plays out: A couple of nights ago my mind started ruminating on an experience I'd had earlier that day at my job as a professor. A student had become belligerent in class, insulting another student and, when I intervened, the belligerent student directed their anger at me. It wasn't something I'd previously encountered in over two decades of teaching, and it unsettled me.

That night, when I was trying to fall asleep, my mind kept replaying what had happened in class—wondering what I should have done to change the situation. Of course, you can't change what's already happened, so my mind kept spinning in circles, getting itself worked up.

In the past, an unsettling incident like this would have led me into a vicious cycle of insomnia, complete with rapid-fire internal dialogue that might have gone something like this:

> "Why is this still bothering me? I need to go to sleep. I have a big day tomorrow. It's stupid to keep thinking about this."
>
> "But why did that happen? Maybe if I can figure it out, it'll go away."
>
> "It's not going away. Stop thinking about it. You need to go to sleep."
>
> "That's why I have to figure this out—so I *can* go to sleep."
>
> "There's nothing more to figure out. You've gone over what happened dozens of times and you've learned all that you can from it."
>
> "Then why does it still bother me? There must be something I'm missing. Something I can change. If I could just fix the situation, it will stop bothering me."
>
> "You can't fix it. What's done is done. Now go to sleep!"
>
> "I can't go to sleep. I'm too upset. I need to make this go away."
>
> "This is insane. You keep messing things up—just like earlier today when everything went wrong in class…"

Needless to say, such inner dialogues rarely result in useful answers or a refreshing night's sleep.

But this time, things went differently. I noticed my mind ruminating, and instead of getting frustrated, trying to stop it, failing, and increasing my frustration, I simply accepted it. From the observer consciousness perspective, I even found it amusing. "Now this body is ruminating over what happened in class today," I said to myself. "Look at it go. Now it's upset about getting upset and not going to sleep. How funny."

Even while my body/mind became upset, on the observer consciousness level of awareness I wasn't upset. I was amused. Consequently, I was able to appreciate the experience of my mind ruminating and stay relaxed. I even fell asleep after a few minutes (in the past, the vicious cycle of insomnia and frustration about my insomnia would have kept me awake for hours).

That's just one simple example of what adopting an observer consciousness perspective can be like, although the deeper benefits are more subtle and pervasive. When you're the knowing, you still have difficult experiences, but you're not carried away by them. You're able to observe what's happening, learn what you can from things, and move on without getting stuck in reactive cycles. A nice side effect of this is that the difficult experiences don't happen as much, last as long, or feel as difficult. These days, I feel content most of the time in a way that never seemed possible to me before—blissful, even when my body/mind is not.

On the one hand, nothing has changed. I still go through life very much like I used to. On the other hand, everything has changed. Chopping wood and carrying water feels pretty amazing now, and I'm probably better at it, too.[64]

---

[64] It's important to realize that having a blissful, fulfilling life doesn't mean you're whistling to bluebirds and dancing with forest creatures all the time. A somber day can be a great day (and the experience of it can serve us), just as a somber movie can be a great movie and useful to watch. It doesn't all have to be rom-

It takes constant reminding to go through life this way. The ego will always try to drag you back to some version of the small self. Changing mental habits so that you don't get stuck in the reactive ego mind is like making new paths through deep snow. It takes many footsteps, and many times walking the same path before the snow gets packed down and traveling the new path becomes easier. But the benefits of walking such paths make the work well worth it.

---

coms and action flicks. That would be tedious. True unconditional happiness involves embracing all conditions—all emotions and experiences.

On Acceptance

Legendary Japanese swordsman and philosopher Miyamoto Musashi listed as his number one precept for life, "Accept everything just the way it is." The recognition of the importance of acceptance is nothing new (Musashi wrote down his 21 precepts almost 400 years ago).[65] Nevertheless, acceptance can be a difficult concept to understand and actualize. Personally, I fiercely resisted acceptance for decades before I finally got a sense of what it actually means, and why it's important.

Hopefully, the importance of accepting *what is* seems clear in the surfing and kayaking metaphors we've discussed. If you don't accept the wave as it is, you can't surf it very well. If you don't accept the river as it is, your actions will most likely be ineffective or counterproductive. However, in life, people often

---

[65] Marcus Aurelius, another great warrior philosopher, also wrote about the importance of acceptance: "Accept whatever comes to you woven in the pattern of your destiny, for what could more aptly fit your needs?"

resist acceptance because the ego asserts that accepting what is means doing nothing, becoming passive, and supporting things you don't agree with.

For me, it wasn't until a breakdown helped me sever my attachment to my ego that I was able to experience acceptance enough to realize that it doesn't mean being passive, agreeing with something you'd normally oppose, or being a doormat. You can, for instance, accept that some people believe the sun revolves around the earth. That doesn't mean that you have to agree with them (acceptance also includes accepting your own desire to disagree). But as long as you deny their perspective, or refuse to accept that they hold such views for reasons that seem sensible to them, you won't have much of a chance of changing their perspective.

On the other hand, if you accept that people believe what they do for reasons that seem sensible to them, while also accepting that you disagree for reasons that seem sensible to you, then you're more clearly seeing the currents in the river and can work with them. With acceptance, you're able to understand why people believe what they do. And when people feel genuinely heard, accepted, and understood, they're more likely to listen to you as you share with them other views of reality.

Likewise, acceptance is crucial for doing effective creative work and loving the process. Accepting when a piece gets rejected, for instance, doesn't mean that you give up. It means you enable yourself to move on and submit the piece to other places, or you use the rejection to help revise the piece, or to help you create new stories. With acceptance, the rejection can become part of the process—something you learn and grow from. Without acceptance, you're fighting against the currents, unable to progress.

Writers, for instance, often waste tremendous amounts of time and energy denying the internal and external voices that point out how something in a draft isn't working. Such feedback can come from helpful critical readers, or from your own story sense. I've spent months resisting such critical voices by trying to convince myself that something is working, only to write hundreds of pages that I later realize are misdirected crap. Maybe I needed to write those crappy pages to figure out why something wasn't working. Still, if I'd accepted what the critical voices were saying sooner and recognized what was useful in such criticism, I could have revised and discovered better alternatives sooner.

The quicker you can accept what is, the quicker you can address it, move on, and discover new possibilities (more on this in the chapter on revision). Rather than being a passive, apathetic thing to do, acceptance is a powerful transformative practice. As Rumi put it, "the moment you accept what troubles you've been given, the door will open."

The Power of Radical Acceptance

Here's a challenge that can help you experience the transformative power of acceptance: **spend five minutes each day imagining what it would feel like to completely accept everything.**

Note: you don't need to *actually* accept everything (your ego probably won't allow that). Instead, start by simply imagining *what it would feel like* if you did accept everything as part of the perfection of being.

To do this, it helps to sit in a quiet place and focus on your breathing. Let your mind settle (see the "Meditation Quick Start Guide" in the Addendum for ways to do this). Then imagine what it would feel like to let go of all your judgments and resistance, and completely accept everything.

Accept the noise of traffic, the exhaust from trucks, and the current political divide. Accept the rejections you've received, the frustrations of work, and the birds flying past. Accept your desire to procrastinate and the fears you feel. Accept the sweet smell of lilacs in the air and the allergies they give you. Accept that people are making love to each other right now, and people are yelling at each other right now. Accept your doubts and pain. Try to imagine what it would feel like to completely accept all aspects of existence as parts of the perfection of being.

Remember, acceptance applies to yourself as well. Therefore, accepting what is includes accepting your own desires, even your desires to change things. After all, the mind's desire to speak out and create change is part of the perfection of being. And if your mind strongly resists the idea of acceptance, accept that too. Know that after these five minutes, you can go back to struggling against everything you dislike. But for these five minutes, simply focus on acceptance.[66]

Go on—set a timer for five minutes, take some deep breaths, and imagine what it would feel like to completely accept everything. In this present moment, everything is perfect as it is.

Did you do it? If so, what did you notice?

Maybe judgments kept creeping in. Maybe part of you (your ego) kept resisting some things or kept saying "I want this and not that." Maybe there were things you refused to accept. Or maybe part of you wanted to argue with things and assert why something was wrong and unacceptable. That's okay. Acceptance is hard. The ego likes to push back against it. But if you could do it, or even just imagine for a moment what it would feel like to do it, you might have noticed a few things.

One thing that happens as acceptance grows is that the ego's influence naturally dissolves, and then your need to see

---

[66] It can be challenging to grasp what acceptance actually means—that it's consciously aligning yourself with being so you can live without resistance. This brief acceptance meditation gives you an opportunity to experience what that might feel like.

things as good or bad, wanted or unwanted, pleasant or unpleasant falls away. This is because **the ego is fundamentally a judgment machine**. It constantly needs to judge, criticize, compare, agree, disagree, desire, and reject to draw firmer lines around itself and perpetuate its existence.

When you accept what is, your ego's limiting grasp lessens allowing the self to expand and embrace everything in a way that feels open, joyous, whole, peaceful, and perfect. It's a *Yes! Yes! Yes!* chorus of appreciation that's blissful and energizing.

With this experience of blissful acceptance comes the awareness that your ego is not what you are. Instead, your ego is what divides, isolates, and limits you from fully experiencing what you are and how you're part of being.

In case this sounds like a bunch of starry-eyed idealism, here's an everyday example of how acceptance works. I often practice radical acceptance as part of my meditation habit. In the past, I used to struggle with sitting still for long periods of time. My internal dialogue would go something like this:

> "My back hurts."
>
> "Ignore it. You need to focus on meditating."
>
> "I want to focus on meditating, but my back really hurts."
>
> "It's not that bad."
>
> "Maybe, but it's getting worse."
>
> "Don't think about it."
>
> "How can I not think about it? It's a screaming cauldron of pain. I think my vertebrae are exploding."
>
> "Don't move."
>
> "Look, you've already lost a couple minutes thinking about this back pain. Just move and fix it."
>
> "I'm supposed to be meditating, not fidgeting around. Meditating is doing nothing. Letting the mind go still."
>
> "All you're doing right now is focusing on your back pain. Rub your shoulder so you can move on."

"But..."
"DO IT NOW!"
"Fine. Satisfied?"
"No. It still hurts..."

That's how it feels to struggle against the currents. What we resist persists. The back pain doesn't go away, it just gets worse until you have to address it. And even then, it doesn't go away. The cycle simply repeats with renewed vigor.

Now, here's what the internal dialogue looks like with acceptance:

"My back hurts."
"I accept that my back hurts. This experience is part of this perfect moment."
"Okay. It still hurts."
"I accept that I'm still thinking about how my back hurts. Everything is exactly as it should be. I am the knowing."

Oddly enough, that's usually it. When I accept that my back hurts and stop struggling against what is, my aching back becomes one more sign of being aware and part of existence—of being the knowing. On a deeper level, such reminders of existing can even be gratifying. Often, when I accept that my back hurts and stop resisting what is, the ache of my back is no longer painful or distracting, and the hurt itself soon fades away.[67]

---

[67] Roman Emperor and stoic philosopher Marcus Aurelius expressed something similar nearly two thousand years ago when he wrote, "Reject your sense of injury and the injury itself disappears." Although it's hard to "reject" the sense of injury, by fully accepting an experience (in this case a back ache), you can turn a negative experience that you're resisting into a peaceful experience of being. Then the "sense of injury" naturally fades away.

Then my mind moves on to other things, and other thoughts arise. For instance, I might think:

> "This meditation is taking forever. Has it been twenty-five minutes yet?"
> "This body's eagerness to get up is part of the perfection of being."
> "I have so many things I need to do today. Sitting here is silly."
> "I accept that this body constantly wants to do things."
> "I suck at meditating. I'm too distracted."
> "I accept that thoughts keep arising. These thoughts are part of this perfect moment."

What's hard to show in this dialogue is how the more I accept things, the quieter such egoic objections become until they disappear entirely. Each objection, as it arises, can be a pleasing embrace of existence. It's how you know you are the knowing.

Resistance causes you to become stuck in exhausting spirals of struggle, frustration, and disappointment. Acceptance gives a way out of such vicious cycles. By accepting things, they no longer have power over you. Acceptance is liberating because it allows you to recognize, acknowledge, and move on.

This applies, most importantly, to yourself. What you refuse to accept in yourself will hold you back. Acceptance is the way to step beyond your egoic self and your current limitations. Not only is it hard to change what you don't accept, **you cannot transcend what you refuse to accept.**

If you keep up a daily practice of radical acceptance, over time you'll find that rather than struggling against the currents and resisting life, you're seeing things more clearly and working with what is. You might even start embracing what is.[68]

---

[68] Embracing what is, at its highest level, means loving what is—even your enemies. Sound familiar? To love everyone and everything—that's been the message of many prophets, sages, and

When this happens, you'll feel lighter, happier, and more open to the creative energy of the universe.[69]

---

religious figures for thousands of years. Love, like acceptance, is transformational.

[69] It can't be emphasized enough that the power of acceptance can only be known through direct experience. If you didn't try it before, take five minutes and try it now. In the Addendum, you'll find a short, enjoyable acceptance meditation that's easy to do. Acceptance is the key to unconditional happiness.

When to Worry

The creative path can be a perilous one. The dangers might not be as external or obvious as in some occupations, but that doesn't mean they're less severe. Putting yourself and your creations out there for people to engage, ignore, or criticize is hard, and the internal struggles that come with the creative path can be devastating. The percentage of those making their living in "arts related" jobs who've died by suicide has been shown to be several times greater than average in some national studies. It's important not to underestimate the toll that doubt, struggle, and rejection can take.

The techniques we've discussed in this book for staying creative and transcending the ego—including embracing failure, loving the process, letting go of the illusion of control, developing observer consciousness, increasing awareness, and accepting what is—aren't easy things to do.

Sometimes we get lost. Sometimes, in the dark night of the soul, we become distracted and lose our sense of the bigger picture. Sometimes the currents pull us under. Even the best kayakers need to be rescued from time to time.

Remember, there are good reasons why the creative path is hard. Real transformation—with the death and rebirth this entails—is never easy. The old self doesn't want to die, and the ego doesn't want to be transcended. It will keep pulling you back to your worries, doubts, and fears. It will keep trying to block you from connecting with the creative energy of the universe and becoming conscious of being more than the limited, separate self the ego wants you to fixate on.

So far we've looked at how struggle, doubt, rejection, and failure are part of the process. When you feel these things, accept them as part of the process and move on. You might even find ways to appreciate them for what they reveal to you. But despair—that's something to look out for. Despair is a whirlpool that sucks you under and holds you there. You can accept that you feel despair, but don't stop there. When you feel despair, get help. Despair isn't something to live with or deal with alone.

One of the most harmful myths for artists is the one of the suffering creative genius—the idea that to be the next Van Gogh (or Kurt Cobain, Sylvia Plath, Virginia Woolf, Ernest Hemingway, etc.), you need to be lonely, tormented, and cut off your ear. It simply isn't so.

You don't need to suffer to create great art. Creating through joy, openness, and connection are far more effective ways to bring new things into existence. That doesn't mean that everything is going to be unicorns and roses. But it does mean that you don't need to seek out the dark, wallow in despair, or heighten your suffering to do creative work. As the Buddhist saying goes, "Pain is inevitable. Suffering is optional."

If you find that you're obsessing over critical thoughts, engaging in self-destructive behaviors, experiencing thoughts of worthlessness, suicide ideation, or feeling hopeless and lost—tell someone. Take steps to get yourself out of the dark whirlpool of despair you're caught in. Your creativity won't suffer. On the contrary, it will get better when you're feeling better.

A lot of times people avoid getting help because they think they can handle it on their own. Smart people often trick themselves into thinking they've got everything under control. And very smart people are experts at tying themselves up into very smart, difficult knots. No matter how smart you are, **you can't untie the knot when you are the knot**.

The question to ask yourself isn't "Do I need help?" but "Can my life be better?"

If your life can be better, why not take the steps to make it so? There are people out there who want to help you. Sure, it can take some effort to find a good counselor. Fortunately, many counselors don't charge for the first session, and you can try out several until you find someone who works well with you. Good counselors will be able to help you untie the knots that are holding you back and dragging you under. They'll help you gain perspective and become more aware of the river so you can enjoy the journey.

You're never in the river alone. We're all in this together, and what you add to existence can only be added by you.[70]

---

[70] Sometimes what leads to self-destructive behaviors and suicide ideation is a relentless feeling of disconnection from being, coupled with the subconscious recognition that you're causing your own suffering (that's what ate away at me). Such a recognition can feel hopeless and dire, like falling into a dark pit of your own making. After all, when what you think you are is causing you to suffer, it makes sense to think the only way to end suffering is to eliminate yourself.

The instinct isn't entirely wrong. It's just distorted by an overactive ego that's keeping you isolated, unaware, and unable to experience your essential connectedness to being when in reality all aspects of being—from the air you breathe, to the people you know, to the ground you walk on—embrace your presence. Rather than eliminating yourself, the solution is to let go of attachment to the ego mind that's causing you to suffer. To do this, it helps to know that the pit is actually a tunnel, and the far side can be reached.

Anytime you get lost in the dark and can't see a way out, here's a good number to keep handy: The National Suicide Prevention Lifeline, 1-800-273-8255. There are people there 24/7 who want to talk with you. Just know, the voice that says you can't reach out—that's your ego. You don't need to listen to it.

Hearts Get Broken Open

Let's explore the difficult aspects of the creative path a little more. Creating things and putting those creations out in the world for others to experience frequently involves heartbreak. We get emotionally invested in what we create, and inevitably things go differently than we expected. Occasionally, the world gives us a better reception than we anticipated, but often we're disappointed since it's ambition's job to exceed reality.

Editors and agents might reject your brilliant manuscript. Some readers will post cruel reviews. It's possible that only two friends and your mom will show up for your art opening or album release party (and maybe they won't even come). The world could meet your creations with brutal negativity, or ignore them entirely. Such difficult experiences are frequently part of the creative process. Although you can accept and even love the process, it's not easy to love harsh criticism and rejection. It takes a bit of alchemy to change what hurts into growth experiences.

We've looked at how failure can be used to dissolve the ego's limiting grasp and expand one's ability to connect with the creative energy of the universe. Critical reviews and comments can do this too, as long as you don't get stuck on how wounded you are by them and retreat into yourself, or use them as egoic excuses to stop creating. Accept that great art always attracts harsh criticism (just look up some of the brutally negative reviews that classics like *The Catcher in the Rye*, *To Kill a Mockingbird*, and *The Great Gatsby* have received).

Criticism doesn't change the reality of what you've created, who you are, or the work you're doing. Just because hundreds of ego-driven reviewers have torn *The Catcher in the Rye* to shreds online doesn't change the fact that it's delighted millions and helped generations of readers feel less alone. Any innovative, challenging work of art is going to be embraced by some and vehemently criticized by others.

Some criticism can even be useful. **To differentiate between criticism that's destructive and criticism that's useful, ask yourself if you can learn something from the criticism that might help you create what you're called to create**. If not, then view the criticism as a barrier to the creative process. When someone criticizes you or your work for egoic reasons, chances are they're saying what they are to make themselves feel superior, or to prevent you from doing what you're called to do because they perceive your creative success as a threat to their ego. Such criticism is about *their* ego, not you or your work, and is best understood as such.[71]

---

[71] Frequently, what such ego-driven criticism reveals is how a person is struggling with their own relationship to creativity. When someone harshly criticizes creative work, it can help to remember that their criticism probably has more to do with them and their doubts, fears, and frustrations, than with the work itself. All criticism is ultimately self-criticism.

On the other hand, if the criticism is revealing something which can help you learn, grow, and create what you're called to create, then the criticism can be useful (as long as you don't let the fear of criticism stop you from continuing to create). This is why some Buddhists call their enemies their "most special teachers."

Despite all this, harsh criticism can be devastating. There's no way around it—if you take the creative path, at times your heart will get broken. As creators, it's important to remember that if we're afraid of heartbreak, avoiding it will cause us to become protective and closed off. We might distrust others or stifle our creativity to avoid the pain of heartbreak. We might become brittle, defensive, and disconnected.

Conversely, when we're able to accept and embrace heartbreak as part of the process, we can experience heartbreak as a potent gift. The pain of heartbreak can propel us into a profound state of openness and compassion. As a friend of mine eloquently put it, "hearts don't just get broken. They get broken open."

The experience of heartbreak enables us to understand each other's pain better and become more aware and connected. And the experience of heartbreak can dramatically open us up to the creative energy of the universe. Many artists have entered their most creatively productive periods through the gateway of heartbreak.

Notice, heartbreak is different from despair. Despair is when you fall into a dark pit and think you'll never get out. It involves giving up hope that you'll ever feel something good again. But heartbreak involves hope and feeling intensely. One can even be heartbroken and joyful at the same time (in fact, the two are often linked). Where despair disconnects us and causes us to isolate ourselves, heartbreak opens us up to new connections and greater compassion.

Through heartbreak, we can experience a pain that enables us to better understand each other's pain. We can become more open with each other, humble, and more con-

nected to the creative energy of the universe.

A teacher once told me that a bodhisattva walks through the world with a broken heart. In the Mahayana Buddhist tradition, a bodhisattva is someone who seeks the complete enlightenment of *all* sentient beings. Instead of simply seeking enlightenment for their small self and transcending the cycle of death, rebirth, and suffering (known as samsara), a bodhisattva vows to stick around to help everyone out. The heartbreak a bodhisattva feels comes from being deeply compassionate and experiencing the suffering of others. Such profound compassion is part of transcending the small self and being more connected to others. Hearts get broken open.[72]

One living example of what such compassionate heartbreak looks like is the 14th Dalai Lama. Although the Dalai Lama is famous for his infectious joy and laughter, he's no stranger to heartbreak. He had to leave his family to begin his monastic education when he was six years old. In 1950, China invaded and violently took over the Dalai Lama's home country of Tibet. During this crisis, when the Dalia Lama was only fifteen years old, he was called upon to assume political leadership for his people. A few years later, after China's brutal suppression of a Tibetan uprising, the Dalai Lama had to flee Tibet to survive. He undertook a two-week journey by foot over the Himalayas, traveling at night to avoid capture, before finally arriving in India.

At twenty-three, he'd lost his country, and he'd seen many loved ones and countrymen killed. Since then, he's lived in exile for most of his life. But rather than becoming angry or vengeful from this experience, the Dalai Lama frequently talks about how it opened his heart and connected him to the world. Because

---

[72] Before you think that bodhisattvas must be sad sacks who go around wallowing in everyone else's suffering, consider that those fat "Laughing Buddha" statues that many Americans think depict Buddha actually depict a bodhisattva known as Budai (or Hotei in Japan). If those little statues are any indication, clearly you can be compassionate *and* wonderfully joyful.

he's an exile, he's had to live outside his country and speak with citizens and leaders around the world. He's become more well-known globally than any previous Dalai Lama. In 1989, he was awarded the Nobel Peace Prize for consistently advocating non-violence, even in the face of extreme aggression. In interviews, he's frequently said that the difficulties he experienced helped him become more compassionate and empathetic.

It's not only the Dalai Lama who demonstrates how hearts get broken open. Studies have shown that lower-income people are significantly more charitable than wealthy people—44% more generous in some studies. Researchers have suggested that, because lower-income people have suffered more, they've developed more empathy and compassion for the suffering of others. On the other hand, wealth can feed a person's ego, which causes their sense of entitlement ("I deserve everything I have") and their fear that others will take away what they have ("Other people are lazy and undeserving") to grow. In this way, wealth can cause people to become more closed off and disconnected from others.

There's a growing stack of research that shows that our sense of connection to others leads to happiness, purpose, and longer, healthier lives, while being disconnected leads to depression, anxiety, and negative health effects. For happiness, feeling connected to others is essential. So, if you want to be happy, be wary of that which causes you to become closed off, and embrace that which helps you become more connected to others, even if such experiences are painful. Let your heart be broken open.

The Secret to Completely Beating the Comparison Game

The comparison game thrives on seeing ourselves as separate from others. Therefore, the ultimate way to beat the comparison game is to transcend the ego-driven illusion of separateness and recognize how we're all interconnected aspects of a greater whole. Although this might sound lofty, there are many practical implications to realizing our essential connectedness.

To understand this, first consider all the fundamental ways we're connected to each other. No one exists alone, and no one can survive for long completely separate from others. We're all interdependent—dependent (at least at one point) on the people who raise us, feed us, educate us, grow our food, and give us clothing and shelter. No adults brought themselves to adulthood on their own, no matter how independent one might claim to be. In addition, we're influenced by those we interact with, read, listen to, and watch. And when we create things, we're using concepts, insights, devices, and techniques developed by others.

We're connected by the air we breathe, the food we eat, and the water we drink. On a purely physical level, our atoms are constantly shifting back and forth. Around 7% of our body mass is exchanged each day through breathing, eating, drinking, and other processes. 7% of "our" atoms are released into the universe, and billions of new atoms become part of us. Each day, atomically speaking, we're at least 7% different. At this rate, it takes about two weeks for as much as our entire body mass to be exchanged, and in one year, according to scientists, 98% of *all* of our atoms are different. In one year, nearly everything we might have thought of as our physical "self" has flowed back into the universe and emerged out of the universe.

In addition, the bodies that we might think of as ours alone are made entirely of atoms that were once part of other things. Most of the atoms that compose us are older than the earth itself. Some are as old as the creation of the universe. For billions of years they've been flowing in and out of different forms. Compared to this, their time forming us is a tiny blip—a drop in an unfathomable ocean.

The molecules that make up your body today could be part of a tree tomorrow, and a butterfly, worm, or blade of grass next week. Parts of what you are right now will become part of something else in a moment, and what you might see as "other" will become you. Who we are is constantly interchanging, and what forms us will continue to do so for as long as the universe exists. We are ephemeral, emerging phenomena.

In any given moment, even the cells that we might think form us and give us our unique genetic signature are likely to be more not us than us, as we're made up of more bacterial cells than human cells. We are ecosystems of cells, constantly interacting with our environments, never separate.[73]

---

[73] Sadhguru once put it this way in an interview: "The individual existence is a fake existence. If you don't understand what I'm say-

In our lives, too, we're constantly interchanging ideas, thoughts, emotions, images, and visions. Our self only seems separate to the ego—and it's that illusion of separateness that the ego clings to and desperately tries to protect. But as soon as we start to question where an idea, thought, image, or concept came from, it immediately gets tangled up with the ideas, thoughts, images, and concepts of others.

The very language we use to think and communicate comes to us from others and is given meaning by others. Words only have significance in their interchange. We swim in an ocean of consciousness, and are only a tiny part of that ocean. The water of existence flows through us but is never ours alone.

We need these connections. We thrive on them—so much so that psychologists consider solitary confinement to be torture. To artificially sever a person's ability to connect with others is a cruel punishment that leads to insanity. The basic truth of our existence is that we're connected to each other in more ways, and more deeply, than we often allow ourselves to realize.

Ego-driven torments like the comparison game can only persist when we see ourselves as separate and disconnected from others. When we recognize our essential connectedness, such destructive comparisons crumble. Unfortunately, this is hard to do. The ego constantly works to perpetuate the illusion of a separate self. It draws an arbitrary boundary around a tiny swirl of thoughts and forms to separate what it thinks it is from what it thinks it isn't. As a result, we often feel isolated and alone in our experiences, and driven to compete with each other to survive.

---

ing, close your mouth and hold your nose for two minutes and see what happens. You will understand that without the larger atmosphere around you, you cannot exist for a moment. What the trees exhale you are inhaling. What you exhale the trees are inhaling... One half of your breathing apparatus is hanging out there. If you experience this, do I have to tell you not to cut down the trees?"

Logically recognizing our essential connectedness is only the beginning. To really beat the comparison game and see beyond the illusion of a separate self, new perspectives and practices are required so that new habits of mind can be formed. In the next few chapters we'll explore practical ways to do this.[74]

---

[74] As Thich Nhat Hahn elegantly put it, "We are here to awaken from our illusion of separateness." However, it's not only spiritual leaders who've emphasized the importance of realizing our essential connectedness. Here's what Albert Einstein wrote on the subject: "A human being is part of a whole, called by us the 'Universe,' a part limited in time and space. He experiences himself, his thoughts and feelings, as something separated from the rest—a kind of optical delusion of his consciousness. This delusion is a kind of prison for us, restricting us to our personal desires and to affection for a few persons nearest us. Our task must be to free ourselves from this prison by widening our circles of compassion to embrace all living creatures and the whole of nature in its beauty."

Slay the Comparison Game with Mudita

One of the best ways to develop a more connected perspective (and eliminate the comparison game) involves something Buddhists call *mudita*.

Mudita is a Sanskrit word that has no corollary in English, but it's often translated as "sympathetic or vicarious joy." Think of it as the opposite of jealousy. Practicing *mudita* means rejoicing in someone else's happiness. When someone you know achieves a significant success, award, or accomplishment, rather than creating a comparison between yourself and them that leaves you feeling lesser, try feeling their joy and sense of accomplishment as if you were them. We're all essentially connected. We're all in this together. And we're all part of one existence. When someone brings something wonderful into existence, we're all made greater by that.

I know this might sound strange at first—especially for those of us raised in a highly competitive culture where we're taught to make comparisons and judge everyone (including ourselves) by such comparisons. In the culture I grew up in, it was often made clear that there are winners and losers, and no one wants to be a loser. But ask yourself, how fun is this perspective? What has it gained you? If you want to feel like a winner all the time and end destructive comparisons, practice *mudita*.

Try it in small ways first. When you hear about someone's success or achievement, imagine how they feel. Then let yourself experience their joy, satisfaction, and gratitude with them. Empathetically explore their experience and celebrate it. You can do this with difficult experiences, too, but that can be more challenging. (You might be surprised, though, by how healing it can be to focus on empathetically feeling what someone else is feeling in a difficult situation, rather than immediately trying to "fix" the situation.)

If the person is someone you know well, feeling the joy they feel may be easier, so start with people you're close to. As a teacher, for instance, I feel joy when one of my students publishes a book or wins an award. As a parent, it's easy to practice *mudita* with my children, too. However, it's important to recognize that *mudita* is different from egoic pride. Rather than experiencing joy for someone's success because it reflects well on you or elevates your status, practicing *mudita* means genuinely and unselfishly wanting others to flourish in their own ways, and rejoicing when they do.

Once you can practice *mudita* with those you know well, try extending your practice to those you're only loosely associated with. Practicing *mudita* requires openness and envisioning our essential connectedness. The more you do this, the better you'll get at it, and the more you'll experience the rewards of *mudita*. Instead of feeling diminished by others' accomplishments, when you practice *mudita* it becomes increasingly enjoyable to learn about the incredible things other people are doing.

Not only is *mudita* far more enjoyable than playing the comparison game, there are several pragmatic advantages to practicing it. When we become more joyful, we're better able to persevere in our own creative endeavors and attract beneficial experiences our way. We rise and fall through our connections with each other. No one succeeds alone (although some may pretend that they do), and people like to help those they feel connected to.

I've noticed that writers, for instance, tend to grow and publish together. This runs counter to the popular notion of writers as solo creators typing away in their basements. Although I spend hours a day writing in my basement, the most important aspects of writing happen through connecting with others. After all, a story isn't just ink on a page. Stories exist through an intimate and miraculous process of collaborating with other minds that we commonly refer to as reading.

Connecting with others is vital for publishing as well. In my experience, the most important step for publishing is finding a helpful critique group of writers who are at a similar stage of development because writers usually grow and succeed together. Often, when one person in a writing group gets published or experiences growth, others in the group will soon have similar experiences.

That's what happened with the first serious writing group I was involved with. After completing an MFA program in fiction, I knew I still had a long way to go to develop my craft, so I teamed up with other recent grads who were interested in giving each other feedback. We met twice a month, read each other's essays and stories, and gave each other pages of comments. We also organized readings and helped each other find publishing opportunities. We were all writing different things, but we supported each other's projects and genuinely wanted to help each other flourish.[75]

---

[75] The stated goal of our little writing group was to "rule the surface world." To this end, we created a Vend-O-Prose machine out

After about a year and a half of working together, one of the group's members was doing a reading at a conference when an agent heard his work and liked it. The agent introduced himself afterward and asked to see what my friend, Steve, was working on. Steve sent him a collection of essays, and the agent (he turned out to be an extremely well-connected agent) offered to represent him. A few months later Steve had a contract from Simon and Schuster for his memoir, *The Guinness Book of Me*.

As a young writer, I was thrilled to see someone I'd traded manuscripts with get a book picked up by a major publisher. I naturally felt happy for Steve and celebrated his success (practicing *mudita*).

What I didn't realize then was how Steve's success would impact me. Not long after Steve secured a book contract, he suggested that I send the manuscript I'd been working on to his agent (it was a YA novel he knew well since he'd given me feedback on it). I sent off the manuscript, and Steve's agent recommended that I send my manuscript to another agent he knew who represented books for young readers. That agent liked my manuscript and offered to represent me. A few months later, I signed my first book contract with Scholastic Press.

In the months and years that followed, other members of our writing group had similar experiences. Now, several of the writers from that group have published with excellent houses, and it was *mudita*—genuinely celebrating and supporting each other's achievements—that helped get us there.

This story isn't unusual. I've met dozens of writers who've described similar paths to publishing. They were working in a critique group, each of them struggling for their first publication, when one got a lucky break and within a few months or years other members of the group also got published. It frequently happens this way because writers often grow together, and because personal connections in publishing, as in most endeavors,

---

of an old tampon vending machine that we refurbished to distribute tampon-sized scrolls of prose in coffee shops and bars.

can lead to new opportunities.

Practicing *mudita* will not only help you overcome the comparison game and feel better, it's the secret to calling good things your way.

Want to take things a step further?

The next time you hear about someone's success, take a few minutes to practice *mudita*:

- Imagine what it would feel like to be them, and to experience what they're experiencing.
- Try to sympathetically and unselfishly feel their joy.
- Reach out to celebrate with them. See if you can express genuine joy and gratitude with them for their experience.

Note: Sometimes, under the guise of being humble, we don't allow ourselves to fully appreciate the positive experiences we get to have. It's important to recognize that one can be thankful, joyous, *and* humble. By genuinely celebrating a positive experience with someone, you can help them more fully realize and appreciate the experience they're having.

What About Competition?

If you're competitive by nature (I am) you can still experience the benefits of competition without the negative effects by practicing *mudita*. In competitions we frequently talk about showing "good sportsmanship"—being a gracious winner or loser. Although good sportsmanship is important, practicing *mudita* goes deeper than this. **Genuinely rejoicing in another's success (even if you're competing with them) transforms the limiting paradigm of competition as a zero-sum game (where to be the winner others must lose) to a cooperative paradigm where one person's success enhances the whole.**

Competition itself is simply a tool for motivation. It doesn't need to be an internecine battle. We can use competition to inspire ourselves to exceed our previous limitations. Great athletes often talk about how their competitors helped them improve, and we often learn the most from those we see ourselves as being in competition with. In healthy competitive relationships, we can push each other while supporting each other and rejoicing in each other's accomplishments.

With creative endeavors, it's especially important to remember that it's not a zero-sum game. I've met writers who've caused themselves tremendous anxiety by thinking that there are only a limited number of books that can be created and shared, so every writer who creates and publishes a book reduces their chances. Such perceived limitations are the fear-provoking susurrations of the ego.

In truth, **there is no limit to creativity or to how much can be created**. As writers and artists, it's frequently advantageous to assist and support each other because the more people engage in creative activities, the more they tend to support other creative endeavors. **Creativity loves creativity.**

Competition that divides us and causes us to see ourselves as disconnected and separate is ultimately harmful. But competition that's based on a foundation of connectedness and cooperation can be a wonderful thing. Practicing *mudita* is a powerful way to foster enriching competitive relationships. After all, when a close competitor is successful, a great deal of that success may be connected to you. It makes sense to celebrate it.

Three Fun Ways to Experience Essential Connectedness and Expand Consciousness

The next time you're out in a public space or driving somewhere try this: Observe a stranger and imagine that you're them. (Writers ought to be good at this since we do something similar when we write stories with characters who are different from ourselves.)

Situate yourself in someone else's perspective. Envision their concerns, worries, and thoughts and imagine that you're experiencing such thoughts. If they're rushing off somewhere, imagine what it feels like to be them, needing to rush to get to someplace else. What needs or desires are prodding them on? What are they heading toward? What are they leaving behind? Who did they just say goodbye to? Who else is present? Are they talking to someone? How are they holding themselves? What sort of mood do they appear to be in? Imagine that you feel their joys and sorrows.

This is a fun game to play when you're stopped at a light, observing people around you. First, try to imagine yourself in their vehicle and situation. Then try to situate your awareness in their body and perspective.

Expanding your perceptions like this takes practice, but the more you do it, the easier it becomes.

Or, the next time someone does something that upsets you, rather than reacting with anger, try this: Let go of your emotional reaction for a moment and imagine that you're the person who upset you, with all of their worries, concerns, fears, and desires. Put yourself in their perspective, feeling what they feel. Rather than blaming them, accept them. Accept that they're driven by countless cause-and-effect relationships (just like you). Can you step into their shoes? Can you see yourself through their eyes? What's it like to be in their situation?

You might notice a powerful alchemy happens when you imagine that you're the "other" who has upset you. It's hard to give someone the bird for cutting you off when you're experiencing what it's like to be them. Your anger will momentarily dissolve (you can always get it back later if you like). Often, when you put yourself in their place, their anger will dissolve as well. You might both feel, for a brief moment, your essential connectedness.

Here's one more consciousness-expanding game: The next time you're in a crowd, look at the people around you and, one by one, extend your awareness toward them. Notice how they're holding their bodies. What do their expressions say? Imagine that you see what they're seeing and feel what they're feeling. How does it feel to be each person? How deeply can you open your awareness to others? How fully can you imagine that you're different people?

Now take things a step further: Imagine that you're the whole crowd. Rather than just experiencing things through one perspective, can you sense being many people at once—many parts of a whole? Can you feel being a hundred-eyed fragment of existence experiencing itself?[76]

In each of these exercises, it's important to recognize that the things you imagine about a person might be inaccurate (sometimes wildly so). Then again, I'm often amazed by how effective intuition, imagination, and empathy can be at inferring what

---

[76] Not long ago, when I was at a poetry reading where I had a good view of most of the crowd, I started playing this game. I extended awareness to one person, then the next, imagining what it was like to sit the way they were sitting, see what they were seeing, and sense what they were sensing (their curiosity, boredom, and exhilaration as they held hands with someone in public…). As I did this, my awareness expanded until I no longer felt limited to my own body. Instead, I experienced the reading from multiple points of view. I felt the beat of other hearts and the rise and fall of other chests. Then I had the sensation of being many people at once, taking a collective breath.

I'm not sure how much time passed, but when the reading ended and the audience clapped, I returned to my singular perspective, only for the rest of the evening (and even a bit of the next day) I was filled with intense happiness. I couldn't stop smiling. Instead of feeling confined, my whole body tingled with the residual sensation of being connected to others in ways my ego couldn't imagine.

To some, this experience might sound absurd. All I can say is that it's an experience worth having. To this day, it remains one of the most amazing experiences I've ever had.

someone is experiencing. As Ramana Maharshi famously replied when asked how one should treat others, "There are no others." Exercises such as these can help us practice empathy, expand consciousness, and become more aware of our essential connectedness.

Developing compassion is another beneficial byproduct of imagining you're others. It's hard to act selfishly and be unkind to people when you imagine that you're them and their experience is your experience.

Likewise, it's hard to be cruel to other creatures, or to ignore the burning of rainforests, the death of coral reefs, and the destruction of ecosystems when you recognize how you're connected to the suffering such destruction causes. As consciousness expands it becomes increasingly clear how impacts to what the ego thinks of as distant entities actually affect the whole.[77] Developing awareness of our essential connectedness can help you become a more effective systems thinker which leads to better decisions and better outcomes for everyone.

At the very least, you might get some good character insights from trying out these exercises. Why experience only one life when you can experience many?

As Rumi urged, "Stop acting so small. You are the universe in ecstatic motion."

---

[77] This notion of essential connectedness doesn't just exist in Hinduism, Buddhism, and Sufism. Jesus talked about it, too. Check out Matthew 25:40 for one example: "Truly I tell you, whatever you did for one of the least of these brothers and sisters, you did for me." Or The Gospel of Thomas 4: "For many of the first will be last, and they will become a single one."

The Ego Strikes Back

Your ego will keep returning, which is why it might be useful to review how the ego impacts creativity before we move on.

Your ego wants you to forget that you're part of a greater whole. It wants to keep you focused on your limited, small self. It wants you to procrastinate, doubt, and avoid taking risks because it fears failure. It wants to keep you in an addictive cycle of achievement, comparisons, and "if onlys." It wants you to go after fame, fortune, and other superficial notions of success. It wants you to be miserable, because then you'll be fixated on yourself. It wants and wants and wants.

Above all, the ego wants to preserve what it thinks it is. That's its job. It's not inherently malicious or evil. On the contrary, it often serves a necessary protective function. But it's also extremely limiting. And the more you identify with it, the harder it becomes to reach beyond your ego-limited small self and connect with creativity. Which is why, to actualize your immense creative potential, it's vital to work on dissolving your ego's limiting grasp. You'll not only be more creative this way, you'll be happier as well.

Don't worry about completely dissolving attachment to the egoic self. If you do that, you'll become like Buddha, Jesus, or other enlightened figures who transcended their small selves and embodied a conscious awareness of the greater whole, becoming infinitely compassionate. For most of us, though, egoic attachments will keep coming back, so don't waste one second worrying about letting the ego go. All you need, as a friend once told me, is just enough ego to look both ways before you cross the street.

Too much attachment to the ego, on the other hand, is an affliction that causes great harm to ourselves and the world we share.[78] I owe it to Leo Gura for pointing out that essentially the ego is selfishness—it's that which keeps us focused on our small selves and satisfying our shallow, temporary, ego-driven desires. Although this may seem obvious, there are profound implications to recognizing this. In almost every story, for instance, the villain is the one who serves their ego the most. Which means that, in an ego-driven society, the villain often works to protect the status quo. Villains simply do what an ego-driven society tells them to do: They look out for number one.

Conversely, the hero is often someone who puts the pursuit of a greater good (be it truth, love, justice, the environment, the collective whole, or serving others) above the desires of the ego. Which means that the hero is usually seen as a threat to the ego-driven status quo because the hero rebels against the supremacy of the ego.

Stories depict this epic struggle between serving the ego and transcending the ego because it's a struggle that plays out in

---

[78] As the Buddha stated over two-thousand years ago, "The root cause of suffering is attachment." This seems especially true when considering attachment to the ego.

each of us every day. Since transcending the ego is the hero's work, it makes sense that the hero's journey is all about facing challenges that dissolve egoic attachment, with the climax being the thing the ego fears most—the death of the ego-bound self (or ego-bound ways of thinking), and the birth of a new self that's more conscious of existence beyond the ego.

This is what creativity requires. To bring something new and significant into the world, one must reach beyond the constant demands of the ego and connect with something greater. Artists who put serving the ego above the call to create are often seen as "selling out" because they're sacrificing their creative visions for money, fame, or other egoic demands. When satisfying the ego becomes the main focus, the hero's story ends tragically. But when the hero transcends the ego, transformational creative leaps can be made.

That's what I hope for you—that through your creative practice you'll keep finding ways to liberate yourself from your ego. That's what I hope for all of us because, like windows in a dark hall, no one has a complete view alone, and all of us are made brighter by the light we let in.[79]

---

[79] BTW, it's not unusual to experience an "ego backlash" once you start to dissolve egoic attachments, as (like the villain in a story) the ego gets more desperate to maintain control. If you experience an ego backlash, don't be discouraged. It means you're making progress. Keep it up! Two steps forward and one step back still moves you forward.

Revision and the Hero's Return

Of all the stages in the creative process, revision might be the trickiest to love—and the most important. Personally, it took me over a decade to learn to love revision, but this is where the magic happens.

There's a reason why Joseph Campbell focused six whole stages of the hero's journey on the hero's return from the special world. This return, which sometimes involves what Campbell referred to as the "elixir of Imperishable Being" (or the wisdom of the gods attained through the difficult experience of death and rebirth), corresponds with the territory of revision in the creative process. It's where you bring back the visions you've been granted and fully enact them for others to see.

To make peace with revision, it may help to adjust your expectations. In Campbell's depiction of the hero's journey, the return from the special world is around one third of the entire journey. For me, revision usually involves much more than that.

I typically spend three times as long revising a book as I do writing the first draft. If the first draft (giving myself some clay to work with) takes six months to complete, I'll spend eighteen months or more revising that book (shaping and reshaping the clay) before the story becomes what it needs to be and the project reveals to me what I need to learn.

What makes this stage in the process tricky is deciding which internal voices to listen to and which to disregard. Some whispers might claim that everything you've created is worthless and you were a fool to spend so much time working on a project. Other whispers might claim that everything is perfect and you shouldn't change a word. And some whispers will tell you that a certain scene isn't working, a character isn't clear, or parts of the story are missing and still need to be discovered.

Not all of these whispers are accurate or helpful, but they all sound convincing. In addition, doubt often accompanies these voices and accumulates until you might doubt every sentence you've created. A little doubt can be useful for revision, but how do you decide which voices and which doubts to listen to?

One technique for navigating the tricky process of revision is to ask yourself, **"Is this voice coming from my ego, or is it coming from the creative source?"** (This is similar to the question you might ask yourself when others criticize your work—**"Is their criticism coming from their ego, or from a genuine desire to aid me in bringing this creation into existence?"**).

Often, the voice that says what you're working on is terrible and should be abandoned is coming from your ego. Oddly enough, so is the voice that tells you everything is brilliant, don't change a word (think of the "Stupid," "Brilliant," "Moron," and "Genius" torpedoes in the Lynda Barry graphic essay we discussed). Although these voices might seem contradictory, they both have the same goal—to get you to quit the creative process. The ego fears risk, change, and bringing new things into existence. It clings to what it already knows, so it uses both shame and pride to convince you to give up and leave things as they are.

The third whispering voice—the one that asks questions and whispers doubts about specific scenes and narrative elements—that's often the creative source telling you that what you're creating isn't yet what it needs to be. It's the voice that points out where your ego has gotten in the way and caused you to attempt to force things to be what *you* think they should be instead of discovering what the story requires. It's the voice that implores you to dig deeper because there's more to uncover and more to realize. Essentially, it's the creative source letting you know that you haven't fully enacted the vision for others to see. Think of this as the **voice of productive doubt**. By listening to it, a writer or artist can enter into a dialogue with the creative source about the creation that's emerging.

Another technique for getting beyond the ego and fostering connections with the creative source while revising is to **switch from telling to asking**. If you're telling a story or creation "I want you to be this," chances are you're letting your ego direct the revision and confining a creation to the limits of your ego mind. Instead, revise by asking the creation, **"Are you what you need to be?"**

One of the hallmarks of being stuck in an ego-driven telling mode is defensively justifying or explaining something in a story (or other creation). When a creation is fully realized, it won't need any defensive justifications or explanations. Therefore, if you encounter parts of your story that are loaded down with convoluted explanations, try letting go of what you think needs to happen at that moment and instead ask the story what it wants to happen. Then stay open to new possibilities.

For example, you might ask, "What am I missing? What needs to be changed, developed, or shown?" You might write a new scene and ask, "Is this it? What about this?" Or you might ask a character, "What am I getting wrong about you?" Then let the character respond in their own voice.[80] By switching from telling to asking, you can lessen the controlling influence of your ego and open yourself up to discovering what else a piece could be until the creation fully reveals itself.[81]

George Saunders (a Man Booker Prize and McArthur "Genius" Award-winning author) focused on revision in his essay "Process and Spirit." In addition to paying attention to the characters in a story, Saunders emphasized paying attention to the reader, and imagining where a reader might feel engaged and connected to a story, and where a reader might become bored or disconnected. As Saunders put it, revision is "an active way of continually improving our relation to the reader." By imagining the characters *and* the reader as real people, and paying attention to both, the revision process becomes a way of respecting and elevating the characters and the reader in the author's mind so that the author can put their needs before the author's controlling intentions. When this process is done effectively, "The imagined entity (the characters) appears in more detail, without the taint of overt authorial intentionality."[82]

---

[80] This ended up being the key question to unlocking a novel that I'd previously spent four years revising. Earlier drafts weren't working because I kept trying to make the main character do what I would do. It wasn't until I let go of what *I* wanted the story to be and asked the main character to tell me *his* story that the book came together in a surprising and satisfying way, and got published.

[81] There's a powerful change that happens when you go from asking if a piece is what it wants to be, to knowing it has become what it needs to be. Then the focus of the creative process shifts from *enacting* to *communicating*. Sometimes a creation isn't ready for the world, so the world will send you back to work on it more. Other times the world isn't ready for a creation. All you can do then is lovingly introduce your creation to the world, and keep creating.

[82] Later in this essay, Saunders writes, "We story-tell, in a sense, to 'untell' a delusional tale we are all born telling: the tale of our own permanence, centrality, and separateness."

Critical feedback from others is essential to developing one's sense of how to connect with readers. You might think a story is complete and fully present on the page, but often it's not until you get feedback from readers that you see what your ego has kept you from seeing—where a vision hasn't yet been fully enacted for others to experience, and where you still have more to figure out.

This process of getting feedback from others is one of letting go of what your ego mind thinks something is and opening yourself up to the discoveries of revision. And revision is often where the best discoveries are made. Staying connected to the creative source, and open to what it tells you, are crucial to doing this well.

To ease your worries during this tricky stage, think of the final steps in the hero's journey. These steps (and once again I'm borrowing names for them from *The Hero with a Thousand Faces*) provide a map to follow through a challenging revision. The stage Campbell calls the "refusal of the return," for instance, is similar to a refusal to revise. The ego doesn't want you to enact something for others to see. You might have become comfortable in the special world—the world of imagination and creativity. To attempt to bring something back from there for others to see requires risking failure, criticism, and rejection—all things the ego hates. But if you don't return, the process isn't complete. Enacting your visions for others to see is how you fully realize a vision, add to existence, and grow.

Once you move past the refusal of the return, you might encounter what Campbell calls "threshold guardians" blocking your return. These can be distractions, doubts, harsh critics, or other obstacles that attempt to get you to abandon a project. It's hard to return with the new awareness you've gained and share it with others. People might not want to see what you've created. They might not be open to it, or they might view your creativity as threatening to their egos. Several threshold guardians might stand in your way during revision.

On the bright side, you might also encounter allies during this stage—people who believe in a project and want to see it fully enacted. Such help correlates to what Campbell referred to as "rescue from without."

The reward for completing the process and enacting things for others to see is becoming what Campbell referred to as the "master of two worlds" and gaining the "freedom to live." Such freedom is attained by experiencing the difficult process of death and rebirth, thereby freeing yourself from the fear of death.[83]

For creators, the "freedom to live" describes what happens when you learn to love the process. By experiencing the struggle, doubt, failure, and rebirth that accompanies bringing something new and significant into existence, you can realize that there's no need to fear the process. Instead, you can embrace every step of the journey, appreciating all the ups and downs and what they have to teach you. That's how you become "master of two worlds" (the known world and unknown world from which creations emerge) and return with the "elixir of Imperishable Being."

That's how you persevere without suffering and stay blissfully creative.

---

[83] What the ego fears most is death—the end of what it thinks it is. The more you can see beyond the illusion of separateness, the more this ego-driven fear of death will fall away. Imagine that you're a ripple in an infinite ocean. Death, to this ripple, means losing its sense of being a separate, individual wave. But of course the ripple is never really separate. It's always part of the ocean, and when it "dies" the water that forms its essence doesn't vanish. It continues to be part of the infinite ocean of existence.

Now imagine that you could become fully aware of being part of the ocean of existence before dying. You would then know that death is only the death of the ego—the death of that ephemeral delusion of being a separate wave. As Eckhart Tolle put it, "The end of illusion—that's all death is. It's only painful as long as you cling to illusion." To shed this illusion gives you the "freedom to live," because it frees you from the constant burden of fearing death and loss.

A Confession

All this is just the beginning.

Becoming aware of the blissful path is one thing. Staying on it is another. Accepting what is, loving the process, and staying open to creativity day after day can be a challenge. It takes dedication and practice.

Some days I get caught up in the things my ego wants me to feel—the insecurities, doubts, and inadequacies. I doubt my ability to do what I'm called to do, so I procrastinate. Or I get overwhelmed by what I fear is going wrong, and all that I haven't accomplished—the "if onlys" that my ego, with its endless siren's song of desire, keeps urging me to pursue.

When this happens, I like to imagine Van Gogh painting in a field. He must have looked like an eccentric failure to his neighbors—a lost cause who kept creating odd paintings no one wanted to buy. Certainly, he didn't paint to make money or gain fame. He simply created what he felt called to create. Visions wanted to exist, and they could only come into existence through him. Perhaps his genius was due in part to his lack of commercial success. Perhaps the heartbreak he experienced cracked him wide open, enabling a flood of creativity to pour through him.

When I get discouraged, I remind myself that there's nothing to do except be. I see myself as the character in the moment, facing the challenges I need to face. I remind myself that I only think I'm a separate self, when in truth I'm part of something infinitely greater.

The more I become aware of this, the more foolish and inconsequential the worries that consume me seem. What I'm experiencing is exactly what I need to experience, and what I'm learning is exactly what I need to learn. My life story, which is part of a much greater story, is exactly what it needs to be. I'm part of being, and in being all things belong.

Then, like a sunflower opening at daybreak, I open to the resplendent creative existence I'm part of, and all is well.

Steps on the Path to Lifelong Creativity

We've come a long way in this book—from examining the perils of chasing after commercial success, to exploring creativity and the creative process, to delving into existential questions and enlightenment practices as ways to transcend the ego, connect with creativity, and make persevering more enjoyable and sustainable. A great deal has been covered. To put it all together, a quick overview of some key concepts might be useful. So here it is, a thirteen-step guide to walking the blissful path of lifelong creativity:

1) Recognize toxic success myths. They lead us astray by causing us to focus on the wrong things. Playing the comparison game and working to achieve "if onlys" are part of this. There is no end to the comparison game. Although it might seem a good way to motivate yourself for a time, it will ultimately exhaust you and crush your creativity.

2) Redefine success as being happy on the deepest, most fulfilling level you can conceive of. Rather than creating to get things and staking your happiness on future achievements (conditional happiness), focus on being intrinsically motivated and unconditionally happy in the present. Not only is this a better notion of success for a joyful and fulfilling life, if you make unconditional happiness your guiding star, you'll be far more likely to succeed in other ways because the ones who succeed are the ones who persevere, and the best way to persevere is by doing what you love and loving what you do.

3) Learn to love the process (all the stages, including the hard stuff). It's much easier to fall down seven times and get up eight when you've adopted a perspective that enables you to appreciate falling and appreciate getting up. Learning to love the process is the secret to persevering effectively, blissfully, and sustainably.

4) Instead of *trying* to create things, *be* creative. If you create, you're a creator. Accept that this is who you are and what you're called to do. Know that the things you're called to create, only you can create. They will not exist without you. The world will be lesser without them. Simply create what you're called to create as honestly and authentically as possible.

5) Understand what creativity actually is. Rather than coming from you, creativity flows through you. Envision creativity in a way that allows you to connect with it freely and avoid creative stinginess. There's no limit to your potential as long as you stay open to creativity and let it flow through you without resistance.

6) Recognize the ego and how it's getting in the way. Beware of that which feeds your ego and makes you ego bound, cutting you off from creativity. Fighting your ego won't help. Instead, become conscious of your ego and step past it. Use healthy creative habits to transcend your ego's limiting grasp and connect more fully and freely with creativity.

7) Embrace doubt, struggle, rejection, fear, and even failure as parts of the process. These experiences have valuable lessons to teach you. They show you how your ego is getting in the way and causing you to suffer. To overcome egoic barriers to creativity, practice developing awareness and dissolving egoic attachments.

8) Stories provide a map for moving beyond your limited ego mind. Look to the stages in the hero's journey for guidance in the transformative process. Know that real, significant change requires the death of the ego-bound self (or ego-bound ways of perceiving) so that a more aware self can emerge and new ways of perceiving and being can be realized.

9) Develop observer consciousness. This is a powerful way to lessen attachment to the ego and appreciate all the stages in the process. See the bigger story. Be the reader of this story and the knowing of your being. The greater your awareness, the more effective your actions will be, and the less you will suffer.

10) Let go of the illusion of control and surf the wave. One of the main ways the ego limits you is by claiming it's in control and causing you to struggle against what is. Rather than trying to control things that are ultimately beyond your control, accept what is and work with it, just like a surfer on a wave or a kayaker in a river. Use observer consciousness to broaden your perspective, scout the river, and notice possibilities. By accepting the whole river and your situation in it, you can align yourself with life, gracefully surfing the waves and using the currents to navigate the rapids.

11) Let go of the illusion of separateness and recognize how we're all connected. There's no need to make comparisons—that's just the ego trying to limit you. You're bigger than that. Practice *mudita* and experience essential connectedness. This is the key to beating the comparison game, being happier, and calling good things your way.

12) Stay open to creativity and what it can teach you (especially in revision). Approach creativity as a way to constantly develop and expand consciousness. Don't worry about how others react to what you create. Keep creating what you're called to create—that's how you buy more lottery tickets and increase your odds of having something take off, and that's how you keep learning and growing while enjoying the intrinsic benefits of creativity.

13) Let go of all attachment to the suffering artist myth. Bliss is a better place to create from than suffering. Appreciate the experiences you get to have. Where you are is exactly where you need to be. What you're learning is exactly what you need to learn. You're part of infinite awareness and infinite creativity. Something wonderful wants to exist through you. Stop clinging to your small self and embrace what is. You're more than you think.

Some Mantras

I'll admit, I used to think mantras were cheesy (but that was just my ego talking). I've since found mantras to be useful. Basically, they're simple ways to remind yourself of beneficial practices so you don't get lost in the dark. At the risk of sounding ridiculous, I'll share a few of the mantras I've used.

The mantras I've found most helpful might be different from some personal affirmations in that they're not focused on trying to make a certain future come true or convincing one's self that things are other than what they are. Instead, they're ways of helping my mind focus on accepting what is so I can love the process.

Different mantras might work for you at different times, depending on your stage of consciousness development. Sometimes mantras become stale. When that happens, try another one that relates to where you're at and what you're working on.

It's good to develop your own mantras to remind yourself of specific mental habits you want to adopt. But... choose your mantras wisely. For a long time, I'd repeat to myself "I will my voice to be heard." Although at first this mantra inspired me to keep writing and keep sending my writing out into the world, it ended up causing me to suffer when the outcome of my efforts wasn't what I wanted it to be. I felt there must have been something wrong with me—after all, I'd said this mantra to myself for years and what I kept willing to happen didn't happen. Telling myself this phrase also kept me trapped in my small self, because of the focus on the "I" and on "my" voice and my "will." When "my" voice wasn't heard (or wasn't heard the way *I* wanted it to be heard), I felt frustrated and alienated from existence.

After a time, I changed this internal mantra to "I will *this* voice to be heard" which was better, since instead of being egoically focused on "my" voice, the words reminded me that I'm part of a larger whole and channeling something into existence. This eased some of my creative blocks, but the mantra still kept me focused on the "I" struggling to "will" something to be different than it was.

In time, the constant struggle to "will" this voice to be heard started to exhaust me. I realized that the mantra was feeding an expectation for something to happen in the future (this voice being heard), which prevented me from recognizing and appreciating the present. It's much more effective and sustainable to embrace what is and surf the river.

Now the mantra I use when I want to focus on bringing something new into existence is simply "This voice is heard." By telling myself "This voice is heard" I'm able to take away much of the anxiety I feel about getting a voice (or a vision I feel called to enact) to be heard. I know the voice is being heard—I hear it. And when my anxiety about getting a voice to be heard falls away, I'm able to bring things into existence more openly and effectively.[84]

I've since started to use other mantras during various stages in the creative process (some of which are shared below). These simple phrases can be used to give yourself reminders and directions. Or try constructing your own mantras (and if you come up with helpful ones, I'd love to hear them).

When developing mantras, here are a few suggestions:

1) Have the mantra focus on the present.

2) Have it focus on what is rather than on what your ego wants to be true.

3) Construct it to encourage habits of mind you'd like to adopt.

4) Avoid negative constructions. Telling yourself to "embrace what is" works much better than telling yourself to "stop resisting what is" (a phrase that can throw your mind into a spiral by causing you to resist resistance).

5) Keep it short and easy to recall during challenging times when you need it most.

---

[84] An unexpected benefit of this mantra was that, after I started using it, I began to notice how "this voice" was being heard—for instance, how books I'd written had impacted others. Previously, when I wanted my voice to be heard, I focused my attention on what I thought *wasn't* happening, instead of what was. After using this mantra, I started to notice and appreciate comments from readers in ways I hadn't been able to before.

Here are some mantras you might try:

- This is what I'm called to create.
- This is the experience I get to have.
- Let go of the struggle to control.
- Be rather than try.
- Create from bliss.
- I'm called to create things. What others make of it is up to them.
- This is my creative path. It's full of unexpected twists and turns.
- Channel the creative energy of the universe.
- I'm more than I think.
- I'm part of infinite creativity.
- Respect the Muse.
- This voice is heard.
- Love the process.
- Enjoy the experience.
- Embrace what is.
- Be the knowing.
- Surf the river.
- We're all in this together.

The Cup in the Flames

The creative work you're doing is incredibly important and incredibly challenging.

We've explored how creating things is a transformative process, both for ourselves and for those who encounter our work. Don't underestimate how important this is.

Stories—whether told through art, music, writing, or other means—shape the ways we think and act. Stories are how we know ourselves, find meaning in our lives, and construct our identities. Stories can change our perspectives, increase empathy and understanding, and elevate consciousness. Stories form our history and shape our future.

I'd like to end this book with a brief story. It's part of a very old tale, and one you might have heard before. It's the story of the Wounded King, or at least a version of it. Here's the story as it came to me today:

Once there was a wounded king who, while huddled before a fire on a cold winter night, had a vision of a golden cup in the flames. A voice told him that this cup would heal his wounds and make him a mighty king who'd have a prosperous reign over the land.

The king, full of ideas of glory, power, and greatness tried to grab the cup. But as soon as he reached for it, it vanished. Instead of getting the golden cup, the king burned his hands in the flames.

It took the king months to recover, and it was a long time before he dared to look into the flames again. When he did, he saw the golden cup in the fire, and he desired it mightily. Once more he tried to grab it and burned his hands.

So it went for several years. The king became obsessed with the thought of claiming the cup to prove that he was a great king, worthy of his kingdom. But every time he reached for it, the cup vanished and the flames burned his hands. The more this happened, the more his wounds deepened, and the more angry and bitter he became.

Without the steady hand of leadership, the kingdom fell into strife and despair. The king knew he needed to claim the golden cup to heal himself and his kingdom, but he no longer saw the cup in the flames. All he saw now was the pain he'd experienced when he'd reached for it. Desperate, he sent his best knights out to find the golden cup. They searched for many years, driven by notions of glory and riches, but none could find it.

Finally, the king's wounds became too much for him to bear and he gave up. He shut himself in his castle to die, miserable and alone.

One day, a fool wandered into his room. The fool didn't see a king. Instead, he saw a suffering man. So, the fool asked him what was wrong.

"I'm thirsty," replied the king.

The fool grabbed a cup and filled it with water.

As the king drank, his wounds were healed. Only then did he realize that he was drinking from the cup he'd so long sought to pull from the flames.

"How did you get what neither myself nor any of my knights could?" asked the king.

"I don't know," the fool answered. "I only knew that you were thirsty."

My wish for you is this: **Be that fool**.

In this world, many are suffering. Many are wounded. Many are thirsty. More kings and knights searching for glory, greatness, and treasure won't solve this. What we need are more compassionate, creative fools.

One of the greatest gifts a person can receive is the call to bring something new into existence. May you hear the call, and when you do, may you respond with openness, awareness, courage, and compassion. Then, without thinking of glory or riches, greatness or doubt, do what you're called to do: reach for the cup, fill it at the creative wellspring, and boldly share it.

Addendum

Want to Take Things a Step Further?

The approaches in this book align with teachings that have their roots in several nondual spiritual and philosophical traditions going back thousands of years, including Stoicism, early Christianity, Gnosticism, Jainism, Hinduism, Buddhism, Sufism, Taoism, Kabala, Tantra, Zen, and Advaita Vedanta.

Basically, a lot of wise monks, sages, philosophers, mystics, and enlightened teachers have come to similar conclusions about attaining unconditional happiness and living a virtuous, fulfilling life, and they've been sharing advice about this for thousands of years. The advice may come in dramatically different packages and it may be framed in different ways, but the essence of nondual teachings is surprisingly similar. It goes something like this:

You're more than you think you are. The mental construct of a separate self that you're clinging to is causing you and others immense suffering. The way to free yourself of this misperception and the suffering it creates is to transcend the ego mind that's keeping you separate and unaware of the wholeness of being. Stop resisting life and embrace what is. This is a far more blissful, effective, fulfilling way to live.

Practices that help you lessen attachment to your ego, see past the illusions of separateness and control, and expand your awareness will not only make you happier and more compassionate, they'll help you become more creative and successful by enabling you to step out of your own way and connect more fully with the creative energy of the universe.

Such practices are sometimes the focus of what's referred to as self-actualization, higher consciousness work, and personal development. Some self-actualization guides combine approaches from psychology, neuroscience, philosophy, and traditional nondual enlightenment teachings. Therefore, if you want to take things a step further, I recommend looking into self-actualization, higher consciousness, and personal development practices that incorporate nonduality. Spiral Dynamics and Integral Theory are two other areas of study that I found helpful.

Scienceandnonduality.com is one online community you might want to explore. There you'll find hundreds of videos and podcasts, book recommendations, and ongoing discussions with people interested in consciousness development and ways to further self-actualization.

Please know, this book isn't in any way affiliated with Scienceandnondulaity.com, and I don't endorse everything you'll find there. There are many paths for personal development. What works for others might not work for you. But, if you want to take things a step further, this site is full of free resources and insights that might help you get started.

Rupert Spira, Alan Watts, Eckhart Tolle, Byron Katie, Shunryu Suzuki, Ram Dass, Thich Nhat Hahn, and Robert

Wright are a few other authors I'd recommend checking out to continue personal development and higher consciousness work.

Working with a counselor, therapist, or personal development guide can also be extremely helpful, although finding a counselor, guide, or teacher who's aware of nonduality and right for you can be a challenge.

It's vital to recognize that books, videos, teachers, and even language itself can only take you so far. To truly understand many of the concepts in this book, direct experience is necessary. Language can only nudge you closer to such an experience, but it cannot describe what's ultimately ineffable.

To apply the concepts in this book, develop consciousness, and expand awareness, one must be willing to leave words behind and experience things directly. That's where meditation comes in. **Adopting a meditation habit is perhaps the single most effective way to quiet the mind, lessen the grasp of the ego, and become more consciously aware of being** (see the "Meditation Quick Start Guide" for more on this). As the poet David Young put it, "Names, get between me and the things I fear. Names, for godsake tell me who I am. Nothing and everything. The time comes when you shut the door, step off the porch, and walk across the fields without a word."

Meditation Quick Start Guide

Why meditate?
Meditation is a time-honored practice to quiet the mind, develop consciousness, and become more aware of being. Research shows that those who practice meditation for 10-20 minutes a day experience a myriad of benefits including reduced stress, better health, less anxiety, increased happiness, improved cognitive functioning, and an increased sense of well-being.

Because meditation is a powerful way to lessen the limiting grasp of the ego, your ego probably won't like it much. It might tell you that meditation is a waste of time, pointless New Age stuff, good for other people but not necessary for you, or nice in theory but impossible to make time for in your busy schedule. Don't listen to your ego's protests. It's lying. Meditation is a powerful way to expand awareness and improve your life—that's why monks and sages have been doing it for millennia.

The only way to get the benefits of meditation is to meditate. If you don't already have a meditation habit in place, start now. It's important to make meditation a habit and not simply something you do when you feel like it because no matter how much you enjoy meditating, your ego will find excuses not to do it. Also, your ability to meditate (and the benefits you experience) will increase dramatically with practice.

What's the goal of meditation?

This is a tricky question because the point of many meditation practices is to do nothing. Just be present—that's the goalless goal.

If you want to dig into this further, think of it this way: your mind incessantly wants to do things, and the constant chattering of your mind obscures the experience of being, much like constantly talking obscures the sound of the wind whispering through tree branches. The quieter your mind becomes, the more you might become conscious of what's beyond your mind. As Rumi put it 800 years ago:

> This silence, this moment, every moment, if it's genuinely inside you, brings what you need. There's nothing to believe. Only when I stopped believing in myself did I come into this beauty. Sit quietly, and listen for a voice that will say, "Be more silent." Die and be quiet. Quietness is the surest sign that you've died. Your old life was a frantic running from silence. Move outside the tangle of fear-thinking. Live in silence.

Meditation is how you "move outside the tangle of fear-thinking," stop focusing on your egoic self, and "come into this beauty."

Becoming consciously aware of being feels awesome (in the truest sense of the word). The greatest bliss I've experienced didn't come from fancy dinners, expensive cruises, or other things people spend thousands of dollars on thinking it will bring them happiness. My greatest experiences of bliss came from sitting in meditation and doing nothing. Therefore, the short answer to the above question is that the goal of meditation is to feel awesome.

But don't seek bliss. If you're seeking bliss, or meditating to feel awesome, then you're doing something. Bliss happens when you stop trying to do things and simply experience being. You can't think or force your way there because your mind is what's keeping you from realizing you are there. That's the whole challenge of meditation.

It's exhausting to constantly try to do things. Let go of that for a little while and see how it feels to do nothing. Be nothing. No mind. No self.

That said, the focused "doing nothing" of meditation isn't the same as sleeping (sleeping is doing something). It's not thinking (that's doing something). It's not figuring things out (that's a mind delusion). It's just letting your mind grow quiet so you can become more aware of being. This can be hard to do, which leads us to the next point.

It's okay to suck at meditation.

I suck at meditation.

Sucking at meditation is partly the point of meditation. Doing nothing is a seemingly impossible task. Also, your ego, in an effort to get you to quit meditating, might tell you that you suck at it and are doing it all wrong. You're not. As long as you're sitting still and letting your mind grow quiet for a little while each day, you're on the right track.

When you suck at meditation, it's working, just like when an exercise becomes hard you're getting the most gains. You're gradually training your ego mind to chill out and not be such an attention hog. Meditate to the point where you suck at it. That's how you develop the ability to quiet the ego mind.

Meditation is a practice, and you only get better at it with practice. Be patient with yourself and meditate every day. It takes time to develop awareness and experience the bliss of being.

Physical techniques:

Place: It helps to find a quiet place where you won't be interrupted. Before I meditate, I tell my wife and kids to pretend that I'm not home for the next 30 minutes. That way if anyone calls or wants my attention, I'm effectively not there.

I also enjoy meditating outside (my favorite places are by rivers and streams), but if there are flies and mosquitoes, this can be challenging. Once you sit, it's best not to move for the duration of the meditation, so make sure the conditions where you sit are conducive for that. It's not necessary to find a perfect place. Barking dogs and buzzing flies can all be part of a blissful meditation session.

Posture: Sit with a straight spine. When I first started meditating, I did it lying down because I have back issues. However, I soon switched to sitting meditation as this keeps one more focused, awake, and open.

You can sit in a chair, as long as you're not slouching. My preference is to sit on a zafu (a thick buckwheat-filled round pillow that elevates your butt and improves your posture). I sit half-lotus and prop a second pillow (or one of my shoes if I'm away from home) under my left knee so my knees are even and my spine is aligned. Some people practice kneeling meditation. The important thing is to find a posture you can hold for twenty minutes without moving. Don't worry if your legs fall asleep, your back aches, or your arm itches. It's unlikely that any harm will come to you by not moving for twenty minutes.

Personally, I like using a zafu so much that I now have one in my office at work, one at home, and an inflatable travel one that I take hiking and on trips so I can meditate anywhere.

Stretch first: To make sitting still for twenty (or more) minutes easier, it's helpful to do a few quick stretches. Usually, when I'm seated in my half-lotus position, I'll lean forward, touch the ground, and stretch my legs and back, then I'll pull my arms across my chest and stretch my arms, shoulders, and neck. After that I'm good to go. (A friend of mine who's a yoga teacher once told me that yoga postures were originally developed to help people meditate longer. I'm not sure if this is true, but if you're having trouble sitting still for twenty minutes, doing yoga or stretching more first might help.)

Set a timer: I use my phone for this. Try starting with fifteen minutes of still meditation. Once this becomes easier, move up to twenty minutes, then twenty-five (or longer). The reason why it's helpful to use a timer is because, when you're meditating, your ego will start protesting that it's taking too long. By setting a timer, you put the decision to stop meditating beyond your ego mind. You'll stop when the timer goes off. Don't let your mind win and think if it complains enough, it can get you to stop before that. Stick to the timer.

As for how long to meditate, here's a common Zen saying: "You should sit in meditation for twenty minutes a day, unless you're too busy. Then you should sit for an hour."

Eyes open or closed? Some folks have strong opinions about this. As for myself, I let my eyes do whatever they want. Sometimes they open, and sometimes they close. Both are good. When my eyes are open, I'm not really looking out at the world because I've let go of the "I" that looks.

It's best, when you're first developing a meditation practice, not to sweat the small stuff (like eyes open or closed or how to hold your hands). Just sit. Do nothing. Let yourself be and observe what happens.

Wait... what about my hands? I like to rest mine in my lap with my left fingers under my right fingers and my thumbs touching. Place your hands wherever you can comfortably leave them without moving for twenty minutes. (There are plenty of other mudras, or hand positions, you can use for meditation, but there's no need to overthink things.)

How should I breathe? Take deep, slow, full breaths. If you can, breathe through your nose (or in through your nose and out through your mouth). Follow your inhale all the way down deep into your lungs. Notice when it switches to exhale. Let this happen naturally.

Some people find it's helpful to visualize breathing in peaceful warm light, and breathing out stress and anxiety. I prefer to focus on the sensation of breathing itself. When I'm meditating, it often feels like *I'm* not breathing at all; rather, the universe is breathing through me.

Mental techniques:

Opening chakras centering practice: This is a subtle body relaxation practice you might do at the start of a meditation session. If you're not familiar with chakras, referring to images (and guides online) can help you develop a sense of where they're located and what subtle energies they're associated with.

Crown Chakra	Spirituality
Third Eye Chakra	Awareness
Throat Chakra	Communication
Heart Chakra	Love, Healing
Solar Plexus Chakra	Wisdom, Power
Sacral Chakra	Sexuality, Creativity
Root Chakra	Basic Trust

Sample chakra placement—photo from Depositphotos.com

I start by focusing on the root chakra. As I take three deep breaths, I focus on opening the root chakra and experiencing the energy of that chakra. Then I move on to the sacral chakra (associated with creativity and sexual energy) for three breaths, then the solar plexus chakra, heart chakra, throat chakra, third-eye chakra, and crown chakra—focusing on each one for at least three breaths, or as long as it takes to feel the chakra open up so that energy flows through it without resistance (like you're a flute with seven holes).

When I complete this subtle body relaxation sequence, I often feel as if a column of light/energy is flowing up my spine, in and out of the seven chakras with every inhale and exhale.

Dealing with discomfort: It's inevitable to feel some discomfort while meditating. Your ego might even enhance the sensation of discomfort to get you to quit meditating. Don't let it win. You're done meditating when the timer goes off.

Since scratching an itch or moving your arms isn't an option (that would be doing something), the best technique I've found to deal with discomfort is to acknowledge, accept, and move on. For instance, if your arm itches, you might say to yourself, "This body's arm itches. It's part of the experience of this perfect moment." By accepting and embracing the discomfort rather than resisting it or trying to change it, it usually fades away. However, for this to work, it's important not to accept something just to make it go away. Genuinely observe and accept any discomfort you feel. It's all part of the experience of existence and how you know you're the knowing. (For more on using acceptance, see "The Power of Radical Acceptance" chapter).

Dealing with mental distractions: In addition to physical discomforts, your ego mind might attempt to keep you from meditating with thoughts. It may come up with pressing concerns or things to worry about. When this happens, you might remind yourself "I'm meditating. I'm doing nothing." You can think about stuff after the timer goes off and you're done meditating. There's no need to worry about forgetting anything. What needs to be remembered will be remembered.

If the thoughts you have are disturbing, simply observe and accept them without judgment as you did with physical discomforts. You might say to yourself, "This body is thinking about being attacked by tigers" (or whatever the disturbing thought is). Accept that's what your mind is doing to distract you, then focus on your inhale and exhale.

Don't get frustrated if your mind keeps coming up with distracting thoughts. Simply observe your mind and return to the focus of your meditation. The more you struggle against your mind, the worse these distractions will get. It's a lot like getting a bowl of muddy water to settle. The more you chase thoughts and feelings around, the more you stir up the mud in the bowl. But if you let the water sit still, the mud will eventually settle and the water will become clearer.

Meditation is how you let your mind become clear so you can deepen your awareness. Sometimes this takes a bit of time. The days when it takes the most time are the days when you need meditation the most.

Dealing with external distractions: There's no need for perfect conditions to meditate. Dogs will bark. Kids will yell. Doorbells will ring. You can meditate just as deeply in a noisy crowd as by a peaceful stream. Simply acknowledge and accept whatever distractions arise as part of the perfect moment. There's nothing to do and no need to respond to any distractions until the timer goes off.

Try it out. Find a place to sit, breathe deeply, and let your mind grow still.[85]

Some meditation practices:

Once you've developed a meditation habit, you might try out different practices. The following are quick descriptions of ones I've found helpful. Most of these are based on traditional meditation practices that have been around for thousands of years. You can also find guided meditations similar to some of

---

[85] "The highest form of meditation is not an activity that is undertaken by the mind," writes Rupert Spira in his wonderful book *Being Aware of Being Aware*. "It is a relaxing, falling back or sinking of the mind into its source or essence of pure awareness, from which it has arisen. This returning of awareness to itself, its remembrance of itself—being aware of being aware—is the essence of meditation and prayer, and the direct path to lasting peace and happiness."

the practices listed below online. The most important thing is to develop the habit of sitting, breathing, and letting your mind become still. There's no need to complicate meditation.

Do nothing meditation: Although this is a basic practice, it's also one of the hardest to do. Let your mind become still and notice what happens. Observe and experience without naming things. When your mind tries to get you to do something (think, describe, worry, complain…) simply tell yourself "I'm meditating. I'm doing nothing." Let go of your attachment to doing things and simply be silent, empty awareness (awareness being aware of itself).

Acceptance meditation: This is one of my favorite practices (mentioned in the chapter on "The Power of Radical Acceptance"). Once you get in a calm meditative state, spend five minutes imagining what it would feel like to completely accept everything. As thoughts and objections arise, accept them as parts of this perfect moment. Imagine what it would feel like to experience no resistance at all. If you can imagine what complete acceptance feels like, stay with that blissful feeling and expand it.

There's no need to judge or reject anything. Accept the doubts that arise. Accept any feelings of inadequacy. Accept the things you dislike and oppose. Accept what upsets you. Accept any pain or discomfort you feel. Accept your fears. Accept them all as parts of this perfect moment. Let go of the ego mind that constantly resists things and imagine what it would feel like to fully embrace what is.

Loving meditation: For this practice, start by focusing your awareness on what it feels like to love someone (I often start by thinking of the love I feel for my daughters). Focus on the feeling of love (not reasons to love, ways to love, or the person you love)—just the raw internal experience of love. Gradually expand the love you feel to yourself until love encompasses you. Then expand your awareness of love beyond you. You exist in an infinite field of love. See how aware of this you can become.

Consciousness meditation: As you meditate, visualize existing in an infinite field of consciousness. Rather than "having" consciousness, imagine that the ground beneath you, the air you breathe, and the sky above you are all consciousness, and what you think of as "you" is simply a swirl in this endless sea of consciousness. Let go of your sense of being a separate self and open your awareness to your infinite existence. You're part of something much larger than your mind can grasp.

Connection meditation: For this practice, it helps to have your eyes open. As you become aware of things beyond yourself (trees, flowers in the yard, flies buzzing, geese flying, squirrels chittering…) open awareness to your shared being. Let your separate self fall away and become more conscious of your essential connectedness with other facets of existence.

Actuality meditation: For this practice, it helps to have a focal object. This could be a stone, leaf, stick, cup—anything physical. As you meditate, keep bringing your attention back to the focal object. Study it and work to perceive its fundamental reality. Rather than trying to understand something conceptually (with theories and ideas) perceive its actual existence. Let go of all ideas and theories. What is your actual experience of the object? Where does this experience exist? Do you know anything other than a sensory experience in consciousness?

Present meditation: This practice involves recognizing that all notions of the past and future are merely concepts. Only the present exists. For this practice, bring your awareness to what's happening in the present moment. Experience the present as directly and fully as possible (the beating of your heart, the blood rushing through your veins, the air moving in and out your nostrils). There's nothing but the present. You cannot experience the present through ideas, thoughts, or concepts (as soon as you describe something, you're no longer focused on the present). Bringing your awareness to the present means that all thoughts and notions of yourself fall away. Keep your awareness in the present experience, on Presence, for as long as you can.

Death meditation: Although meditating on death might sound grim, it's actually a classic practice that can lead to relief from fear and experiencing a greater connection to life. There are many ways to approach death meditations (you'll find several variations and guided approaches online). However, most involve the same basic goal—to let go of attachment to the egoic self you think you are and liberate yourself from fear.

The death meditation I've found most helpful involves bringing your awareness to the billions of people who have died before you (all the artists, writers, musicians, politicians, poets, actors, scientists, teachers, etc.). Accept these deaths. Recognize that existence continues. Next bring your awareness to the billions of people and creatures alive now. All of these selves will also pass. Even the earth will eventually crumble and fade away, yet existence will go on. Accept this. Now bring your awareness of death to the small self you cling to. This too will die. Visualize the passing of your egoic self. There's no need to fear this, because the separate self you're clinging to is not what you are. Let go and die before dying. Experience your true Self as unending awareness. Nothing exists without awareness.

No mind meditation: This one really throws the mind for a loop. The goal of this meditation is to become aware of the empty awareness that is your essence. As thoughts come to you, observe and let them go with as little judgment and attention as possible. Instead, direct your attention to the empty awareness between thoughts. Linger in that space between thoughts. There's nothing to do, nothing to be. You are empty awareness. (Note: The only way to understand what Zen practitioners mean when they speak of "emptiness" or "nothingness" is to experience it. Until then, just know that it's not what your ego thinks it is and it's nothing to fear.)

Sensory deprivation meditation: Sensory deprivation float tanks provide a potent way to amplify the ego-dissolving effects of meditation. Once you've developed a meditation practice, you might see if a sensory deprivation float tank is available in your area (a tank that provides complete darkness, silence, and warm salt-water that suspends your body in a near weightless, body-temperature environment). Doing a 90-minute or longer meditation in a sensory deprivation tank might freak out your ego mind as it's deprived of most of the sensory stimuli it normally reacts to, but once you breathe through this, the lack of stimuli can help quiet the mind and lead to profound experiences.

Self-inquiry meditation/contemplation: This is a hard one to explain since it involves meditation, but is a bit more active than traditional meditation. This is also a more advanced practice, and not one I'd recommend starting out with.

The question "Who am I?" is one that's been used in enlightenment practices for millennia. The purpose of this practice is to attempt to find the self you think you are. After all, if the small self you identify with exists, where does it exist? Shouldn't you be able to locate it?

Once you enter a meditative state, as thoughts and feelings arise, ask yourself "Who is having this thought?" Or "Who is feeling this discomfort?" Or "Who is aware?" Instead of coming up with a theoretical or logical answer, focus on seeking the "I" you think you are. Where does this "I" exist? In your head? Where? In your body? Where? In your thoughts? Where? What are you? Are you an idea or belief? If so, who is having the idea or belief? Are you an experience? If so, who is having the experience? Are you a form? If so, who is perceiving the form? If you perceive yourself, who is the perceiver? If you're aware, who is being aware?

Keep asking yourself variations of these "who is" questions, and keep seeking the source of your sense of self—the knowing of your being. This, by the way, might seem an impossible task, but it's one that's incredibly effective at dissolving attachment to the ego and challenging egoic limitations. Basically, by constantly asking "who is" questions and seeking who you truly are, you can focus your awareness on the source of awareness until you start to awaken to your true Self. (I owe it to Leo Gura for introducing me to one form of this practice with his podcast, "How to Become Enlightened." Rupert Spira has also shared helpful descriptions of a similar contemplative practice using the sacred question, "Am I aware?" in his book *Being Aware of Being Aware*.)

Breathing meditation: This is a return to one of the most basic yet powerful meditation practices. Direct your attention to your breath. Notice that when you're breathing naturally, inhale switches to exhale without any egoic decision to do so. There's just the universe breathing through you, and you are the universe breathing. Sit with this awareness for as long as you can.

Acknowledgements

One of the most damaging myths for writers is that we create alone. I'm grateful to all the folks who helped bring this book into existence. There are more than I can list, but here are some of the friends, mentors, and fellow writers who went above and beyond. My deepest thanks go to:

Laura Resau, Laura Pritchett, Karye Cattrell, Emily France, Tony and Dave, Heather Sappenfield, Big C, Nich Krause, and K for giving this manuscript early reads and crucial feedback.

Eric Easley, Eric Salahub, Nich, and Jon McIntosh for humoring my many philosophical, ethical, and psychological questions.

Matt de la Peña, Lynda Barry, Eliot Schrefer, George Saunders, and many others for their thoughts on writing and creativity.

Kyle Larson, for being a wise, funny friend, fellow traveler, and centering influence.

Ginger Knowlton, my agent, for sticking with me during all the ups and downs. You're one of the brightest stars in this writer's sky.

Emma Nelson and Hannah Smith at Owl Hollow Press for being extraordinary editors who believed in this project enough to guide it through several drafts while carefully shaping it into a book others might read.

My daughters, Addison and Cailin, for always reminding me of what's important in life.

My wife, Kerri, for her incredible support, love, wisdom, laughter, and brilliant insights. You grasped the compassionate advantages of determinism long before I did, and you openly went on this journey with me. I'm a lucky man to get to travel through this life with you.

Finally, I want to thank Chris for being my existential guide at the start of this journey. Even when the ground fell away and all I saw was a black pit of nihilism waiting to swallow me up, you were there to bring me through it. You helped me open a door that I'd been too afraid to open on my own. When I walked through it, I was finally able to see what had been holding me back. Of course, it was me all long.

About the Author

Todd Mitchell is the award-winning author of several novels for young readers and adults including *The Namer of Spirits, The Last Panther, The Secret to Lying, The Traitor King,* and *Backwards*. In addition to writing, he's been a professional speaker and teacher for 25 years, working with every grade except kindergarten. Currently, he serves as the Director of the

Beginning Creative Writing Teaching Program at Colorado State University, where he teaches creative writing and literature, but that's not why you should read this book.

The reason why you should read this book is because Todd struggled with chasing success for decades, failed spectacularly, and experienced a breakdown that led to discovering far more fulfilling and effective ways to practice creativity.

He now lives and writes (happily) in Fort Collins, Colorado with his wife, daughters, female dog, and female guinea pigs. He's basically the lone guy in a multi-species sorority. You can visit him (and learn about his squirrel obsession) at www.ToddMitchellBooks.com.

Notes

Arranged by Chapter:

PART I
 The James Tate quote included at the beginning of this section came from his fabulous poem, "Teaching the Ape to Write Poems," collected in his *Selected Poems*, published by Wesleyan University Press, 1991.

Not Another Annoying Success Story
 For the "Guess the Success Game" biographical items on J.K. Rowling came from magazine articles and interviews, like this one: Rachel Gillett, "From Welfare to One of the World's Wealthiest Women—The Incredible Rags-to-Riches Story of J. K. Rowling," *Insider*, May 18, 2015, http://www.businessinsider.com/the-rags-to-riches-story-of-jk-rowling-2015-5/.

Biographical information on Stephanie Meyer came from several interviews, including the following: Tony-Allen Mills, "News Review Interview: Stephenie Meyer," *The Sunday Times*, August 10, 2008, https://en.wikipedia.org/wiki/Stephenie_Meyer, and Gregory Kirschling, "Interview With A Vampire Writer Stephenie Meyer," *Entertainment*, July 5, 2088, http://ew.com/article/2008/07/05/interview-vampire-writer-stephenie-meyer/.

Biographical information on John Grisham came from his own website bio: http://www.jgrisham.com/bio/. The claim about him being "bored" as a lawyer/legislator comes from this "Biography of John Grisham" by Sean Hosie: https://www.mswritersandmusicians.com/mississippi-writers/john-grisham.

Biographical information on Lewis Carroll (a.k.a. Charles Dodgson) is widely known and can be found in summary here: https://www.britannica.com/biography/Lewis-Carroll.

Information on David Levithan and how he wrote *Boy Meets Boy* came from his own website: http://www.davidlevithan.com/about/.

Information about S.E. Hinton and the writing of *The Outsiders* is available from many sources, including this one: https://en.wikipedia.org/wiki/S._E._Hinton.

The First Problem with Success Stories: They Focus on the Wrong Things

If you want to explore the significance of failure, and how one's attitude toward failure impacts learning, a good place to start is Carol Dweck's book, *Mindset: Changing the Way You Think to Fulfill Your Potential*.

The Comparison Game Will Kill You (It Nearly Destroyed Me)

The pen name Stephen King took on to publish even more books is Richard Bachman. If you want to know more about King's struggles with writing and addiction (and how he barely remembers writing *Cujo*), check out his excellent memoir/craft book *On Writing*.

The Comparison Game is Bigger Than You Think

For a good scholarly overview of social comparison theory, check out this 2011 article from *Theories in Social Psychology*, "Social Comparison: Motives, Standards, and Mechanisms" by Katja Corcoran, Jan Crusius, and Thomas Mussweiler. There's much more to social comparison theory than I was able to go into in this chapter. (BTW: this is where that "fundamental" and "ubiquitous" claim came from. The authors also called making comparisons with others a "robust human proclivity," which has a lovely sound to it.)

However, if you're looking for a less scholarly and more directly applicable discussion of social comparisons, how they make us unhappy, and how to change this, Russ Harris's *The Happiness Trap: How to Stop Struggling and Start Living* is a good book to consult. He briefly explores the evolutionary basis for making comparisons in his "Introduction."

The Trouble with Chasing Success: A Brief Word From Monet

The opening quote from Monet is cited in several articles and biographies. Here's one if you'd like to learn more: https://www.biography.com/people/claude-monet-9411771.

What is Success Anyway?

For more on Richard Davidson's research check out *The Science of Meditation* and *The Emotional Life of Your Brain* (both co-authored by Davidson).

If you want to explore that claim about the so-called "world's happiest man" here are a few articles:
https://www.independent.co.uk/life-style/a-69-year-old-monk-who-scientists-call-the-worlds-happiest-man-says-the-secret-to-being-happy-takes-a7869166.html

https://www.businessinsider.com/how-to-be-happier-according-to-matthieu-ricard-the-worlds-happiest-man-2016-1.

A Better Notion of Success

Leo Gura, life-coach and founder of Actualized.org, has a good video/podcast on conditional and unconditional happiness called "You're Not Happy Because You Don't Really Want to Be." If you want to explore the concept of unconditional happiness further, that's a good place to start.

The Dolly Parton quote came from an interview with her that aired on NPR *Morning Edition*, December 9th, 2018.

Four Common Ways to Beat the Comparison Game (And Why These Don't Work)

Want to know more about the trouble with self-affirmations? Here's one study that shows how such positive self-affirmations can backfire: "Positive Self-Statements: Power for Some, Peril for Others," by Joanne Wood, W.Q. Perunovic, and John Lee, *Psychological Science*, July 1, 2009, http://journals.sagepub.com/doi/abs/10.1111/j.1467-9280.2009.02370.x.

Interested in that Stephen King interview I mentioned? Here's a *Guardian* article on it from February 5, 2009: https://www.theguardian.com/books/2009/feb/05/stephenkingfiction?CMP=aff_1432&awc=5795_1535755697_877c4fa729e00b934659f0ad5d4c8082.

PART II

Why the Ego Makes You Feel Bad...
The completely fabulous Lynda Barry graphic essay described in this chapter was originally published in *McSweeney's Quarterly Concern* in 2004. It can also be found in her beautiful book on creativity, writing, and "the formless thing which gives things form," *What It Is.*

For a more thorough exploration of the ego and how it can get in the way of developing consciousness, check out Eckart Tolle's book *A New Earth: Awakening to Your Life's Purpose.*

What is Creativity?
This chapter begins with a seemingly basic question that turns out to be endlessly complicated. In fact, the more you contemplate "what is creativity," the more you might realize that there is no ground here. However, for the purpose of this chapter, I wanted to represent the general, commonly understood definition of creativity. For this, I took several popular definitions of creativity and worked to extrapolate the common threads. Originally, I settled on "the ability to create something new and useful," but the word "useful" tripped me up. Some great art was created to subvert the notion of utility ("art for art's sake"). Then I came across a Wikipedia definition of creativity which uses the phrase "somehow valuable." Although I think this leads to other problematic questions about what is valuable, and who gets to determine what is valuable, it seemed an improvement over "useful."

There are several journals dedicated to understanding creativity better, and research on how to measure and improve creativity. Two of the most helpful ones I encountered in my research were the *Creativity Research Journal* and *Thinking Skills and Creativity*. There, you'll find research papers like this one on "Measuring and Training Creativity Competencies: Validation of a New Test" by Epstein, Schmidt, and Warfel, http://www.tandfonline.com/doi/abs/10.1080/10400410701839876#.VNPNUWSsX0Q.

If what you're interested in is a general article on creativity, you might want to start here, with this piece from *Newsweek* on "The Creativity Crisis" by Po Bronson and Ashley Merryman from the July 10, 2010 issue: http://www.newsweek.com/creativity-crisis-74665.

What Creativity Really Is

Robert Lewis Stevenson's "A Chapter on Dreams" was originally published in 1888 and can be found in *Selected Essays of Robert Lewis Stevenson*.

For a good introductory exploration of Buddhist notions of the self (and to see the term "small self" in use), check out this article by Jack Kornfield published in *Tricycle*, "Identity and Selflessness in Buddhism: No Self or True Self?" https://tricycle.org/magazine/no-self-or-true-self/.

The Rupert Spira quote on the ego being an activity given in the footnote in this chapter comes from his book *The Transparency of Things: Contemplating the Nature of Experience*.

The Paradox of Creativity, Control, and Intention

Psychologist Mihály Csíkszentmihályi has written a few books on the flow state. The quote in this chapter, though, was taken from a 1996 *Wired* magazine interview with Csíkszentmihályi that can be found here: https://www.wired.com/1996/09/czik.

The potter quote in the footnotes comes from Ram Dass's book *Be Here Now*.

A Brief Excursion into the Difference Between Trying and Being

The Baryshnikov quote comes from a commencement speech he gave in May 2019 reported on in this article from *Pointe*: https://www.pointemagazine.com/baryshnikov-graduation-speech-2637307357.html?rebelltitem=1#rebelltitem1.

How Failure Can Be Your Friend

For more on Carol Dweck's work, check out her book, *Mindset: Changing the Way You Think to Fulfill Your Potential*. Dweck has also participated in more recent research on the importance of failure in learning. Some of her research is outlined in this January 30th, 2017 blog article from *Psychology Today* that can be found here: https://www.psychologytoday.com/us/blog/the-athletes-way/201701/self-compassion-growth-mindset-and-the-benefits-failure.

Research led by Hans Schroder at MSU supports Dweck's findings, and further explores the benefits of failure and focusing on one's mistakes with a growth mindset as a way to increase learning. Here's a reference for that 2017 study: Hans S. Schroder, Megan E. Fisher, Yanli Lin, Sharon L. Lo, Judith H. Danovitch, Jason S. Moser. "Neural evidence for enhanced attention to mistakes among school-aged children with a growth mindset." *Developmental Cognitive Neuroscience*, 2017; 24: 42 DOI: 10.1016/j.dcn.2017.01.004.

Jeff Bezo's quote on failure can be found in several articles. Here's one where you can learn more about his thoughts on failure and innovation: "The Best Business Advice from Jeff Bezos" by Eugene Kim, *Business Insider*, https://www.businessinsider.com/business-advice-from-amazon-ceo-jeff-bezos-2016-4#-3.

Twelve Practical Ways to Get Past Doubt, Procrastination, and Other Ego Blocks

I'm grateful to Charlie Mitchell for pointing out that not everyone can do aerobic activity, and for sharing with me the tensing and relaxing muscle awareness activity mentioned in this chapter as an effective alternative. It's a great activity to try while sitting at your desk.

The Sadhguru quote I referenced in the step further box is a good one to see in context since his presence conveys more than the words on a page. Here's a link to a short video of the interview that can be found on the Isha website (the organization Sadhguru founded): https://isha.sadhguru.org/us/en/wisdom/video/the-first-step-in-spirituality.

What About Talent and Intelligence?

The quote from Calvin Coolidge comes from *The Autobiography of Calvin Coolidge,* published in 1929, and is entirely available in the public domain.

The Study That Will Forever Change How You Look at Commercial Success

I've heard the claim that seven out of ten titles do not earn back their advance repeated by a few editors in private discussions and at conferences. However, getting comprehensive research to back this up is tricky since publishers don't tend to make such information public. To show you that this is a commonly held notion about publishing, here's one example of that claim being used in the *New York Times Sunday Book Review*, "About That Book Advance..." by Michael Meyer, April 10, 2009, http://www.nytimes.com/2009/04/12/books/review/Meyer-t.html.

For more on the Salganic, Dodds, and Watts study explored in this chapter, here's the research paper they published on their work in *Science:* Salganik, M., Dodds, P., & Watts, D. (2006). "Experimental Study of Inequality and Unpredictability in an Artificial Cultural Market." *Science, 311*, 854-856 DOI: 10.1126/science.1121066.

And here's a reference to the 2013 interview I quoted Salganik from: *Harvard Business Review* interview with Matthew J. Salganik: https://hbr.org/2013/11/was-gangnam-style-a-fluke.

I also quoted Salganik from this interview on Salganik's research that was part of NPR's *Morning Edition* in 2014: https://www.npr.org/2014/02/27/282939233/good-art-is-popular-because-its-good-right.

Out of curiosity, I looked up *52Metro's* "Lockdown" (the song that was ranked #1 in one world, and 40th out of 48 in another). When I found it on YouTube while writing this book, it had 25 views (26, thanks to me). You can find it here and give it a listen (who knows, maybe in this reality something will happen that will cause it to rise to number 1): https://www.youtube.com/watch?v=1JJ6YiTGNvg.

Take Away Two: Undiscovered Van Goghs

Two of the sources I found most useful for information about Van Gogh and how Johanna van Gogh-Bonger helped bring his works into the world are the Van Gogh Museum in Amsterdam (https://www.vangoghmuseum.nl/en), and this article from the *Smithsonian Magazine*, "The Woman Who Brought Van Gogh to the World" by Jess Righthand, November 1, 2010: https://www.smithsonianmag.com/arts-culture/the-woman-who-brought-van-gogh-to-the-world-66805589/.

The rejection and sales numbers for the books listed in this chapter come from the following sources:

https://www.npr.org/sections/thetwo-way/2017/04/24/525443040/-zen-and-the-art-of-motorcycle-maintenance-author-robert-m-pirsig-dies-at-88

http://mentalfloss.com/article/62736/12-fantastic-facts-about-wrinkle-time

http://www.writersdigest.com/online-editor/60-rejection-letters-didnt-stop-kathryn-stockett-and-her-best seller-the-help.

But Perseverance Isn't Fun

Joseph Campbell's wonderful "follow your bliss" quote comes from the Bill Moyer's *PBS* interviews with Joseph Campbell that were later collected in the excellent book *The Power of Myth*.

PART III

Transform Your Characters, Transform Yourself

These next few chapters refer frequently to stages in what Joseph Campbell termed "the monomyth" (now commonly referred to as the hero's journey) that Campbell first mapped out and explored in his seminal 1949 book, *The Hero with a Thousand Faces*.

The stages in the hero's journey that Campbell depicted have since been explored (and renamed) by countless other works on story structure and plot. Most notable in shaping my own understanding of story structure (and essential reading for any writers out there who want to understand narrative structure better) are Robert McKee's *Story*, Blake Snyder's *Save the Cat*, Christopher Vogler's *The Writer's Journey*, and Nancy Kress's *Beginnings, Middles & Ends.*

How I Died (and Found a Better Way to Be)

I didn't want to clutter this chapter with a philosophical debate that's ultimately unresolvable, but if you really want to get into the weeds, look up whether existentialism as described by Sartre (we are "condemned to be free" and one must choose to give life meaning) is compatible with or undermined by determinism.

One way to circumvent this debate is to recognize that generally determinism is concerned with metaphysics (how things work on a fundamental level), and existentialism is concerned with psychological philosophy (how we understand things on a human level), so they're talking about different aspects of existence and can be both compatible and contradictory depending upon the perspective you view them from.

The Far Side of the Tunnel

If you talk with ghosts, you might think you're crazy until you meet someone else who's met the same ghosts. For me, that was what reading Eckhart Tolle's *The Power of Now* felt like. I'd avoided reading Tolle's books until after I'd finished a draft of this book (if I think a book might tread similar territory as one I'm working on, I try not to read it until I've completed my version of things so I can avoid any imitative influence). However, the other day when I was revising this book, I took a break and read a bit of *The Power of Now*. I was both surprised and pleased to discover Tolle's eloquent descriptions of several experiences that had seemed deeply personal to me (including many of the changes described in this chapter). Upon revising, I worked a few of Tolle's quotes into this book to tip the hat in his direction, and because Tolle has a knack for stating challenging concepts in elegantly clear prose.

On pages 133-135 of *The Power of Now* you can find Tolle discussing "Other Portals" to awakening. The three portals he discusses are strikingly similar to three of the other doorways I discuss in this chapter: present moment awareness, the cessation of thinking, and letting go of "mental-emotional resistance to what is" because, as Tolle puts it, "Inner resistance cuts you off from other people, from yourself, from the world around you. It strengthens the feeling of separateness on which the ego depends for its survival."

Essentially, each portal provides a way to transcend the ego mind and experience the essence of existence which the ego mind obscures. To me, seeing such similar things discussed in Tolle's book (as well as in many Buddhist, Zen, Sufi, Hindu, and early Christian texts) reinforced the notion that my experience wasn't a uniquely personal occurrence, but simply an aspect of existence that's been encountered and described by many.

The Ego Mind Is a Box

Philosopher Eliot Deutsch wrote an interesting passage on the inability of the mind to think beyond the mind in *Advaita Vedanta: A Philosophical Reconstruction*. As he put it, "there is no way to open to the mind to deny logically the results of its own functioning; that is, to deny the reality of its own contents" (page 83).

On Writing Your Life

The two Rupert Spira quotes given in the footnotes in this chapter come from his books *The Transparency of Things: Contemplating the Nature of Experience* and *Being Aware of Being Aware* (respectively).

A Simple Practice for Unlocking Observer Consciousness

I want to thank my counselor friend, Christopher Roney, for introducing me to the "Now this body is…" practice and to its connection to a lineage of Tibetan Zen Buddhism.

There are several studies that explore the gap between when our brains decide to do something and when we consciously think we decide to do something. Benjamin Libet originally pioneered this work in the 1980s with EEG machines. More recently, researches have used fMRI machines and intracranial recording techniques to further explore how decisions work. Although most of the research shows that our brains decide to do something seconds (sometimes as much as 10 seconds) before we consciously *think* we make a decision, some researchers have recently explored whether the decision is really made then, or whether the brain is simply preparing to make a certain decision. Recent research suggests that we have the ability to veto a decision up to a fraction of a second before the decision is made. Then our brains pass a "point of no return" and the decision is essentially made. Regardless, almost all the neurological research shows that we make decisions *before* we're consciously aware of making them. If you want to explore some of the research on this, here are a couple papers you might want to start with:

Soon, Chun Siong; Brass, Marcel; Heinze, Hans-Jochen; Haynes, John-Dylan (2008). "Unconscious determinants of free decisions in the human brain." *Nature Neuroscience*. 11 (5): 543–5.

Fried, Itzhak; Mukamel, Roy; Kreiman, Gabriel. "Internally Generated Preactivation of Single Neurons in Human Medial Frontal Cortex Predicts Volition." *Neuron*. Volume 69, Issue 3. 10 February, 2011. Pages 548-562.

For more on "affect labeling" (mentioned in one of the footnotes in this chapter) and the dozens of studies that show that affect labeling increases emotional regulation, decreases fear, and lowers stress, I suggest starting with a broad overview of the research, like this article by Tom Valeo, published in *Brain Work*, "When Labeling an Emotion Quiets It," September, 2013. Or this scholarly article on affect labeling by Matthew Lieberman and Jarred B. Torre, "Putting Feelings Into Words: Affect Labeling as Implicit Emotional Regulation" published in *Emotion Review*, Vol. 10, No. 2, April 2018.

If you want to read the tarantula study mentioned in the footnotes, here it is: K. Kirkanski, Lieberman, and Craske, "Feelings Into Words: Contributions of Language to Exposure Therapy." *Psychological Science.* 23(10):1086-91, August 2012.

When to Worry

The figure on people who work in "arts-related" jobs being several times more likely than the national average to die by suicide comes from a study done by the British Office of National Statistics, published in 2017. The study covered England from 2011 to 2015. Similar comprehensive national statistical data on the suicide rate of those who work in the arts or arts-related jobs in the United States wasn't available. For more on the above British study, visit: https://www.telegraph.co.uk/news/2017/03/17/people-artistic-professions-likely-commit-suicide-ons-study/.

Hearts Get Broken Open

The biographical information on the 14th Dalai Lama came from a variety of sources. However, one of the best sources I found for learning about the Dalai Lama was the Dalai Lama's own website, www.dalailama.com. Also, if you're interested in reading several interviews with the Dalai Lama and the Archbishop Desmond Tutu, I recommend *The Book of Joy*.

The statistic quoted in this chapter about lower-income people being more charitable than wealthy people comes from this study: Piff, P. K., Kraus, M. W., Côté, S., Cheng, B. H., &

Keltner, D. (2010). "Having less, giving more: The influence of social class on prosocial behavior." *Journal of Personality and Social Psychology.* 99(5), 771-784.

You can learn more about this study, and hear a conversation with one of the authors, on this piece from NPR's *All Things Considered:*
https://www.npr.org/templates/story/story.php?storyId=129068241.

The Secret to Completely Beating the Comparison Game

Researchers in the 1950's did a study (published in 1953 in the *Annual Report of the Smithsonian Institution*) that used radioactive atoms to determine that 98% of our atoms get replaced each year. For more on that, check out this NPR story from 2007 on the subject:
https://www.npr.org/templates/story/story.php?storyId=11893583.

The claim about 7% of our body mass being exchanged each day through eating, drinking, respiration, sweating, and other processes comes from napkin calculations I did assuming average intake of water, food, and air for an average-sized individual. It's probably an underestimate. When I calculated how much I tend to eat, drink, and breathe per day, I found that I might exchange closer to 9% of my body mass per day.

There are several studies that show that the average human body contains more bacterial cells (or other organisms) than human cells. In the past, it was thought to be nearly a 10:1 ratio. However, more recent research on this shows that bacterial cells only slightly outnumber human cells in most people. One 2016 research paper on this, done by Sender, Fuchs, and Milo is titled "Revised Estimates for the Number of Bacterial Cells in the Human Body."

The Sadhguru interview I quoted from in the footnotes can be found here: https://www.youtube.com/watch?v=7qnmaD6Kl1g.

If you want to know more about the psychological harm caused by solitary confinement, here's a good article to start with: https://io9.gizmodo.com/why-solitary-confinement-is-the-worst-kind-of-psycholog-1598543595.

The Ego Strikes Back

The Leo Gura reference in this chapter about ego essentially being selfishness comes from a podcast and YouTube video Leo did on the ego. Leo Gura has posted over 300 free videos and podcasts (available on *iTunes* and other platforms) about various elements of personal development and self-actualization. Most can be found on *Actualized.org*, an online organization he founded.

Revision and the Hero's Return

The George Saunders essay I quoted from in this chapter, "Process and Spirit," was published in the September 2018 issue of *The Writer's Chronicle*. I highly recommend reading it in its entirety—it's both funny and wise.

All of the Joseph Campbell titles and terms I used in this chapter come from Campbell's *The Hero with a Thousand Faces*, published in 1949.

ADDENDUM

Want to Take Things a Step Further?

David Young was my poetry teacher at Oberlin College way back in the 90's. I remember he circled the word "woods" once in a poem I'd written and told me to consider why I used that word instead of "forest." It took me 24 years to figure out the deeper difference.

The lovely lines at the end of this chapter come from a poem by David Young, "The Names of a Hare in English," collected in a book of the same title, published by the University of Pittsburg Press in 1979. Words, once released into the world, can live a curious life.

Thank you for reading!

If you found this book useful, please let others know about it. Posting a short review on Amazon, Goodreads, or other sites can make a huge difference for writers like me.

Reviews need not be long. Even one sentence helps to spread the word and support creativity.

Write on!

For more information about Todd Mitchell and to discover other titles by Owl Hollow Press, find us here:

Website: owlhollowpress.com
Twitter: @owlhollowpress
Facebook: Owl Hollow Press
Instagram: owlhollowpress

www.ingramcontent.com/pod-product-compliance
Lightning Source LLC
Chambersburg PA
CBHW022058120526
44592CB00033B/133